GROUP
PROCESS
and
GANG
DELINQUENCY

JAMES F. SHORT, JR.
and
FRED L. STRODTBECK

THE UNIVERSITY OF CHICAGO PRESS
CHICAGO AND LONDON

Library of Congress Catalog Card Number: 65-14434

THE UNIVERSITY OF CHICAGO PRESS, CHICAGO 60637
The University of Chicago Press, Ltd., London W.C. 1

Preface

In November of 1958 a small group met in the offices of the Young Men's Christian Association of Metropolitan Chicago to discuss the present state of knowledge concerning "delinquent gangs" and a detached-worker program recently embarked upon by the Association. The discussion was excited and eager. After more than two decades in which new knowledge about the behavior of adolescent gangs had scarcely replaced what was being forgotten, new theoretical perspectives and empirical investigations were being combined with experimental action programs. Prospects for further gains seemed bright. Albert Cohen discussed his by now classic formulation of conditions accounting for the emergence of delinquent subcultures. Lloyd Ohlin spoke of "Delinquency and Opportunity" long before the book bearing the same title was published. Walter Miller brought the perspective of lower class culture forcefully to bear at a time when little was published by the Roxbury Youth Project. Philip Hauser, who chaired the sessions, related the historical concerns for the demographic and ecological forces which shape cities to newer cultural and social organizational perspectives.

The YMCA "team" at this meeting was distinguished by a practical capacity for innovation, as well as concern for the traditionally humanitarian goals of the organization. The late, deeply loved Lloyd McClow, General Secretary of the Chicago YMCA, found time to give his personal attention to the scientific reports and discussions. Frank Anger, President of the Chicago National Bank, then serving as President of the Association, attended faithfully, as did Ed Emery, President of the Chicago Rawhide Manufacturing Company, Treasurer of the Chicago Association, and Chairman of the lay committee responsible for the Program for Detached Workers. Anger and Emery both gave unflagging support to the detached-worker program from the very beginning, and encouraged the associated research efforts. Also present was Richard W. Boone, Director of the Program for Detached Workers, who had come recently to the YMCA from a broad background in police and correctional work. Boone's genius for experimentation and effective work in the midst of powerful and often contradictory forces sparked the program's philosophy and implementation, both within the YMCA and in relation to other agencies. John Root, present General Secretary of the Chicago Association, the "traditional" YMCA secretary whose untraditional ideas and action nourished a small but vital program as the basis for change on a much larger scale within the YMCA, was also a member of the "team." These men, along with a few others, were responsible for a virtual revolution within the Y. They had agreed to call this small group of academicians together because they wanted to know what they were getting into—what their chances of success were likely to be. They wanted a research program to accompany their newly formed action program, as a basis for evaluation and the accumulation of knowledge for further implementation.

There were others who sat in on some of the meetings—detached workers, YMCA committee members, Catharine Richards from the Welfare Council of Metropolitan Chicago. They were all curious about the new program, wondering what research had to contribute to these problems, and wanting to know whether academicians were, after all, concerned with "real" problems.

The academicians were welcomed warmly and for two days the floor was theirs. Presentations were brief and discussion spirited. Questions were raised and research designs suggested. In the end, YMCA representatives and observers must have been puzzled at the exhilaration of the academicians, for despite fundamental disagreements and admitted ignorance in certain areas, there was an atmosphere of consensus. The academicians have continued their association with the project since that first meeting. Personal respect and camaraderie have reduced the doubts and suspicions arising from conflicting intellectual positions.

When the YMCA first approached the Department of Sociology at the University of Chicago for consultation on their new program, Philip Hauser had referred them to Fred L. Strodtbeck of the University's Departments of Sociology and Psychology, and it was Strodtbeck and Boone who planned that first meeting. James F. Short, Jr., of Washington State University was one of those invited.

At the close of the first meeting the essential design was clear. We were to open a window on the gangs being worked with by the detached workers and, among other things, collect observations in Chicago to test propositions of the type we had reviewed at the two-day meeting. Short was asked to draft a research proposal based on our discussions for submission to the Behavior Science Study Section of the National Institute of Mental Health. The final version was prepared with Strodtbeck. The proposal was acted upon favorably, and in June, 1959, Short took a leave of absence from Washington State University and joined the faculty of the University of Chicago as Visiting Associate Professor of Sociology. He recruited the staff and gave detailed day-to-day direction in problems of conceptual focus, instrument design, and data collection.

No research team ever enjoyed a better relationship with its "client" than ours with the YMCA. We are profoundly grateful for this, for the support from our colleagues such as we enjoyed at the University of Chicago, and for the extended leave granted Short by Washington State University. The original National Institutes of Health research grant (M-3301) of three years was supplemented and extended for an additional two-year period after Short's return to Washington State. Further support was received from the YMCA, the Ford Foundation, and the Office of Juvenile Delinquency and Youth Development, U.S. Department of Health, Education, and Welfare. The confidence of these institutions was, of course, crucial and very much appreciated.

The happy "accident" of our respective roles at the first meeting, the many discussions of the research findings, and the joint attack on problems of analysis led to the series of papers comprising, in large part, this volume. Readers familiar with earlier steps of our enterprise will find that this book brings together previously published work in a form which reveals the interplay between our method and theory. It is a "natural history" of the way in which the research findings opened new theoretical perspectives to us. In this sense, it is reminiscent of Edwin Sutherland's account of the development of the theory of "differential association."[1]

Plan of the Book

The plan of the book may be seen from the ordering of its contents. Chapter 1 treats the theoretical traditions which were the

[1] Albert Cohen, Alfred Lindesmith, and Karl Schuessler, eds. *The Sutherland Papers* (Bloomington: Indiana University Press, 1956).

basis for our approach to the study of delinquent gangs, ideas concerning research design, and decisions made in this respect. Chapter 2 represents something of a departure from conventional notions of research strategy and illustrates an approach which we have found useful.

Complementary to the basic group-process perspective of the book, Chapter 3 explores the implications of data on the values of gang and non-gang subjects for various theories of gang behavior. Similarly, Chapters 4 and 5 are concerned with the empirical validity of theories in the delinquent subculture tradition, with their treatment of the nature of the behavior for which an explanation is sought.

Chapters 6 and 7 present our efforts to decipher the puzzle of self-conception in relation to behavior among the boys studied. In particular, we focus on boys' self-conceptions *in the context of their groups* and on how these are related to behavior, and to cultural and social structural factors such as social class and race.

Chapter 8 describes one of the early group-process "discoveries" of the project, namely, that delinquent episodes are related to status-maintaining mechanisms within the group. Chapter 9 extends the discussion in several ways, by exploring further implications of group norms for the nature of group responses to status threats, conceived more broadly than in the previous chapter. Chapter 10 follows up the status-threat notion by exploring social disabilities among the gang boys, which may account for the specifically delinquent nature of portions of their behavior—a hypothesis drawn initially by Robert A. Gordon from further examination of the values data introduced in Chapter 3. Chapter 11 returns to the argument introduced in Chapter 2 that certain aspects of delinquent episodes involve a calculus of decision-making for which the term "hedonism" is inadequate, and continues the stress on the nature of group process. Chapter 12 summarizes the development of the group-process perspective and places it in the context of recent theoretical formulations, particularly concerning social exchange.

The publication of this set of our completed papers does not represent a termination of the enterprise; many aspects of the perspective of the book continue to develop in the thinking and subsequent research of both of the authors. It is hoped that our enthusiasm for neglected approaches and the development of new perspectives and research methods will find acceptance with other delinquency investigators. We feel that the group-process perspective here stressed contains solid leads for revised theory—leads which to our regret, we have not, in many instances, been free to follow as far as we would like.

Acknowledgments

To Albert K. Cohen, Philip M. Hauser, Walter B. Miller, and Lloyd E. Ohlin—the other members (for we are members, too)— of the "advisory group," we are grateful for much inspiration, counsel, and friendly debate—past, present, and future; and to colleagues at the University of Chicago and Washington State University who have suffered through numerous versions of the chapters, in seminars, "brown bag" luncheons, at staff meetings and parties—wherever we could corner them. Because they were especially "victimized"— as methodological or editorial advisers, and as advisers on theses— special mention should be made of Jack Sawyer, Mayer Zald, Rita James Simon, James A. Davis, Peter H. Rossi, Peter Blau, and C. Arnold Anderson.

Colleagues from many other institutions have been generous with their time and critical talent. We are especially grateful to Albert J. Reiss, Jr., Stanton Wheeler, Howard S. Becker, Meda White, David Bordua, Solomon Kobrin, Henry D. McKay, Harold Finestone, Hanan Selvin, Clarence Schrag, Donald Garrity, Don Gibbons, Marshall B. Clinard, and Irving Goffman.

Staff members and secretaries have labored with us in so many ways, most of them at graduate student "slave wages." We have recognized several research assistants by name in the text which follows, but dozens of observers, interviewers, coders, clerical and secretarial aides, computer programmers, laboratory assistants, and students in classes who aided us in innumerable ways must remain anonymous. Secretaries Jane Schaeffer, Ruth Robinson, and Catherine Chapman did a great deal to keep the enterprise moving, by countless telephone calls and details of co-ordination, and by their patience with instrument and manuscript preparation. Following the program's move to Washington State University, Bernice Dayton's fresh perspective on the data and our interpretations and her critical eye and care in manuscript and index preparation have been invaluable.

Special recognition beyond their citation in individual chapters must go to co-authors of papers previously published and included here with minor revisions. Desmond S. Cartwright, Robert A. Gordon, and Kenneth I. Howard have at various times been part of the "executive team" of the research program. Ellen Kolegar was a long-time research assistant to Strodtbeck, and Ray A. Tennyson was senior research assistant to Short as director of the program from its inception. His role as collaborator in other phases of the research continues.

Our debt to the YMCA cannot go unacknowledged; yet full acknowledgment is impossible. Their leadership in Chicago and their willingness to expose themselves freely to objective inquiry are rare, indeed, in an age of almost frantic competition for the welfare dollar. Without them we could not have launched this particular effort, and it is doubtful that under any other auspices the close observation of several of Chicago's most delinquent gangs would have been possible. Special thanks, in addition to those recognized in the Introduction, are due the staff of the Program for Detached Workers, who served as eyes, ears, and reporters of much of the experience we have sought to record and analyze. Fred D. Hubbard and Charles N. Cooper have been especially helpful in making possible the entree we have required into many situations, and as sources of data in their own right. Every worker helped in so many ways. They are cited by name in appropriate places in the manuscript, but citation cannot begin to acknowledge our indebtedness to them.

Finally, it is impossible to acknowledge fully our debt to the hundreds of gang and non-gang boys, but especially the former, who allowed us the privilege of entering into their lives, sometimes very intimately. It is to them that we dedicate this volume.

Contents

List of Tables

CHAPTER I

Delinquent Subcultures, Groups, and Research Designs

The gang as a form of human association and a social problem, an object of curiosity and commentary is at once ancient and contemporary. Probably no generation has been without its detractors, and each younger generation's antics in collective form have been especially vulnerable in this respect. What is new, apparently, is the extent to which *gang delinquency* has become a problem of major proportions in many countries since World War II. Even this is not new in some countries, such as the United States, but here the *forms* of gang delinquency appear to have changed somewhat.

United Nations and other reports suggest that collective forms of delinquency have become cause for alarm in such widely separated areas as Western Europe and the Iron Curtain countries, the Far East, in Australia, and in such rapidly changing underdeveloped countries as Ghana and Kenya.[1] Picturesque names establish the public identity of these young people and no doubt add an important increment to their private identity as well—names like "zoot-suiters" and "boppers" in the U.S., "Teddy boys" in England, "blousons noirs" in France, "vitelloni" in Italy, "Halbstarke" in Germany, "bodgies" (boys) and "widgies" (girls) in Australia and New Zealand, "tsotsio" in South Africa, "mambo" boys and girls in Japan, "hooligans" in Poland and Russia, the "tap-karoschi" of Yugoslavia, and the "lui-mang" and "tai-pau" of Taiwan. Names the youngsters give themselves are even more intriguing—consider these *noms de plume* of lower class Negro gangs in Chicago: Jewtown Egyptian Cobras (a gang in the area of the old Jewish open-market on Max-

---

[1] See, for example, Wolf Middendorf, *New Forms of Juvenile Delinquency: Their Origin, Prevention and Treatment* (New York: U.N. Department of Economic and Social Affairs, 1960); Council of Europe, *Juvenile Delinquency in Post-War Europe* (1960); and T. R. Fyvel, *Troublemakers: Rebellious Youth in an Affluent Society* (New York: Shocken Books, Inc., 1961, 1962).

well Street), and the Cobrettes (their "ladies auxiliary"); the Vice Lords and Vice Ladies; Racketeers and Lady Racketeers; and by contrast (in name only) the Chaplains, Imperial Chaplains, Roman Saints; the Nobles and the Mafia; Vampires and Braves; Navahoes and Sioux (pronounced Sī-ox!); or the anomaly of the German Counts with a swastika as their mark. The list is literally endless because new gangs are formed and old ones change, sometimes dissolving into anonymity, in a constant procession. It would be hazardous, indeed, to attribute precise meaning to these symbols—however tempting their dramatic nature—beyond suggesting that they provide some sort of common identity and perhaps a reaching out for status on the part of group members, individually and collectively.

Knowledge of the extent and nature of these phenomena has not kept pace with public concern, nor can it ever, one suspects, by virtue of the slow, painstaking nature of research and theoretical endeavor. Still, some of the most exciting developments in the behavioral sciences in recent years have been concerned with these problems, and it has been our privilege to observe and in some measure to participate in them. In this first chapter we will review the main currents of thought that have guided our inquiry and describe the research program we hope will contribute to their further development.

The discovery by sociologists of the old "Chicago school," the now commonplace knowledge that juvenile delinquency and many other social problems were concentrated with poverty in the central areas of Chicago and other large cities, is a landmark in behavioral science. So, too, the discoveries that most delinquent youngsters committed their delinquencies in company with one or more peers and that adolescent gangs were concentrated in much the same manner as was delinquency.[2] Taken together these findings are an important foundation for much delinquency theory of the past thirty years.

The first finding—having to do with the ecological correlates of delinquency—has been the basis for the greatest divergence in theoretical interpretations of delinquent behavior. The second has almost been taken for granted, though much disagreement exists as to *why* it should be so that delinquent behavior so often occurs in the company of peers.[3] It was in part to test competing interpretations, and

[2] Clifford R. Shaw *et al.*, *Delinquency Areas* (Chicago: University of Chicago Press, 1929); and Frederic M. Thrasher, *The Gang* abridged ed. with new introduction, 1963 (Chicago: University of Chicago Press, 1927).

[3] From the "birds of a feather flock together" interpretation of the Gluecks, to Sutherland's classic statement of "differential association" and more recent the-

to focus more specifically on the nature of gang interaction and behavior, that the present research was undertaken.

The ecological findings and research and theory concerning the nature of social stratification focus attention on the impact of the social-class structure on social life generally and on adolescents in particular.[4] Two fundamentally opposing viewpoints have been expressed: the impact of *relative* position and of *absolute* position in the social structure. Relative position is stressed by Robert K. Merton, who argues that a society with an open-class system which indoctrinates all groups with high aspirations for "success," but denies equal opportunity for achievement of these aspirations, generates *anomie* among those who are disadvantaged in the struggle for success. Anomie, the breakdown of regulatory norms, may result in various modes of individual adaptation such as resorting to criminal means (innovation) and drug use (retreatism). Merton's discussion of the relation between poverty and crime is especially appropriate for our purposes.[5]

. . . our egalitarian ideology denies by implication the existence of noncompeting individuals and groups in the pursuit of pecuniary success. Instead, the same body of success symbols is held to apply for all. Goals are held to transcend class lines, not to be bounded by them, yet the actual

---

ories treating the emergence of delinquent subcultures. See Sheldon and Eleanor Glueck, *Unravelling Juvenile Delinquency* (New York: Commonwealth Fund, 1951); Edwin H. Sutherland, *Principles of Criminology*, revised by Donald R. Cressey (6th ed.; Philadelphia: J. B. Lippincott, 1960); Albert K. Cohen, *Delinquent Boys* (Glencoe: The Free Press, 1955); Richard A. Cloward and Lloyd E. Ohlin, *Delinquency and Opportunity* (Glencoe: The Free Press, 1960); and Walter B. Miller, "Lower Class Culture as a Generating Milieu of Gang Delinquency," *Journal of Social Issues,* XIV (Summer, 1958), 5–19. For a more extended discussion of the "sociology of delinquency" than is necessary or appropriate in the present context, see Albert K. Cohen and James F. Short, Jr., "Juvenile Delinquency," in *Contemporary Social Problems,* Robert K. Merton and Robert A. Nisbet, eds. (New York: Harcourt, Brace and World, Inc., 1961).

[4] Ratios of boys to girls appearing before U.S. courts have dropped from 50 or 60 to 1 in the early 1900's to 4 or 5 to 1 at mid-century. Research and theoretical attention to the girls is increasing. See Cohen's statement in this regard in *Delinquent Boys, op. cit.,* and its sequel, Cohen and Short, "Research in Delinquent Subcultures," *Journal of Social Issues,* XIV (Summer, 1958), 20–37. Miller's research is concerned with girls as well as boys. The Youth Studies Program, from which this volume emanates, has been concerned primarily with boys' gangs, but reports on their female "auxiliaries," and on control groups of lower and middle class non-gang girls, will be forthcoming.

[5] Robert K. Merton, *Social Theory and Social Structure* (rev. ed., Glencoe: The Free Press, 1957), pp. 146–47.

social organization is such that there exist class differentials in accessibility of the goals. In this setting, a cardinal American virtue, "ambition," promotes a cardinal American vice, "deviant behavior."
. . . Poverty as such and consequent limitation of opportunity are not enough to produce a conspicuously high rate of criminal behavior. Even the notorious "poverty in the midst of plenty" will not necessarily lead to this result. But when poverty and associated disadvantages in competing for the culture values approved for *all* members of the society are linked with a cultural emphasis on pecuniary success as a dominant goal, high rates of criminal behavior are the normal outcome.

Following the Merton tradition, Albert Cohen directs attention to characteristics of delinquency in American society which appear to be less "rationally" and economically motivated than crime as it is conceptualized in the Merton schema. Cohen attempts to account for the emergence of "the delinquent subculture" in terms of *status problems* which are involved in the discrepancy between culture goals and institutionalized means. Juvenile delinquency, he points out, consists largely of violence and property destruction or appropriation in which goods stolen have little or no intrinsic value to the thief, illicit sexual behavior, and consumption of alcohol. The bases for conceptualizing delinquency as "subcultural" are the familiar ecological and demographic findings—it is largely a male, working-class phenomenon, and it takes an organized and collective form.

When we speak of a delinquent subculture, we speak of a way of life that has somehow become traditional among certain groups in American society. These groups are the boys' gangs that flourish most conspicuously in the "delinquency neighborhoods" of our larger American cities. The members of these gangs grow up, some to become law-abiding citizens and others to graduate to more professional and adult forms of criminality, but the delinquent tradition is kept alive by the age-groups that succeed them.[6]

The delinquent subculture emerges, says Cohen, as a response to status problems experienced by working-class boys. The granting of status is governed in large part by adult representatives of the middle classes, in institutional contexts such as school, church, and business community. By virtue of their socialization in working-class families

[6] *Delinquent Boys, op. cit.*, p. 13. Here Cohen follows the earlier work of Sutherland, Shaw and McKay, and others. See Albert K. Cohen, Alfred Lindesmith, and Karl Schuessler, eds. *The Sutherland Papers* (Bloomington: Indiana University Press, 1956); and Clifford R. Shaw and Henry McKay, *Juvenile Delinquency and Urban Areas* (Chicago: University of Chicago Press, 1956).

and communities, many youngsters are ill-equipped to succeed in terms of the criteria of these persons and institutions, criteria such as "good manners," ambition, thrift, neatness, and self-restraint. As a result of failure to measure up to the standards of the "middle class measuring rod" these youngsters experience loss of status and of self-respect. The subcultural nature of delinquency arises by virtue of the fact that youngsters who are similarly disadvantaged join together to *reject* middle class criteria of status and establish their own criteria in terms of which they can succeed. Their alternative status system, says Cohen, takes the form of a "reaction-formation" *against* the middle-class criteria in terms of which they are found wanting. It is this which accounts for the non-utilitarian, malicious, and negativistic character of the delinquent subculture. Cohen notes that status is, by definition, the granting of respect by others; hence the response of these youngsters "makes sense" only as a group response. He suggests further that by virtue of their repudiation of convention and the consequent even greater loss of respect from others, participants in the delinquent subculture become all the more dependent for status upon one another. The extremity of gang behavior is related to the fact that "group interaction is a sort of catalyst which releases potentialities not otherwise visible."[7]

Cohen has recognized the existence of "more or less distinct delinquent subcultures" and, with Short, has attempted to delineate and explain the emergence of conflict, semiprofessional theft, and drug-oriented subcultures from the parent or "garden variety" of delinquent subculture which he had previously described.[8] The most ambitious and systematic theory to account for varieties of delinquent subcultures, however, is *Delinquency and Opportunity: A Theory of Delinquent Gangs* by Richard Cloward and Lloyd Ohlin. These men add to Merton's basic premise concerning relative accessibility of legitimate means the notion of differential availability of illegitimate means, and they develop more fully the implications of the theory specifically for subcultural delinquency. It is their contention that delinquent subcultures are formed by lower class youngsters who are blocked in their ambitions for improvement in economic position. These youngsters are not oriented toward changes in life style, however. Cohen's delinquents, they say, seem likely to be drawn from youngsters who are oriented toward membership in the

---

[7] *Delinquent Boys, op. cit.*, p. 136.

[8] Cohen and Short, "Research in Delinquent Subcultures," *op. cit.*

middle class and who may or may not be oriented toward improved economic goals. In any case they, too, are blocked in their efforts. Whyte's "college boys" presumably would be oriented toward improvement both in social class and in economic position, while his "corner boys" would be non-aspiring in both areas.

From this basic typology, Cloward and Ohlin assume, with Merton, that legitimate means to success goals are limited and, hence, that intense pressures are exerted toward deviant behavior. Merton had suggested that "Al Capone represents the triumph of amoral intelligence over morally-prescribed 'failure,' when the channels of vertical mobility are closed or narrowed *in a society which places a high premium on economic affluence and social ascent for all its members.*"[9] Cloward and Ohlin point to the fact, documented by Sutherland and others, that illegitimate means are not equally available to all.[10] Their availability is conceptualized as varying with the extent of integration of adult carriers of conventional and criminal values in urban areas. Kobrin earlier had discussed variations in delinquency areas along this dimension.[11] In integrated areas relations between legitimate and illegitimate adults are held to be accommodative; there is reciprocal participation of each in the value system of the other. By contrast, in unintegrated areas the aims of these adults conflict, and neither group is effectively organized. Opportunities for learning and performing criminal roles are available in integrated areas, unavailable in unintegrated areas. In integrated areas social control originates and therefore is effective in both legitimate and illegal structures, while it is ineffective in unintegrated areas.

Youngsters who have "a sense of being unjustly deprived of access to opportunities to which one is entitled,"[12] say Cloward and Ohlin, seek opportunities for advancement by illegitimate means. Under the varying circumstances described above, however, their delinquent adaptations take different forms. In integrated areas rational, disciplined, crime-oriented behavior emerges as the boys learn by example of their elders and by doing, and as they seek legitima-

[9] Merton, *op cit.*, p. 146.

[10] Edwin H. Sutherland, *The Professional Thief* (Chicago: University of Chicago Press, 1937).

[11] Solomon Kobrin, "The Conflict of Values in Delinquency Areas," *American Sociological Review,* XVI (October, 1951), 653–61.

[12] Cloward and Ohlin, *op. cit.*

tion in the eyes of powerful adults. In the absence either of legitimate or illegitimate opportunities, however, expressive behavior in the form of the conflict subculture emerges in unintegrated areas.

Cloward and Ohlin see the resort to drug use and other "kicks" as an escapist reaction on the part of youngsters who are failures even in available illegitimate avenues to achievement, that is, crime in integrated and violence in unintegrated areas. These "double failures" form "retreatist" subcultures.

Merton, Cohen, and Cloward and Ohlin thus see universal goals of American society as responsible for problems of adjustment of lower class, and thereby disadvantaged, adolescent youngsters. *Relative* position in the social order is a major contributing factor to the delinquent solutions chosen. Strong issue with this point of view is taken by Walter Miller, who argues that lower class culture, "a long established, distinctively-patterned tradition with an integrity of its own"[13] exerts the most direct influence on gang delinquency— that is, *absolute* position in the social order rather than position relative to others in a universal and competitive system of goals and means to their achievement.

Miller describes features of lower class culture which explain the prevalence of gangs and their involvement in delinquency. Socialization in "female-based households" creates identity problems that are worked out on the street with the gang. Six lower class focal concerns and two focal concerns of the lower class adolescent street-corner group are hypothesized to bring about much delinquent behavior. Concern over "trouble," "toughness," "smartness," "excitement," "fate," and "autonomy" are general among lower class persons, says Miller, and at a somewhat higher level of abstraction, concern with "status" and "belonging" characterize male adolescent corner groups. The latter goals often are achieved via fulfilment of the more general areas of concern.

And so the controversy is engaged. On the question of the impact of social position—whether simply belonging to the lower class or being disadvantaged relative to others higher in the social order is most important in the production of gang delinquency—it seems fair to say that all recognize that the truth lies somewhere between the extreme positions taken by these theorists, however polemic the arguments.

13 Miller, *op. cit.*, p. 5.

Research Designs

It is generally agreed that theory and research which seek to isolate and explain patterns of delinquent behavior homogeneous in important respects, and differentiating one delinquent population from another, are superior both to simple sovereign propositions which purport to explain the entire spectrum of behavior that falls under the heading of delinquency and to theoretically undisciplined "multiple-factor" studies. This has been the major thrust of recent theoretical development concerning juvenile delinquency, by psychologists and psychiatrists, as well as in sociology. Indeed, the investigator who seeks guidance for empirical inquiry soon finds that he is confronted with an array of classifications which overlap, contain gaps, and intersect in confusing ways.

Our decision to study lower class gang delinquency and lower class gang delinquents occurred first of all as a result of a research opportunity provided by the YMCA of Metropolitan Chicago. Choice of the theories reviewed as major guidelines for empirical inquiry and further theoretical development was indicated by the fact that each is concerned with explaining the nature of lower class gang delinquency. While the theories do not address precisely the same questions, and they are difficult to operationalize in ways which will permit testing of the relative merits of each, they do present alternative explanations of behavior which in important ways are the same. Research design decisions were governed by considerations such as the extent of overlap among the theories, the clarity with which basic concepts could be defined in such a way as to facilitate their use for empirical operations, availability of relevant subject populations, and, of course, the inevitable problem of optimal utilization of available resources.

The first criterion caused no great difficulty. The theories were similar enough in terms of the phenomena they wished to explain and basic explanatory concepts, and that a research design which would permit testing of one theory likely could be employed for the others. Other criteria were more troublesome. A research design which would accommodate study of the influence on adolescents of the relative integration of adult carriers of criminal and legitimate values could, providing the proper observations were made, also shed light on such matters as "position discontent" with respect to status and economic advancement and the impact of socialization in female-based households. By adding a racial variable, ethnic variations could be studied (Fig. 1.1).

The research problem then would be to study the adaptations of adolescents in these communities and to account for variations within and between communities. Study of the degree of integration of adult carriers of criminal and legitimate values is itself a major empirical problem, however, which if pursued would have occupied a major portion of the resources available to us. A solution to this problem might have been possible based on selection of communities for study which on a prima facie basis possessed the desired characteristics, were it not for difficulties related to the availability of communities with these varying characteristics. Integrated communities, or "areas" (for Cloward and Ohlin somewhat beg the question as to just what local unit is appropriate for their theory) in Chicago were

Relations between Adult Carriers of
Criminal and Legitimate Values

Race	Integrated	Unintegrated
White		
Negro		

FIG. 1.1.—Research design: integration status by race.

not readily available to us. This is the case in part because it is in these communities that the Chicago Area Project has come to play a major role in community organization and delinquency-prevention activities.[14] We were restricted also by the fact that the YMCA detached-worker program was not at this time a community-oriented effort. These problems did not prevent us from studying youngsters in integrated areas, but they did alter the basic design from that suggested above.

Designs such as this also are inadequate because virtually all of the relevant variables *are variables* rather than attributes, and the

[14] See, for example, the recent research reports by Solomon Kobrin and his associates: Solomon Kobrin, Joseph Puntil, and Emil Peluso, "Criteria of Status among Street Gangs," paper read at the annual meetings of the American Sociological Association, 1963; and Brahm Baittle, "Psychiatric Aspects of the Development of a Street Corner Group: An Exploratory Study," *American Journal of Orthopsychiatry*, XXXI (October, 1961), 703–12; and Solomon Kobrin, "Sociological Aspects of the Development of a Street Corner Group: An Exploratory Study," *American Journal of Orthopsychiatry*, XXXI (October, 1961), 685–702.

extent and nature of their variation is not well understood. This is especially true of such basic independent variables (in the theories) as the relative integration of communities in the Cloward and Ohlin usage, the extent and nature of "position discontent" among lower class youngsters, and of variation in lower class culture.[15]

There were other, more positive considerations which helped us to reach a decision concerning basic research designs. The first of these was our relationship with the YMCA program. The value of the "service" legitimation which this program provided the research effort was as great in this respect as was the quality of the data the workers came later to provide. We would argue, with Kobrin, that "Fruitful observation of such a group is possible only when the observer is accepted by the subjects in a role which they perceive as meaningful in relation to their needs and problems."[16]

The great strength of the YMCA program, from the standpoint of research design, was its ability to establish contact with delinquent gangs such as those with which the theories were concerned, and to establish quickly relatively intimate relationships with them. Furthermore, the YMCA was willing to work with gangs with a variety of behavior adaptations because they wished to share knowledge of such adaptations and to experiment with delinquency prevention techniques among them.

We determined, therefore, to select broadly from among Chicago's delinquent gangs groups of boys which appeared from early contact to represent the variety of behavior adaptations with which the theories were concerned. Purposive selection—as opposed to methods of probability sampling—was dictated by the very nature of the phenomena we sought to study. There was, to begin with, no list of gangs from which probability samples could be drawn. Even if such a list had been available, we were assured by competent observers from the police and youth-work fields that it would have been obsolete from the day of its completion, so shifting in membership and identity are these groups. We were, in addition, interested not merely in broadly representative groups, but in the varieties of subcultures which had been posited by Cohen and Short, Cloward and Ohlin, and others. For theoretical reasons we expected the conflict, criminal, and "retreatist" subcultures to be rare as compared with the more

15 Each of the theorists reviewed recognizes these problems and in fact urges their systematic study.

16 *Op. cit.*, "Sociological Aspects. . . ."

ubiquitous "parent" delinquent subculture out of which the former were hypothesized to emerge. This hypothesis is based upon the assumption that extensive drug use is not a generally supported gang activity; moreover, community areas where carriers of criminal and conventional values are integrated in such a way as to produce adolescent criminal subcultures occur relatively infrequently.[17] Despite the good offices of the police and other youth-serving agencies, and a concerted effort by the detached workers and the research staff, *finding* gangs whose primary activities and norms were oriented around drug use or rational, systematic, economically motivated criminal activity, proved to be a major problem.

It is important to realize that the search for gangs with the "proper" orientations was carried out with the full co-operation of the action agency, its administration, and its field staff. We spent many hours in the field for this purpose. The results were oftentimes humorous, sometimes a little frightening, always interesting. The night the White Sox won the American League pennant—their first in forty years—the directors of the research and action programs spent conferring in a small bar-cafe (where fortunately the game was telecast!) with an ex-convict who was in contact with two groups of boys reported to be engaged in rational systematic theft. One lead proved false. The other was correct but shortly after making contact with the group their ranks were decimated and their activities disrupted by the arrest of several key members. After this they became much less interesting to us! Shortly after this the detached worker with these boys reported excitedly that he had located a group of pot (marijuana) smokers in the same general area of the city. We were elated and so was he. His parting shot as he left the research offices after his usual weekly interview was, "Don't worry, Doc, I'll keep them on the stuff until you can study them!" Unfortunately for the research effort, these boys proved to be only casual and occasional users and so did not qualify for an ideal research design.

In dramatic contrast, Negro conflict gangs were plentiful. When the research project began in June, 1959, one white and six Negro gangs were assigned detached workers by the YMCA. All of these had been chosen because of their involvement in conflict with other gangs, harassment of local community institutions, or their reputa-

---

[17] Cf. Cohen and Short, *op. cit.*, "Research in Delinquent Subcultures"; Cloward and Ohlin, *op. cit.*; and Isidor Chein and Eva Rosenfeld, "Juvenile Narcotics Use," *Law and Contemporary Problems*, XXII (1957), 52–68.

tions for toughness and troublemaking among local adults, police, and other agency representatives. Though we could not be certain, it appeared that each was to a considerable degree a carrier of some form of conflict subculture. None of these groups were being worked with primarily because of their criminal or drug-use activities. Much marijuana smoking was found in several groups, and heroin and "pills" were experimented with by many boys, always in concert with other boys; but these were not major activities or normative emphases of the groups. It took more than a year of extensive inquiries among police and local community adults, coupled with field investigations, to locate a clearly drug-oriented group.

Although much criminal activity was found in nearly all groups, criminally oriented gangs such as those hypothesized by Cloward and Ohlin were equally difficult to locate. An incident related to our search for criminally oriented groups illustrates some of the limitations as well as the advantages of working with an action program such as the YMCA. We had begun to work with and study a gang of Negro boys who showed some "promise" of being drug users when it was discovered that theft and armed robbery were specializations of several of the boys, particularly of its leadership clique, known as the "Big Seven," and that drug use was quite incidental as a group activity. In the interest of further pursuing the nature of their theft activities, contact with the group was maintained. Shortly after this the worker reported that the leadership clique had outlined an elaborate "syndicate" type of organization of youngsters in the immediate area of the housing project where some of them lived, and they were in the process of attempting to carry out their plan. Each member of the clique was to be responsible for collections from gangs in his assigned territory. In return for "protection" from other gangs and counsel based upon their own expertise, the "syndicate" was to be paid a proportion of each gang's "take" from various illegal enterprises each week. This turn of events delighted us, but the plan was nipped in the bud by effective action by the worker and the police. The YMCA program did not hesitate to inform us what was happening, but, not surprisingly, they felt obligated to intervene. If the proposed syndicate had been an on-going reality, we would have had ample opportunity to observe it in action. Plans are a good deal easier to disrupt than are established patterns of behavior. Observation of group activities seldom was compromised as dramatically as in this instance. This is not to say that delinquent behavior by this group did not continue to be a problem—the armed robberies were not effectively contained until jobs were secured for the "Big Seven," and even then serious problems remained—only that the "syndicate" did not get off the ground. With respect to the total detached-worker effort, even large-scale gang conflict, which was sharply curtailed by the program in short order, remained a serious problem as a result of "cold war" tactics and occasional guerilla warfare between groups which threatened whatever uneasy equilibrium had been secured by the detached workers.

The failure to locate a full-blown criminal group, or more than one drug-using group, despite our highly motivated effort to do so, is a "finding" of some importance, for it casts doubt on the generality of these phenomena, if not on their existence. Our subsequent search for gangs to fit a research design based upon the typology of conflict, criminal, and retreatist gangs, and the analyses presented in this volume must be viewed against this background. We were led in the end to seek groups not primarily oriented around fighting, but with extensive involvement in the pursuit of "kicks" or various forms of theft. We hoped that systematic study of these groups would permit more precise identification of the nature of delinquent subcultures, either on the basis of between- or within-group behavioral differentiation. A partial report of these efforts is found in later chapters in this book.[18]

For the purpose of delineating behavior patterns of gang boys, then, we had gangs worked with by the Program for Detached Workers of the YMCA of Metropolitan Chicago over a period of three years from June, 1959, through August, 1962.[19] As gangs were added to the Program, always after consultation with the research team, we studied them through their detached workers and by various means of data generation. It was not possible to carry out the full range of these procedures on all gangs contacted. A few gangs broke up before we could learn much about them. One of these, a white gang in a racially transitional area, simply dissolved as a result of the fact that the boys' families moved out of the area to widely scattered locations

[18] See especially Chapters 4, 5, 6, 7, 9, and 10.

[19] The advantages and problems of action-research collaboration are discussed at greater length in James F. Short, Jr., "Notes on Action-Research Collaboration: Research Design and Some Not-So-Technical but Vital Problems," *Conference on Research Planning on Crime and Delinquency* (Youth Studies Center, University of Southern California, October, 1962, mimeographed).

in the city. A Negro conflict-oriented gang split into several cliques and various isolated individuals after "putting it down" (ceasing gang-conflict activities). The YMCA withdrew its worker with this group because it did not wish to reunite the boys, several of whom had left gang life altogether and were making conventional adjustments. Some gangs came into the program too late to receive the full "data treatment." In a few instances detached workers were unable to arrange for research operations to be carried out among the boys. Acceptance and co-operation in the field (and therefore field observation) was possible in all cases. Bringing the boys in for personality assessment or arranging for interviews and completion of paper and pencil tests sometimes proved to be extremely difficult.

The most detailed observational data were collected on 16 gangs ranging in size from 16 to 68 members and totaling 598 boys. Eleven of these gangs, with 464 members, were Negro; five with 134 members were whites. For these boys detached workers were our informants and they served as judges of which boys were members of the gangs at any given time. Additional data were gathered on other boys affiliated with these and other groups, for a total of twelve Negro gangs with 504 members in all and ten white gangs with 191 members. We shall return to the question of which data were collected from which gangs at a later point in the chapter.

Investigation of complex theories such as those discussed above requires more than study of gang boys. If we find that gang boys behave and perceive the world as one or another of the theories suggests, it may also be the case that non-gang boys do the same; or perhaps they behave differently but have the same types of backgrounds, aspirations, expectations, self-conceptions, and perceptions of opportunities as do gang boys. What, then, of the theories' explanatory powers? And what of youngsters in middle class sectors of the city? The theories are not always explicit as to how relevant variables should behave for middle class subjects, but differences certainly must be predicted and can be inferred from various positions.

Designs for study of questions such as these were complicated, again, by the nature of gangs and design decisions made in this respect. If gang youngsters could not be compiled into a list, neither could non-gang youngsters. After consultation with detached workers and personnel in other youth-serving agencies, and with colleagues in research, it was decided that selection of non-gang boys could be accomplished most efficiently and with reasonable validity by study-

ing the clientele of youth-serving agencies in the gang areas. Thus, non-gang boys in the Maxwell Street area, the "home" of one of our gangs, were selected from the Maxwell YMCA and a Chicago Boys' Club branch located one block from the main street of our gang. The gang boys in fact frequented both agencies when they were allowed to do so—a practice which was facilitated by the Program for Detached Workers. Personnel of these agencies agreed to produce for study boys who were not members of gangs and who were roughly of the same age as the gang boys. Detached workers confirmed at least the *current* non-gang status of boys so selected. Whether or not a boy is a member of a gang may, of course, change from time to time. For very few non-gang boys selected was there any evidence of prior gang membership, however. Findings from our research, some of which will be discussed at later points in this volume, suggest that these boys were likely not to affiliate with gangs at any future time, though this, of course, is open to conjecture. In any case, non-gang boys were selected from YMCA's, Boys' Clubs, Settlement Houses, Park District field houses, and other youth-serving agencies in the same areas where gangs we were studying were located. In all, 165 Negro boys from 14 groups and 117 white boys from four clubs or agencies were contacted. The number of clubs need not correspond to the number of gangs for matching purposes, since more than one gang or club may come from the same area. The number of boys contacted for processes of data collection in both gang and non-gang categories varied from time to time despite our efforts to maintain continuity in study populations. Comparative study of the variety of data collections undertaken suggest that the bias thus introduced is not a serious problem for interpretation of findings, as demonstrated where appropriate in later chapters.[20]

An ideal research design would have included both gang and non-gang middle class boys, as well as lower class boys in these categories. Gangs of middle class youngsters apparently are rare, however, despite mounting public concern over middle class delinquency.[21] We

[20] Preliminary analyses of data not covered in this book provide further encouragement on this point. See, for example, Ramon J. Rivera and James F. Short, Jr., "Occupational Goals: A Comparative Analysis," *Juvenile Gangs in Context: Theory, Research, and Action,* Malcolm Klein and Barbara Myerhoff, eds. (Conference Report, Youth Studies Center, University of Southern California, 1964).

[21] See, in addition to numerous references in the mass media, the theoretical, or more aptly pretheoretical, statements in this connection in the following

could not, in any case we did not, locate middle class gangs for study.[22] Hence, our design is without a "gang" category under middle class, as in Figure 1.2.

Selection of non-gang middle class subjects was governed in considerable measure by procedures followed for gang and non-gang lower class boys. It seemed desirable again to select club members rather than isolated or randomly located boys. For this purpose YMCA Hi-Y Clubs in middle class areas served admirably. Consultation with the Program Secretary of the Metropolitan office, and with executive secretaries of local associations resulted in the selection of

Social Class and Gang Status

RACE	LOWER CLASS		MIDDLE CLASS
	Gang	Non-Gang	
White			
Negro			

FIG. 1.2.—Research design: race by social class, by gang status.

two white and two Negro clubs, totaling thirty-four Negroes and fifty-four whites.[23]

Demographic data for the community areas from which our sub-

articles: Cohen and Short, op. cit., "Research in Delinquent Subcultures"; William C. Kvaraceus and Walter B. Miller, Delinquent Behavior: Culture and the Individual (National Education Association of the United States, 1959); Ralph W. England, Jr., "A Theory of Middle Class Delinquency," Journal of Criminal Law, Criminology, and Police Science (March–April, 1960), pp. 535–40; Robert H. Bohlke, "Social Mobility, Stratification Inconsistency, and Middle Class Delinquency," Social Problems, VIII (Spring, 1961), 351–63; Howard L. and Barbara G. Myerhoff, Field Observation of Middle Class "Gangs," Youth Studies Center, University of Southern California, 1962 (mimeographed).

[22] Although we did not know it at the time, Greeley and Casey report the existence during a portion of our period of study of a middle class gang in the same general area from which our middle class white subjects were selected. See Andrew Greeley and James Casey, "An Upper Middle Class Deviant Gang," American Catholic Sociological Review (Spring, 1963), pp. 33–41.

[23] The clubs were chosen from one YMCA with a white clientele. Racially integrated YMCA's were not considered for this purpose, since we wished to match the racially homogeneous lower class samples. We are indebted to John O. Root, Walter F. Worrill, and Leigh W. Kendrick for their considerable aid in reaching middle class boys, and especially to the boys themselves who co-operated so wholeheartedly.

jects were drawn are presented in Table 1.1. Differences in community milieu of subjects in lower and middle class categories and by race are quite apparent. Perhaps the most notable features of the data are the complete lack of overlap between white and Negro lower class areas in median income and the great advantage by any criterion of the white middle class community. The Negro middle class community clearly is "better off" than the Negro lower class communities, but they are more like lower class white communities than the white middle class insofar as socioeconomic characteristics are concerned. It is also the case that one of the two white middle class clubs consisted of the "cream of the YMCA crop." They would, individual-

TABLE 1.1

SELECTED DEMOGRAPHIC STATISTICS FOR
NEIGHBORHOODS OF SIX SAMPLES

SAMPLE AND COMMUNITY AREA FROM WHICH IT WAS DRAWN	STANDARDIZED PUBLIC ASSISTANCE RATE PER 1,000 PERSONS, 1952	MEDIAN INCOME FAMILIES, 1959	MEDIAN GROSS RENT, 1959	PERCENTAGE OF MALE WORKERS IN PROFESSIONAL OR TECHNICAL OCCUPATIONS, 1959
	Lower Class and Gang			
Negro:				
C.A. 8..............	71.1	$ 3,734	$ 69	2.7
C.A. 28.............	109.1	3,241	69	1.8
C.A. 29.............	46.6	4,860	98	1.0
C.A. 35.............	163.3	3,614	68	5.7
C.A. 36.............	165.5	3,417	72	1.0
C.A. 68.............	30.0	5,189	101	4.2
White:				
C.A. 7..............	18.5	6,195	78	11.2
C.A. 68.............	30.0			
Tracts 882, 883....		6,487	90	5.3
C.A. 69.............	19.2			
Tract 894.........		6,238	79	6.5
	Middle Class			
Negro, C.A. 44.....	6.1	7,054	119	7.4
White, C.A. 72.....	2.0	$11,437	$140	23.2

NOTE: All data for Negroes, except public assistance rate, given for non-whites only. Data for lower class and gang whites, except public assistance rate, corrected for proportion of non-whites in area, so that they apply more nearly to white neighborhoods. See Philip M. Hauser and Evelyn M. Kitagawa (eds.), *Local Community Fact Book for Chicago, 1950*, Chicago Community Inventory, University of Chicago (1953). Data for 1959 provided through the courtesy of Karl E. Taeuber.

ly and collectively, constitute ideal types of the white, middle class, protestant variety. Quite aside from racial differences, the Negro middle class boys varied considerably from this ideal-typical model.[24] These differences will be important to various phases of analyses to follow.

The diagram in Figure 1.2 accommodates research designs involving lower class gang and non-gang, and middle class comparisons for both Negro and white subjects (row comparisons) as well as racial comparisons for any social class and gang-status category (column comparisons). These designs, and comparisons of between- and within-gang variations as discussed above, lend themselves to study of various theoretical and empirical questions.

Precisely which questions are to be addressed is a major problem for every research project. For this too, of course, we were dependent in part on the theories of subcultural delinquency. As we began to consider specific questions raised by the theories and their operationalization for research purposes, it became apparent that the theories are couched primarily at one "level of explanation," namely, the *environment* of lower class youngsters. That is, they seek explanations for the boys' behavior in terms of the culture and social structure of the larger society (in the case of Merton, Cohen, Cloward and Ohlin) or of lower class culture (Miller). Other levels of explanation creep into their analyses, but they are largely ignored, assumed, or regarded as determined by the environment. Personality variables, for example, for all practical purposes are ignored. To the extent that group variables are treated at all in these theories, they are viewed as resulting from what Homans has called the "external system" of the group, i.e., relations among group members which solve the problem of survival in the environment.[25] For example, gang norms are explained by virtue of the operation of culture or in reaction to cultural and social structural forces. Their modification and the process by which they become translated into behavior through the internal development of the group are not dealt with. The "catalytic" nature of group interaction is suggested but not explored. Indeed, despite emphasis on the gang as an important context for delinquent behavior,

[24] For a recent discussion of ideal types, see Don Martindale, "Sociological Theory and the Ideal Type," *Symposium on Sociological Theory,* edited by Llewellyn Gross (Evanston: Row, Peterson & Co., 1959).

[25] George C. Homans, *The Human Group* (New York: Harcourt, Brace and Co., 1950), pp. 90 ff.

none of the theories explores systematically or abstractly the etiological importance of gang interaction.

These reflections on the theories we sought in some measure to address led us to focus—not always abstractly or systematically, but empirically in any case—on other levels of explanation in addition to the external system. Specifically, we sought by various means to discover the nature and the role of the following types of influences on gang boys and to a lesser extent—because we lacked the important resource of the detached-worker program for them—on non-gang boys:

1. *The environment*—the local and larger community of adults and institutions, backgrounds, perceptions of opportunities, aspirations and expectations of the boys. For this purpose field observation by detached workers[26] and the research team[27] provide broad documentation, as do demographic and ecological data.[28] Interviews of boys with this purpose as a primary objective were undertaken at the close of the first and throughout the second years of operation.[29] Weekly interviews with detached workers began early in the project and continued until August, 1962.[30] Reports by field observers extended over the same period.

[26] Detached workers interviewed most extensively over the three-year period of most intensive contact with the YMCA program were: Gene Anderson, Charles Brown, Lee Deering, George Dryden, William Gillmore, Fred Hubbard, Robert Jemilo, John LaMotte, Edgar Mitchell, Glenn Powell, Mike Riley, Benjamin Ross, and Albert Smith. Less extensive, but nonetheless important, interviews were held with Henry Bach, Lonnie Dillard, Paul McGuire, James Morita, Veronica Shaw, Leon Walker, and Henry Young. Field contact was maintained also with administrative personnel, including Richard W. Boone, Charles N. Cooper, and Kenneth Vallis. These and observers from the university research team served as cross checks on one another and supplemented and complemented each other in important ways.

[27] Field observers from the research team for the duration of the project were Lawrence Landry and Whitney Pope. They were joined for varying periods by Laura Thomasson Fishman, Jonathan Freedman, John Moland, and William Wright, and during the summer of 1961 by Frank Cherry.

[28] Daniel Parrish and Ray A. Tennyson provided valuable assistance in the analyses of demographic and ecological data.

[29] Ramon J. Rivera supervised construction of the interview schedule, interviewer training and interviewing, and coding of the data. Interviewers were drawn from NORC rosters and from other projects, and were especially trained for this project.

[30] Ray A. Tennyson did most of the interviewing of detached workers, with occasional supplementation by the Director and various other staff members of the research team. See Ray A. Tennyson, "Detached Workers as Sources of Data," paper read at the annual meeting of the Society for the Study of Social Problems, 1960.

2. *Characteristics of individuals*—Self-concepts of the boys were explored by means of a paired-comparison instrument which was part of a battery of paper and pencil self-reports administered in the field during the spring of 1960 and throughout the following year.[31] Assessment of values, motivations, intelligence, and personality characteristics was undertaken in research headquarters at the University of Chicago late in the summer of 1960 and continued for approximately a year and a half.[32]

3. *Norms of the group*—Field observations are our most valuable guide to group norms. These are supplemented by various sociometric devices in combination with study of individual characteristics.

4. *Group process*—The rich literature of small groups research and theory has not been applied or followed up with respect to gang behavior. We sought a measure of redress for this situation in an effort to determine the processes by which variables at the three levels of explanation, above, become translated into behavior. As our analysis has proceeded these have been conceptualized chiefly in terms of status-maintaining mechanisms of the group. Their investigation has been largely through analysis of behavior episodes reported by detached workers and observers from the research team.

The total number of boys under observation and contacted for various research purposes is impossible to determine due to the shifting nature of the field situation and because we did not ask workers and observers to compile lists of boys observed each time they were in the field. The number of boys for whom bodies of more specific data were collected is listed in Table 1.2. In addition to those discussed earlier, a "baseline assessment" of gang boys and a police record search of all boys is included. The baseline assessment consisted of a series of questions which the detached workers were asked to answer regarding each member of their gang(s) upon two occasions—during the fall of 1959 or after a minimum of six months' contact, whichever occurred later, and in late winter and spring of 1961,

---

[31] Self-report instruments were drafted by members of the Youth Studies staff in meetings with the Director. Field observers, with assistance from detached workers and other agency personnel when appropriate, administered the battery of self-reports. Patricia Hodge coded the reports and, together with Ellen Kolegar, carried out much of the data analysis. Jack Sawyer provided valuable consultation concerning data analysis.

[32] Desmond S. Cartwright supervised construction and administration of the assessment of values, intelligence, motivations, and personality traits. Kenneth I. Howard assisted in all phases of the project and assumed direction of test administration and, in consultation with Cartwright, directed analyses of all but the values data after Cartwright moved to the University of Colorado. The values instrument was administered and data later analyzed by Robert A. Gordon.

TABLE 1.2

NUMBER OF BOYS IN GROUPS (PSEUDONYMS) INCLUDED IN RESEARCH
DESIGNS OF THE YOUTH STUDIES PROGRAM, BY RACE, CLASS, AND
GANG STATUS CATEGORY AND DATA GENERATION PROCEDURE[a]

CATEGORY AND GROUP	No. of Boys, by Data Generation Procedure				
	Values and Personality Assessment	Interviews	Self-reports	Baseline Assessment	Police Records
Negro Gang					
01 Midget Knights........	24	21	31	68	54
02 Junior Knights.........	....	3	6	55	56
03 Vice Kings............	....	....	....	55	....
05 Senior Rattlers........	23	27	33	58	58
06 Junior Rattlers........	8	6	....	....	....
09 Chiefs................	20	20	24	29	42
10 Garden Gang..........	32	35	38	44	44
11 Mighty Peewees........	12	12	10	19	19
15 Southside Rattlers.....	19	24	17	48	57
20 Vandals...............	19	25	27	46	47
21 Midget Vandals........	19	15	16	21	28
23 Navahoes.............	10	17	15	21	22
Subtotal.............	186	205	217	464	427
Negro Non-Gang					
31 Knights Area Guys.....	10	....	....	....	2
33 Vandals Area Guys.....	1	....	....	....	....
35 Rattler Area Guys.....	5	....	....	....	....
39 Chiefs Area Guys......	2	....	....	....	....
45 Southside Rattler Area Guys.................	4	....	....	....	....
70 Illini Club.............	....	....	9	....	9
73 Boys, Inc.............	....	....	8	....	8
90 Garden Project Guys...	14	16	16	....	18
91 Hawks................	8	9	12	....	12
92 Market St. Y..........	16	15	24	....	26
93 Market Boys, Inc.......	10	10	9	....	11
94 North Project Center...	5	18	30	....	29
97 Menlo................	....	....	8	....	7
98 Freedom Center.......	17	21	19	....	....
Subtotal.............	92	89	135	....	122

[a] Code numbers were assigned to facilitate group identification.

TABLE 1.2—*Continued*

CATEGORY AND GROUP	NO. OF BOYS, BY DATA GENERATION PROCEDURE				
	Values and Personality Assessment	Interviews	Self-reports	Baseline Assessment	Police Records
Negro Middle Class					
95 Alphas..............	15	14	17	....	19
96 Omegas..............	9	12	14	....	15
Subtotal............	24	26	31	....	34
White Gang					
13 Amboys..............	3	22	20	38	43
14 Bengals, Sharks, Cues...	8	17	19	....	26
16 Coyotes..............	16	15	15	....	....
17 Aces................	....	6	15	18	19
18 Ravens..............	4	1	....	16	15
22 Pizza Grill...........	9	19	....	39	40
24 Pill Poppers..........	....	2	....	23	....
25 Triumphs............	8	7	....	....	....
Subtotal............	48	89	69	134	143
White Non-Gang					
12 Park Guys...........	8	12	11	....	21
72 Gresham Y...........	....	12	11	....	30
74 Gary's Guys..........	....	6	9	....	8
81 St. Paul Settlement.....	29	44	51	....	58
Subtotal............	37	74	82	....	117
White Middle Class					
85 Admirals Hi-Y.........	26	34	34	....	34
86 Eagles Hi-Y...........	15	19	20	....	17
Subtotal............	41	53	54	....	51
Total..............	428	536	588	598	894

with the same proviso concerning worker contact.[33] Questions asked concerned specific items of behavior (see Chapter 4), age, roles in the group, friendships, sources of income of the boy and his family, frequency of police, court, and correctional institution experience, and extent and nature of worker contact with the boy. The police record search was conducted during the summer of 1960 on all boys included in any group roster available to us at the time.[34] It will be noted that this procedure is the most inclusive of all. Two gangs, the Vice Kings (03) and Pill Poppers (24), were added to the project after the record search. The Vice Kings were the last group to be included in the baseline assessment, and even this was feasible only because the detached worker with that group knew them exceptionally well by virtue of contact while he was employed by another agency. The Pill Poppers simply proved to be inaccessible except for field observation. We attempted repeatedly to carry out other methods of data collection without success.[35] This was the only gang where such difficulty was encountered. In a few cases boys were trimmed from gang rosters for purposes of the baseline assessment in an attempt to be more realistic concerning gang membership during our period of observation. Similarly, boys were added to rosters as observation suggested they should be, the most notable instance of this being the Midget Knights (01). Two groups, the Junior Knights (02) and Aces (17), were dropped from the project before most data-collection procedures could be carried out with them. Four groups, the Bengals, Sharks, and Cues (14) and the Triumphs (25) were added for various studies—but not the baseline assessment, because our workers did not know them well enough to make such a report—in order to bolster the white-gang cell in our research design.

[33] Ray A. Tennyson conducted the baseline assessment on both occasions.

[34] John Wise was responsible for the police record search. See his Master's thesis at the University of Chicago, "A Comparison of Sources of Data as Indexes of Delinquent Behavior," 1962. Thanks are due Captains Delaney and McInerny of the Chicago Police Department, and to various members of their staffs for permission and assistance in the record search.

[35] The detached worker with this group was an excellent observer in the field, as confirmed by independent reports of two observers from the research team. And, although he occasionally brought boys to the research offices for purposes of observation—usually one of the boys would be under the influence of drugs, at the tail-end of a three or four day "binge"—he was unable, apparently, to motivate them to be interviewed, tested, or to complete paper and pencil instruments. This is not to say that the fault was entirely the worker's. We were likewise unsuccessful.

Once contacted, middle class subjects were the easiest to study. They made and kept appointments despite heavy activity schedules, and they seemed eager to perform any task assigned them.[36] Furthermore, they "stood still" in the sense that it was easy to maintain contact with them from one data collection to another. By contrast, lower class non-gang boys were the most difficult to study and to maintain contact with. We had no detached workers to rely on for this purpose, and other agency personnel tended not to have close personal relationships with these boys such as characterized detached-workers' relations with most of their boys. This varied from group to group, of course. In some instances detached workers also facilitated contact with non-gang boys. This was especially true for values and personality assessment of Negro non-gang "area guys," and for all data collection among the Garden Project Guys and the white Park Guys. A few of these boys were contacted for only one assessment, though in nearly all cases we attempted to maintain continuity from one project to another.

It will be clear from the foregoing that while initial impetus for the study was provided by recent theories which seek to account for the emergence and on-going functioning of delinquent subcultures as a result of cultural and social-structural factors, from the very beginning it was determined not to limit ourselves to investigation of these. This decision was based upon our conviction (1) that too little is known descriptively of the nature of "delinquent gangs," and (2) that existing theories, even if confirmed, left unanswered many questions concerning the behavior of gang youngsters. As a result, we employed two very different research strategies. The first was designed to test in the traditional hypothetical-deductive manner hypotheses drawn from alternative theories in the recent literature. For this purpose instruments and designs were drawn which would bear directly on specific hypotheses. Even with respect to these, however, it seemed necessary to go beyond hypotheses which could be inferred from existing theories. We turned, therefore, to a second strategy which may be broadly described as *retroductive* in nature. That is, we sought to expose ourselves to data not specifically relevant to existing

---

[36] A Youth Studies Program staff member (Whitney Pope) who had been administering the self-report battery to gang subjects accompanied the Director to assist in administering the instruments to white middle class boys. The evening went very smoothly, without "horseplay" or disruptions of any sort. After the session Mr. Pope remarked, "Now I know why there are so many studies of white middle class subjects!"

hypotheses concerning gang delinquency and thereby to stimulate new perspectives and hypotheses. In this respect we have written in an earlier version of Chapter 6:[37]

The old dichotomy between hypotheses based upon theory and radical empiricism is no longer clear. It has become commonplace to use the term serendipity[38] to describe the process of empirically discovering one thing while looking for another. While serendipity is a welcome addition to descriptions of the discovery process, it is not accurate in terms of the objectives of the present study. Our objective has been to expose ourselves over a three-year period to a flow of quite heterogeneous observations of the behavior of delinquent gangs. There is a clear expectation of surprises to be found in the data and willingness to be distracted by such surprises. The essential characteristic of this *retroductive* perspective is that the investigator who exposes himself to a flow of data accepts the responsibility of formulating hypotheses which, if true, would remove the surprise in the observation in question.

This perspective required that we "keep a window open" on gangs with which the detached workers were in contact over an extended period. Weekly interviews with detached workers served this purpose well, and they facilitated also maintenance of working relationships with these men for other purposes, such as arranging for field contacts by observers and interviewers from the research team and bringing in boys for laboratory assessment.

It must be clear, also, that in many instances we were dealing with matters for which standardized instruments did not exist. We were forced to be inventive; hopefully, we were creative. Even when standardized instruments existed, we felt it necessary to test their validity, especially for gang and other lower class subjects, and the substance of some instruments was changed while in others the form was altered.[39]

This book presents analyses principally of field observations by

[37] Fred L. Strodtbeck, James F. Short, Jr., and Ellen Kolegar, "The Analysis of Self-Descriptions by Members of Delinquent Gangs," *The Sociological Quarterly* (October, 1962), pp. 331–56.

[38] See Leo A. Goodman, "Notes on the Etymology of Serendipity and Some Related Philological Observations," *Modern Language Notes,* LXXVI (May, 1961), 454–57.

[39] See especially Chapter 3 for Robert A. Gordon's testing of semantic-differential scales. Desmond S. Cartwright and Kenneth I. Howard have in preparation a mongraph describing their use and in some instances revision of standard personality tests.

detached workers and observers from the research team, and from values, self-reports, and baseline assessments. Occasionally we draw upon data from interviews and police records, and from other sources such as the United States Census. Principal analyses of interview data, which in many instances bear directly on the social-structural theories, are or will be published elsewhere.[40] The chapters in the book are arranged roughly in the order in which they were written. Early chapters, written without knowledge of what might develop in later research, have not been extensively revised. While this mode of exposition makes some imposition upon the reader, it is hoped that the degree to which it has enabled us to report the natural history of our work will make the book of greater value to students of research process.

[40] Preliminary reports of these data include Jonathan Freedman and Ramon J. Rivera, "Education, Social Class, and Patterns of Delinquency," read at the annual meetings of the American Sociological Association, 1962; James F. Short, Jr., Ramon J. Rivera, and Ray A. Tennyson, "Perceived Opportunities, Gang Membership, and Delinquency," *American Sociological Review*, XXX (February, 1965); Rivera and Short, "Occupational Goals . . . ," *op. cit.*; and Ray A. Tennyson, "Family Structure and Delinquent Behavior," *Juvenile Gangs in Context: Theory, Research, and Action*, Malcolm W. Klein and Barbara G. Myerhoff, eds., Conference Report, Youth Studies Center, University of Southern California, 1964; and James F. Short, Jr., "Gang Delinquency and Anomie," *Anomie and Deviant Behavior*, Marshall B. Clinard, ed. (New York: The Free Press of Glencoe, Inc., 1964). The other papers eventually will be published in one form or another.

CHAPTER 2

A Strategy for Utilizing Research Dilemmas: A Case from the Study of Parenthood in a Street-Corner Gang

In the present chapter we shall consider two topics simultaneously. Our main task will be to present three different but interrelated types of observations concerning a street-corner gang and illegitimate parenthood. Our secondary objective will be to share with the reader the dilemmas we encountered in selecting these data and deciding upon an appropriate form in which to communicate them.

Turning first to the secondary objective, we note that as data unfold during a field research project, insights and questions arise which require relatively quick decisions by the investigator. The decisions relate to types of data to be gathered, selection of appropriate methodology, latent interpretations that one has in mind, and indeed the very possibility of findings beyond the intended scope of the original research. The sharpest consciousness of the weight of such decisions comes at times when some of the data are in and one faces the problem of the further allocation of energies. These are short-lived and sometimes painful moments in the research process which give maximum opportunity to make "creative" decisions. Once further commitments are made, the claim to attention of a rejected path weakens rapidly. It is likely not to be reported in research publications, since one wishes to have paths followed seem intrinsically superior to those neglected.

Even research efforts which are self-consciously designed to generate new data often are rationalized and tidied in the final reports

This chapter was published in *Sociological Inquiry*, XXXII (Spring, 1962), 185–202, and was co-authored by Desmond S. Cartwright. It was read originally at the annual meetings of the Society for Social Research at the University of Chicago, 1961.

and thereby stripped of the spirit of discovery. This may be prudent in the final reports for it emphasizes the degree to which systematic, inclusive, closed theories are desired. At the same time, it is also true that there is much to be gained by the examination of partial data from a variety of theoretical perspectives before the requirements of theoretical closure cut off the richness of detail and related possibilities of discovery.

Many investigators find themselves with bits of information from paths of inquiry which they find interesting but do not exploit fully. It is difficult to have such data speak very convincingly for themselves, for on the points of possible excitement, they are likely to lack statistical significance. A fully conceptualized theoretical analysis ordinarily is not possible, because in many instances the concepts being used are very closely related to concrete observations rather than to established theoretical systems.

This chapter attempts to wrestle self-consciously with the role of reports which make available empirical observations that are either unanticipated, or poorly accounted for, by initial research designs or by existent theories. Projects differ in the degree to which an exposure to unanticipated results is courted. The relevance of the present methodological concern is greatest for projects which, like the present one, have theoretical considerations embedded in the original designs, but which also provide for the accommodation of alternative designs on the basis of data encountered in various project phases. This is an aspect of research design which relates to the stimulation of new hypotheses, which if verified, will modify currently accepted theory. In the language of Peirce, and in most analyses of the scientific process, it is an attempt to do something about the *retroductive*,[1] in addition to the *inductive* or *deductive,* logical operations in scientific process.

The argument will become clearer in terms of an example taken from our current study of "delinquent gangs" in Chicago. The data in question serve our methodological purposes well. We shall be concerned with the behavior of only twenty-five street-corner gang members. This forecloses elaborate statistical analysis. In addition, our dependent variable will be whether or not the gang member has become a parent. This type of variable leaves the range of relevant theory both unspecified and almost unlimited. Finally, we are inter-

---

[1] See Fred L. Strodtbeck, "The Case for Pragmatism in Social Psychology," forthcoming in *Sociometry.*

ested in how group process, cultural expectations, and personality differences are implicated in each of the aspects of juvenile delinquency we investigate. The concern about parenthood was not stressed in the original project design, and the information which is available was in all instances collected with other purposes explicitly in mind. Additionally, it seems unlikely that the research program will have resources to pursue the matter much further. We will describe the initial inquiry, introduce the materials bearing on the group, cultural, and personality perspectives, then return to the question of the role of this type of fugitive information in scientific inquiry.

Initial Inquiry

During the summer of 1959, prior to the beginning of the Youth Studies Program, a staff member of the Program for Detached Workers of the YMCA of Metropolitan Chicago interviewed core members of his street-corner group (the Chiefs) concerning the boys' views of family relationships. Specifically he sought answers to three questions: (1) What are the relationships existing in your family as you perceive them? (2) What do you think the ideal family relationship should be? (3) What kind of relationship will you establish as head of a family?

The Chiefs were a "delinquent gang" of twenty-four boys and one girl. This is a group which has had extensive contacts with the police and with institutions for the treatment of delinquents. They were all Negroes between fifteen and twenty years of age at the time of the initial inquiry. The first interviews with twelve core members were carried out by the detached worker in the course of his usual field contacts with the boys in his car, in local restaurants, or in the local park. Questions were not asked formally, but were introduced in the vernacular of the street and in an open-ended fashion when the worker was alone with a particular boy.

The boys described *existing* relationships in a manner familiar to students of lower class Negro families, i.e., mothers were described as being in control of within-family decisions, while fathers often were undependable or inconsistent and domineering in their relations with children.[2] *Ideal* family relationships approached such middle-

[2] See E. Franklin Frazier, *The Negro Family in the United States* (Chicago: University of Chicago Press, 1939).

class standards as small size, job stability, and marital fidelity. The worker's report captures the boys' sentiments:

The father, in each member's opinion, should be a reliable breadwinner. In addition to this, he should exhibit and exercise more interest than did their own fathers in the activities of the children, especially the male children. The majority of the boys felt that the father should be allowed some time which was strictly his own and was not to be accounted for to his wife and family.

Differences of opinion occurred when the question was asked, "What is to be done by the father during this time?" All of the fellows, except the one whose father had been killed in a gambling argument, felt that it was permissible for him to do on his own anything that he would enjoy, providing it did not interfere with his family life. This meant that a father should be allowed to "go out and take a few drinks and get a little high, but not come home drunk except maybe a couple of times a year on holidays or something, and when he comes home drunk, he ain't to mess around with his wife or kids, but he's to go on to bed and sleep it off." This also meant that he could "gamble a little with his partners after he had left the bread (money) for the house and paid all the bills." It also meant, "He could go out and eyeball the broads, and maybe even get a piece every now and then, but he ain't supposed to let one of those no good broads get his nose open (get him attracted) to the point where he is going to fuck over his family."

The boy whose father had been killed differed from the remainder of the boys and held fast to his opinion that a father "shouldn't go out drinking, gambling and fucking around with the broads. If he wants to go into a pool room and shoot a couple of games and bullshit with the boys that's all right, but that's all he should do."

The boys were generally in accord as to the role of the wife-mother of the family. They all agreed that a wife should work until she becomes pregnant. There were two reasons for this advanced by the boys, one of them being that she should do everything she could to help in a financial manner in preparation for the future, and the other reason being well expressed by the boys as, "What the hell is she goin' to be doin' all day while I'm off working?"

All the boys felt that they should have children and they were united in the feeling that the families should not have a large number of children. The boys' objecting to families larger than three or four were based again, on economic considerations. As one boy said, "It's hard enough to keep you and your wife straight without having a houseful of kids to look after."

All the boys expressed more concern about the welfare of the male child than of the female. The attitude most often expressed about the female child was, "I'm goin' to let my wife take care of that."

The attitude toward the male child was mainly expressed as, "I'm goin' to make sure that he don't spend too much time in the pool room and messin' around with wine and that kind of stuff. He ain't goin' to be no sissy or nothin' like that, you understand, but I just don't want him to fuck up too much." All the boys felt that their male children should have some kind of a part-time job while they were in high school. However, they were careful to say that the kids should not work so hard that they wouldn't want to go to school. *Most of the fellows felt that they should do everything possible to make the boys want to go to school;* however, if it appeared that the child was not doing too well or didn't want to go, there would be no objections to his quitting, provided that when he quit he got himself a job. All of the boys were against the proposition of a young boy neither going to school nor working.

In response to the third question, "What kind of relationship will you establish in your family?" the worker found that the boys "stuck to their guns and described this situation in terms of their description of the *ideal* relationship in a family." There was general recognition that their marriages might not work out, due to anticipated *economic* problems. All insisted that the husband should have a "good job" or a "steady job" as a basis for a successful marriage.

There was no anticipation of a marriage without children, nor of the use of contraception to defer their arrival. The worker found the boys to be ignorant of all but the rudimentary forms of birth control involving condoms and withdrawal, and to these they were unreceptive. Recorded comments included: "Man, you ain't always got time," "Sometimes you forget," and "It's better without all that stuff."

As a follow-up to the individual interviews, the worker brought the twelve Chiefs interviewed together for a group session on the same family questions. The results, in the words of the worker, "were rather disappointing."

The group refused to get serious about the subject. Individuals who did attempt to say something seriously were ridiculed and kidded a lot. The worker was able to maintain only a minimum of order during the entire session. For example, one fellow would say something referring to "my wife" and immediately comments would arrive of the nature of, "Who in the hell is going to marry you?" and "You mean that bear that lives down on 35th Street?" No one could continue facing this kind of opposition. The number of boys who were not going to get married rose from the three indicated in individual interviews to five at the group session. Many ideas about the propriety of conduct in husband-wife relationship which had been expressed in individual interviews were not voiced at all. . . . The one boy whose father had been killed and who had rather strict ideas about the duties of a husband toward his family, was conspicuously quiet. He said not a word all during the discussion. The group attitude at this session toward marriage and the family could be described as a "devil-may-care," "rake-hell" expression of male chauvinism.

The worker's interpretation of the boys' behavior was that considerations of status within the group inhibited endorsement of middle class family norms while in the group setting. The group norms clearly were not consistent with the attitudes and expectations expressed in the individual interviews. The worker felt certain that the boys were not "conning" him in the interviews and, at the same time, there is no reason to doubt that, to some degree, they were also expressing genuinely held sentiments and values in the group situation.

We did not know which, if either, of the expressed attitudes would be consistent with courtship behavior. It was possible that the perception of the group position might have been such as to cause each boy to believe that his more middle class ideas about family behavior were idiosyncratic. This would not matter if the boy perceived that the interest of the group was limited to his actions in the group situation. However, if his actions away from the group were to be assessed by the group standards, then behavior demonstrating an exploitative attitude toward females might be important to the maintenance of high rank in the group.

In another similar gang, we know of a boy who acknowledged enjoying a trip to the museum with his girl friend, but who refused to have anything more to do with her after she "squared" him with the group by "telling everybody about it." Causing a girl to conceive, however, may be quite a different matter. If it has no effect on rank in the group, then group process is not likely to influence such behavior. If it has a negative effect, then those who illegitimately impregnate girls may be expected to stop hanging with the group. If the effect is to increase rank in the group, then we may conclude that group process supports illegitimate conceptions as well as the related sexual activities.

Sociometric Concomitants of Fatherhood

At the time of the first interviews, three of the core members of the Chiefs had fathered illegitimate children. One of them was at the time living with the mother of his child at the home of her parents in a relationship which might be classified as a "common-law" marriage. One other had married the girl after the birth of their child. All of the boys had been having sex relations with girls for at least several months.

Eighteen months later, despite movement of members into and out of the group, it was possible to determine which of the Chiefs were known to be the fathers of illegitimate children. This information is summarized for core and non-core members for both the eighteen-month and a two-year period in Table 2.1.

TABLE 2.1

ILLEGITIMACY AMONG THE CHIEFS AT THREE TIME PERIODS

TIME	CORE MEMBERS		NON-CORE MEMBERS	
	Illegitimate Parents	Non-illegitimate Parents	Illegitimate Parents	Non-illegitimate Parents
Initial inquiry......	3	9	2	11
18 months later....	6[a]	6[b]	4[c]	9[d]
24 months later....	8[e]	4[b]	4[c]	9[d, f]

[a] Includes two boys who had joined the armed services since the initial inquiry, and two who were serving short jail terms.

[b] Includes one boy who had left the group after graduating from high school—one year after the initial inquiry.

[c] Includes one boy who was serving a term in prison for manslaughter and one who was in jail for a short term.

[d] Includes three boys who had married and left the group entirely by this time.

[e] Includes two boys who had joined the armed services since the initial inquiry, one of the two who had been in jail (see note a above), and one who had, by this time, ceased association with the group.

[f] At 22 months, an additional two boys were in jail for extended terms and there was one additional boy who only rarely frequented the corner at this time—these three are included along with the three accounted for in footnote d.

There was a continuous increase in illegitimate parenthood between the initial inquiry and the two follow-up periods, particularly among the core members. No stable marriages were found among the boys who remained with the group, though, as noted above, two of the boys interviewed at the time of the initial inquiry had established temporary family relationships with the mothers of their children. Three boys in the non-core group had married and left the group. Only one of the illegitimate core-group fathers had chosen to marry the mother of his child and this marriage was short-lived. The lone female member of the group, who at the time of the initial inquiry was reported by the worker as sexually inaccessible to the boys and "able to take care of herself," had, during the ensuing eighteen months, borne a child out of wedlock by one of the members of the group.

At the time of the twenty-four-month follow-up a higher proportion of non-core than core boys had left the Chiefs, although at this time even the core members had ceased to be very cohesive or to act in concert except under such conditions as an athletic contest. At this time, the summer of 1961, a brief and futile attempt was made at formal reorganization of the group, and new fringe members were given formal recognition as members. This attempt was short-lived, however. Within an additional six months, the Chiefs virtually had lost their identity and their detached worker was concentrating his efforts on two other groups in the area who were beginning to come into their own as troublemakers.

The sociometric assessment was made at two points in this cycle of three summers. The first three-by-five card request to list best friends first, next best, and so on down the line was made three months after the initial individual and family interviews by the group worker. Sixteen boys present at a group meeting were involved. We need not examine these data in detail, except to note that illegitimate paternity, as such, at this time apparently did not confer status nor did it detract from status. Some core members were illegitimate fathers, others were not. Some of the most popular boys were illegitimate fathers, others were not.

Nearly a year later, during the summer of 1960, a second friendship choice test in which unlimited choice was allowed was administered to 21 Chiefs by staff members of our research team. This test indicated that, if ranks are established in terms of most to fewest choices received, the nine illegitimate fathers present at this time received ranks (3, 3, 5.5, 10.5, 10.5, 10.5, 15.5, 18.5, 18.5)[3] which averaged 10.6, a non-significant departure from the expected value of 11.0. Illegitimate fathers did give 28 per cent of their choices outside the Chiefs in contrast with 19 per cent for non-fathers and they also made more choices. However, for the within-group exchange of choices, the percentage of potential choices which were actually utilized did not vary greatly.

From illegitimate parents to: illegitimate parents = 24%
                              non-parents   = 24%
From non-parents to: non-parents   = 15%
                              illegitimate parents = 18%

[3] Allowing for ties.

Thus, on the point of interest, parents and non-parents show no tendency to form cliques.

It is of interest that as of the twenty-four-month follow-up, two of the three non-fathers among the initial core group who remained with the group and one of the non-fathers among the non-core group were "going with," and having sex relations with, girls who were pregnant. It appears, however, that these girls were pregnant at the time these boys began to have sex relations with them. Although the gang knew the facts, they got mileage out of the situation in several ways. For example, the mildest-mannered of the three was being kidded that he was the father. On the other hand, one of the three known to be quite experienced was kidded that he was being "suckered"—particularly after he helped buy baby clothes—to pay for someone else's baby.

The light tenor of the joking about paternity involvements is consistent with the relative lack of relation between paternity status and rank in the group. The anomaly is that making sexual contacts with girls is *not* unrelated to status. That this degree of demonstration of masculinity is necessary may be inferred from the case of the lowest status long-time member of the Chiefs. He was a tall, thin, boyish-looking non-father who had never enjoyed high status in the group and who, for some time, consorted with a well-known local homosexual from whom he received money for his attentions. This boy, the detached workers and some members of the Chiefs have noted, felt the need to "build a rep." The worker reported that *this* boy "would be in seventh heaven if he could get a girl pregnant"—this specifically because of his non-masculine "rep" in the group. For the great majority of the boys, however, the causing of a pregnancy would not be salient to the attainment of higher rank.

The Cultural Matrix

The concern of the corner group with heterosexual activity and the lack of concern with the pregnancies which ensue does not grow in isolation from Negro lower class culture. In addition, it does not seem to develop in opposition to any particular middle class standard. Our analysis is not very different from Walter Miller's, even though we have approached the organization of our observations in terms of the background for group process, instead of using more direct modes of cultural assessment.

The area where the Chiefs "hang," and where most of them live, is an area of high physical deterioration which gradually is being torn down by urban-redevelopment programs. It is an area of high illegitimacy, juvenile and adult crime, and drug use. The worker's description of typical summer evenings gives greater detail concerning the group adaptation.

What happens is during the summer months the boys will come out and sit on the bench and they all sing their "Du-waps." They drink the wine and smoke the reefers and drink beer. Then they'll play with the girls in a rassling sort of fashion. Some of them that are not too juvenile . . . the real lovers like Jake and Billy . . . they just pull the girl off to the side and start rapping to her. As it goes on, the park becomes emptier and the young children and old folks go in. Jake will lay a broad right on the bench but most of them will take the girl off somewhere to one of these junked cars and lay her there, or if Brown (a drug pushing and using young man in the area) is around they might be able to get a key to one of the pads up there. They'll discuss who's fucking and who's not, how much time it takes for this one and how much time it takes for that one.

The permissive character of the adult community can be illustrated by the fact that a father might approach a boy and ask him to "be careful" and not "get the girl in trouble" rather than to stop sexual relations. A "new father" among the Chiefs explained what the girl's parents thought of his being the illegitimate father of their daughter's child by saying, "Oh, they'll go along with the program so long as I bring in milk money." Milk money was defined as "maybe $5 a month." After Aid to Dependent Children assistance has been regularized, the boys sometimes receive small amounts from the mothers of their children.

While adolescent practices do not generally contrast with adult practices, the value of stable legitimate marriages clearly is not shared by the street-corner group. Evidence from the group interview reported earlier may be buttressed by the behavior of a group of Chiefs observed on a spring afternoon in 1960, when a former Chief, now married, walked past the corner with his wife. The worker's account follows:

> . . . Jackson (the former Chief) had the baby in his arms; and such howling, clapping, and carrying on—they were razzing him.
> Q: Razzing him for being a legitimate father?
> A: Legitimate father walking around the street with his baby. Then Billy said, "Let me shut up 'cause I might be out walkin' my baby. You, too, Henry." Henry said, "Not me. I ain't walkin' nobody's baby."

Members of street-corner groups such as the Chiefs often enter directly into the serial monogamy mating patterns which have been described for other lower class segments of the population. Whiting and Miller have used the term "female-based" household to emphasize the potency this pattern confers upon the mother.[4] These mothers keep their children and function as the stable source of authority and resources. Miller notes the rich fantasy life of lower class girls concerning marriage and family life, but reports "for some girls, an almost fatalistic conviction that the ideal could never be realized."[5] The following quote from a detached worker with the Chiefs suggests that when pregnancy occurs, different generations of women in the area exchange pointers on the search for a father.

There are older women in the area—25 to 35 years old—who have really been around and lived a life on the streets. They don't generally have a steady man, but they'll latch on to a younger man, say 18 to 21, and get his nose open (i.e., attract him) for a while so he pays for the groceries while he's living with them. These arrangements don't last long so these women are always on the make. So the younger girls can see this going on and they talk to the older women about how to hook the boys. Pleased to have the younger ones think they know how to make suckers out of men, the older ones talk and talk about how to get a boy to pay for the baby.

It is apparent that this system is relatively free of adult control when compared with the lower class Italian system described by Whyte.[6] It does not force, indeed it does not *allow*, "individual role bargains" in the manner of "polish Parish," as described by Green[7] or the lower class Caribbean area described by Goode.[8] Rather, role bargains concerning sex relations take place within the context of peer-group interaction which is not specifically oriented toward

4 Roger V. Burton and John W. M. Whiting, "The Absent Father: Effects on the Developing Child," paper read at the annual meetings of the American Psychological Association, 1960; Walter B. Miller, "Implications of Lower Class Culture for Social Work," *The Social Service Review*, XXXIII (September, 1959).

5 Walter B. Miller, "Female Sexual and Mating Behavior," *City Gangs: Cultural Milieu, Customary Behavior, and Delinquency*, forthcoming (dittoed).

6 William F. Whyte, "A Slum Sex Code," *American Journal of Sociology*, XLIX (July, 1943), 24–31.

7 Arnold W. Green, "The 'Cult of Personality' and Sexual Relations," *Psychiatry*, IV (August, 1941), 344–48.

8 William J. Goode, "Illegitimacy in the Caribbean Social Structure," *American Sociological Review*, XXV (February, 1960), 21–30.

marriage. Sex is a valued commodity for boys in this street-corner society because sexual prowess is highly valued as an indication of masculinity, ranking with skill in fighting and athletics. For girls, skilful employment of their sex provides prestige, and a way of coping with the physical power of the male-dominated peer society.

Viewed from the perspective of the individual adolescent, Negro street-corner society provides a high degree of sexual stimulation. The sexual outlets are available and contraception costs money and is distracting. While the exposure to conception is high, this is quite different from saying that pregnancies are sought. It is notable that the exposure takes place under conditions in which pregnancy does not carry an implied obligation between boy and girl that they will marry. For the boy we assume there is little anxiety. For the girl there is probably some anxiety each month but when the pregnancy eventually occurs, there are also some rewards.

Goode has suggested that where a high rate of illegitimacy is observed, the stigma suffered by the average illegitimate child cannot be great relative to the legitimate child in his stratum and neighborhood. This is no less true for illegitimate parenthood. Other investigators have found support for this hypothesis in three areas for the lower class Negro girl.

Miller points out that, for the lower class girl in general, "In a situation where girls controlled few really persuasive devices to bring about an agreement of marriage, it was always possible to hope that the knowledge by one's mating partner that he was your baby's father would serve as the critical factor which would tip the scale in favor of such an agreement."[9] In addition, "A girl who felt her acceptance by the community endangered by a worsening 'reputation' as 'cheap' could semi-deliberately court pregnancy, knowing that the advent of a child would reverse the process by which she was being excluded, and would produce active reimmersement in group life."[10] Thus, with regard to the larger community, the baby might land the husband, and, in many cases, it could change a role definition from "bum" to "unmarried mother."

In the home, also, there might be possible gains. Again in Miller's words, he suggests that bearing a child may secure desired attention for the girl, primarily from her mother, her female kin peers, and, also, the female social worker. It may "strengthen affiliation with

9 Miller, "Female Sexual and Mating Behavior," *op. cit.*, pp. 28–29.
10 *Ibid.*

one's mother," reversing a "trend toward increasing estrangement and resolidifying the bond between mother and daughter." In the real politic sense, it is "the single most effective way of actualizing the status of adulthood and the role of female." Motherhood makes of the young female an "equal partner" in the female-based household, complete with her own welfare contribution to support of the family. She is no longer a "little girl," but an adult, with her own child to care for.

Finally, the essential ingredient of the low differential between legitimate and illegitimate status is the lack of economic opportunity[11] for lower class Negro males who are called upon to act as heads of households. The reality of the economic ceiling is emphasized by many writers and the following quote from a gang boy's interview shows that the participants themselves can clearly state the case:

... I was thinking of getting married but, ah—

Q: But not any more?

A: Yeah, I'm still thinking, but I just can't see if I'm going to get married because of financial problems.

Q: What kind of financial problems do you mean?

A: I mean, steady job, you know. Security in other words. Well, where . . . I'm working from day to day, there's no future, you know. Job where there's a chance for probably going up. Stead of staying at the same level all the time, on the bottom.

Q: Why, why just the bottom? When you say the bottom, how low is that?

A: I would say, ah . . . rest of your life making $60 a week.

Q: Uh huh. You think that's the bottom?

A: The bottom.

Q: And how far up is up?

A: Really not living high. Say a job making, say $70, you know, not in no strain all the time, because I feel that to compete with the $50 a week scale, it goes up.

Q: What about if your wife worked, wouldn't she bring in some money?

A: Well, yeah. But you figure, I say ah, I was married a year or two, we had some kids, well she's out of . . . now there is three mouths, but I will be still making that $50 a week.

Even though this evaluation of Negro lower class culture is compounded from hypotheses, observations of others, and of local mate-

[11] Richard Cloward made this point in an address before the 30th Annual Governor's Conference on Youth, State of Illinois, 1961.

rials, it nonetheless provides a consistent picture. There seems to be little reason to conceive of Negro adolescent culture as being functionally opposed to Negro adult culture. Negro adult culture seems poorly organized to effect control of youth, and Negro youth seems not to have the moratorium on adult responsibilities which some see as essential to the development of a youth culture. The economic disability of the adolescent Negro male differs only in degree from that of the adult Negro male—both have great disabilities.

Economic facts combine with cultural considerations to buttress the Negro male's rationalizations of non-performance as a husband. This suggests that illegitimate parenthood would not only differ little from legitimate parenthood in terms of overt social stigma, but there would also be little covert personality maladjustment. The concomitants of illegitimate parenthood upon personality scores can be investigated in a manner parallel to the examination of effects upon sociometric scores.

Personality Concomitants

The preparation to obtain personality measurements was much more complicated than the preparation required for sociometric measures. Because it was recognized that many of these boys cannot read or write, and that they are likely to be impatient with schoolish tasks, performance tests were utilized extensively. The testing situation was made as game-like as possible, hot dogs and soft drinks were made abundantly available to the boys at the laboratory, and no boy refused testing after having been brought to the laboratory. In all, more than four hundred boys from street-corner and related control groups were tested, but it was only possible to test eighteen of the twenty-five Chiefs. Some were unavailable in jail, or out of town, or just not on the street at times when sets of boys were being rounded up.

A very large number of personality measures became available from the four hours of testing. However, we shall only comment upon those which have a manifestly plausible relationship to illegitimate fatherhood. For example, as a ground-clearing first observation, it may be reported that fathers and non-fathers[12] among the Chiefs had virtually identical means in the IPAT "culture-free" intelligence

[12] The lone female member of the Chiefs was not tested.

test.[13] In addition, there were no differences in super-ego strength.[14] Our strongest expectation for differentiation arose in connection with a motivational questionnaire which we constructed to parallel Cattell's earlier work, after having made modifications to adjust the items to correspond to the vocabulary and experiences of the gang boys.[15] This instrument consisted of sets of twelve statements[16] relating to each of five motivational areas, viz., sex, gregariousness, fear, self-assertion, and narcism. The scale scores represent roughly what a person is willing to say he wishes or wants in the need areas in question. Most of the terms are fairly denotative, with the possible exception of narcism, which, in this context, refers to self-indulgence, indicated by agreements to such statements as "The main goal in life is to find comfort," and a rejection of collectivity concerns indicated by disagreement with, "The most important thing in life is to help other people." To illustrate the manifest nature of the content of this instrument, the nine items in the sex score are given below:

+Most men want above all to fall in love with a beautiful woman.
Only girls who attract men can really be happy.
A man needs to make love at least once a day.
The most important thing about a woman is how well built she is.
A book about love and beautiful women is the best kind of book.
—There are better things to do than go out with girls.
Sometimes a guy likes to go to dances just to dig the music.
You can stay away from girls and still be a regular guy.
There's too much emphasis on sex these days.

The ranking of obtained sex scores over the full range of subjects tested found lower class Negro gang boys highest, followed by their non-gang controls, then by lower class white gang boys, their non-gang controls, and finally by Negro middle class boys and white mid-

---

[13] The culture-free intelligence test is published by the Institute for Personality and Ability Testing. See their Handbook for the *Culture-Free Test of Intelligence*, II (1602 Coronado Drive, Champaign, Illinois, 1958).

[14] Taken from R. B. Cattell and G. F. Stice, "The Sixteen Personality Factor Questionnaire" (3d ed.; Institute for Personality and Ability Testing, 1602 Coronado Drive, Champaign, Illinois, 1957).

[15] See R. B. Cattell, A. B. Sweney, and J. A. Radcliffe, "The Objective Measurement of Motivation Structure in Children," *Journal of Clinical Psychology*, XVI (1960), 227–32.

[16] Discriminant item analysis reduced the number of items included in a given score to from five to eleven items each.

dle class boys, in order.[17] It is assumed that the higher the score, the higher the consciousness of unfulfilled need. The greater sex experience of gang boys, and generally of boys with high scores on this test, suggests that need is relevant in this instance not so much to deprivation as to the value placed on sexual behavior. Among the Chiefs tested, both self reports by the boys and the observations of workers indicate that all of these boys had engaged in sex relations over the several months before and during the period of our study. It comes as no great surprise, therefore, to discover in Table 2.2 that fathers and non-fathers among the Chiefs have virtually identical sex scores from the motivational opinionaire.

TABLE 2.2

MOTIVATIONAL OPINIONAIRE SCORES AND PARENTAL STATUS

Dimensions	Non-Parents ($N=12$)	Illegitimate Parents ($N=6$)	"t" Value (p[t .975, 9 d.f.] $=2.26$)
Sex...............	6.6	6.5	.05
Gregariousness.....	9.4	11.9	1.24
Fear..............	13.8	13.0	.51
Self-assertiveness...	4.0	2.3	1.82 p<.10
Narcism..........	6.0	7.2	.96

There are no statistically significant differences in Table 2.2. The frequencies are small, hence this finding of no difference will need to be rechecked when the information is available from our larger sample. It may be noted that the illegitimate parents who made more sociometric choices come out higher on gregariousness. The non-fathers are high on self-assertiveness, though this difference also is not significant at the .05 level. By use of an alternate form completions test based upon the same need areas, we have independently determined that no significant differences exist for these boys. We therefore conclude that our expectation that personality concomitants of illegitimate fatherhood would be absent—given the cultural permissiveness and low relevance to group rank—is confirmed.

Discussion of Substantive Findings

The link between the methodological and substantive concerns in this chapter is the simple one: Were the aspirations for stable family

[17] See Desmond S. Cartwright, Kenneth I. Howard, and James F. Short, Jr., "Psychological Assessment of Street Corner Youth: Motivation," 1962 (mimeographed).

relations a genuine reflection of the boys' desires? If so, why were they performing so poorly in the actualization of them?

Our pursuit of this question was based in part upon knowledge of the theoretical interest in determining the degree to which lower class culture is a distinct value system, as argued by Miller,[18] in contrast with some amalgam of reactions to frustrated striving, as argued by advocates of the Merton deviance paradigm such as Cohen,[19] Cloward and Ohlin,[20] and to some degree, Cohen and Short.[21] It is possible that the importance of the difference between these positions may recede as more documented instances of evaluative behavior are studied in detail.

For example, in the next chapter we demonstrate, for more than three hundred gang and control boys, that they were not differentiated from middle class boys in their evaluation (using Osgood's technique) of middle class images such as *being a good student, reading,* and *saving.*[22] The gang boys were, however, significantly more accepting of *pimping* and *making out* with girls. In an earlier study of differential occupational aspirations between Italians and Jews, no significant differences were found between the willingness to work in high-status positions, but the Jews, the more achievement-oriented group, were significantly less disposed to accept the lesser positions.[23] These findings, along with the present data, suggest that: (*a*) there are many instances in which middle-status and lower-status persons agree on positive goals; yet (*b*) middle-status persons have much greater resistance to accepting compromise solutions. Judging from our observations of gang boys, lower-status persons who become involved in compromise solutions are not characterized by personal rejection of the goals denied them, but the group norms select for em-

[18] Walter B. Miller, "Lower Class Culture as a Generating Milieu of Gang Delinquency," *The Journal of Social Issues,* XXIV (1958), 5–19.

[19] Albert K. Cohen, *Delinquent Boys* (Glencoe: The Free Press, 1955).

[20] Richard Cloward and Lloyd E. Ohlin, *Delinquency and Opportunity* (Glencoe: The Free Press, 1960).

[21] Albert K. Cohen and James F. Short, Jr., "Research in Delinquent Subcultures," *The Journal of Social Issues,* XIV (1958), 20–37.

[22] Robert A. Gordon, James F. Short, Jr., Desmond S. Cartwright, and Fred L. Strodtbeck, "Values and Gang Delinquency: A Study of Street-Corner Groups," *American Journal of Sociology,* LXIX (September, 1963), 109–28.

[23] Fred L. Strodtbeck, Margaret R. McDonald, and Bernard C. Rosen, "Evaluation of Occupations: A Reflection of Jewish and Italian Mobility Differences," *American Sociological Review,* XXII (October, 1957), 546–53.

phasis styles of behavior which are incompatible with attainment of the goals.

There is also a question of the orbit of relevance for status-related behavior. Dollard has indicated how lower middle class men see the regulation of sexual behavior as necessary to the attainment of higher status.[24] This contrasts with the Chiefs, for no member would believe that he could advance in status in the larger society if, by force of self-determination, he stopped having sex relations with girls. On the other hand, a Chief would lose status in the group if he did not continue to be active heterosexually with the easily available set of female partners. Under these circumstances, it is our disposition to look for the linkage between a boy's behavior and the eventual pregnancy (which engages the interest of the larger society) as being mediated by a chance process. We see forces operating which place him in a position of high risk, and whether this position eventuates in conception as an *aleatory* matter.

Something of the risk approach is implied whenever it is stated that sociological explanations explain rates, but not the behavior of individuals. This thinking can be reviewed in terms of illegitimate fathers. It is our guess that if the group had continued to function as a cohesive unit for another year, a high percentage of the non-fathers would have changed classification. In our terms, we suggest that the non-fathers were just lucky—we use this word advisedly and in a technical sense. We note that fathers are a significant year-and-four-months older than non-fathers,[25] and we feel that the shorter period of exposure for non-fathers is a most important determinant of their failure to become parents. It is possible that those boys who get through this period and see their group disband without having fathered illegitimate children have a greater chance of avoiding this pattern. Aging, the break-up of the gang, and the movement of boys into more legitimate statuses, including marriage, interrupt the system of relations we have described.

Fundamental to our argument is the conception of illegitimate fatherhood as a "state" or "outcome" rather than as an action or behavior.[26] A kind of two-stage stochastic process is involved. First

[24] John Dollard, *Caste and Class in a Southern Town* (New Haven: Yale University Press, 1937).

[25] Both fatherhood and age taken as of the time of the personality assessment.

[26] We are indebted to a number of people for critical reading of this chapter. In the following analysis we are especially grateful for suggestions made by Albert K. Cohen.

there is the probability that a given boy will engage in extramarital intercourse with a given frequency. Secondly, there is the probability that these actions will eventuate in illegitimate parenthood. The term "aleatory" refers to the independence between the first and second probabilities.

The first probability is dependent upon the cultural tolerance of intercourse, or—in the present instance—pressure to engage in intercourse, the intrinsic pleasures of intercourse, etc. However the full matrix of costs or payoffs is conceptualized, it is clear that for the class of actions involved in the first step of this process, the outcome of the second step has little consequence. It makes little difference whether or not the boys become fathers, and for this reason, the outcome probabilities of the second stage are given little thought at the time of the first action. In this way, the incidence of illegitimacy becomes a function of the amount of time spent "at risk," and the explanation of variance among individuals is, so far as we can tell, independent of intentions or expectations about parenthood. This result is directly responsive to the original area of surprise, the very loose articulation of family norms with behavior which results in illegitimacy.

Some parts of this approach to the study of illegitimate parenthood may be tested with other types of delinquency. In Chapter 12 we look further into instances of sudden violence. Our study of one instance suggests that, given culturally supported requirements for aggressive responses, such characteristics of lower class life as public drinking, milling behavior, and a high incidence of guns may precondition the occurrence of acts of violence which involve individuals who could not have been differentiated from their peers by any personality assessment, even an hour before the occurrence of violence. The chance process, which caused boy A in contrast with boy B to be implicated in the act of violence is, in many cases like the chance process which causes a 5:05 commuter to be fender-crunched and a 4:15 commuter to escape—it is a matter of exposure to risk. In a social matter such as fighting, the effective social environment must be understood to include the expectation of appropriate behavior. In both fighting and casual sexual activity, group norms create risks for group members which would not exist for non-members.

Discussion of Strategy

The primary "dilemma" which is of interest in this chapter relates to the allocation of resources for the discussion and preparation for publication of unanticipated findings. In the case at point, the inconsistency between family attitudes and behavior was encountered in a study designed to test alternative delinquency theories. These theories did not explicitly bear on the discovered inconsistency. On the one hand, we did not wish to present an analysis which might not be valid; on the other, we did not wish to leave unreported data which might prove of interest. This is but one example of a broader class of dilemmas in which fidelity to one's original concerns (and the allocation of resources to them) becomes pitted against the possible distraction of following extraneous leads. In much research, extraneous leads are likely to be quite limited in number; in research specifically designed to keep a window open on ongoing process, such leads will almost certainly exceed resources available for their exploitation. If, as one of the authors recently has argued, more use needs to be made of experimental research designs in field and institutional contexts, then the management of promising leads becomes of crucial importance to research strategy.

The strategy illustrated in this paper involves two components. First, a heightened desire to invest enough additional energy to produce a publicly reviewable report; and second, an increased willingness to expose ourselves to the possibility that further investigation might disconfirm the original interpretation. This strategy contrasts with an unwillingness to publish before an analysis is confirmed and a great desire to avoid the possibility of disconfirmation.

This strategy is not unique. Paul Lazarsfeld has indicated his sensitivity to it by advocating the establishment of the Brief Reports section of the *Public Opinion Quarterly*. But the strategy calls for more than brief, particularized publications. It seems apparent that behavioral scientists should be encouraged to study more carefully their own decision processes at points when potential creativity is being judged. It requires further that in the conduct of research, careful records be made both of what is reported and what is not. From such records, realistic estimates can be made as to the amount of energy to budget in different types of designs for the exploitation of unanticipated findings (up to the point of a public report). In this way, the confusion of research dilemmas can be reduced and one further aspect of the art of social research can be brought under more rational control.

CHAPTER 3

Values and Gang Delinquency: A Study of Street-Corner Groups

Three recent theories of juvenile-gang delinquency view values as an important link in a causal chain leading from social status to illegitimate behavior.[1] The theories are seemingly in agreement as to what they mean by "values," and they differ only slightly in the content of the values which they ascribe to members of three relatively distinct social categories: lower class gang, lower class non-gang, and middle class non-gang. There are, however, important differences between the theories in the assumptions underlying these values. As a result, competing, if not always mutually exclusive, hypotheses are implied. This chapter attempts to further refine thinking in this area by empirically testing some hypotheses that might reasonably be deduced from the three theories. Accordingly, relevant data gathered from both Negro and white adolescent members of each of the social categories are presented.

This chapter was published in *The American Journal of Sociology*, LXIX (September, 1963), 109–28. Co-authors were Robert A. Gordon, James F. Short, Jr., Desmond S. Cartwright, and Fred L. Strodtbeck. The authors wish to express their gratitude to Kenneth I. Howard for assistance and counsel during all phases of the research, to Albert K. Cohen, Stanton Wheeler, Maria Gordon, and Patricia Leavey Hodge for helpful suggestions, and to Alan E. Hendrickson for programming some of the computations for Univac I.

[1] These theoretical statements are by Albert K. Cohen, *Delinquent Boys* (Glencoe: The Free Press, 1955); Walter B. Miller, "Lower Class Culture as a Generating Milieu of Gang Delinquency," *Journal of Social Issues*, XIV (1958), 5–19; and Richard A. Cloward and Lloyd E. Ohlin, *Delinquency and Opportunity* (Glencoe: The Free Press, 1960). For further elaboration of the Cohen point of view see Albert K. Cohen and James F. Short, Jr., "Research in Delinquent Subcultures," *Journal of Social Issues*, XIV (1958), 20–37. Miller brings his viewpoint to bear on empirical data in Walter B. Miller, Hildred Geertz, and Henry S. G. Cutter, "Aggression in a Boys' Street-Corner Group," *Psychiatry*, XXIV (1961), 283–98.

The Sample

Samples of Negro and white males were drawn from each of the following social categories, making a total of six populations under study.

Gang.—The gang boys studied are members of nine Negro and six white gangs assigned workers by the Program for Detached Workers of the YMCA of Metropolitan Chicago. The samples contain 163 Negroes and 58 whites, and constitute from a third to a half of the total membership of these gangs. Police record data were obtained for all nine Negro gangs and four of the six white gangs.[2] For the total memberships, the number of offenses known to the police per boy averaged 3.17 for Negroes and 2.91 for whites; for boys in the samples these figures are 3.29 and 3.39, respectively. Thus, boys from whom data were collected do not appear to be less delinquent than the average member of their gangs. A comparison of the ages of boys in the samples with those not included reveals that the included Negroes are 0.57 years, and the included whites 0.16 years younger than members of their gangs not included. A check of rosters of gang members prepared in advance of collecting these data gave no sign that detached workers were able to produce only their more tractable gang boys for research. If newspaper headlines are any criterion, these gangs include all but one of the most notorious in Chicago during 1960–61.

Lower class.—Boys residing in the same neighborhoods as the gang boys but not themselves members of gangs were contacted through Y's and settlement houses. Six Negro and two white groups or clubs constitute the samples, for a total of sixty-nine Negroes and thirty-seven whites. The search of police records revealed these boys to have had a moderate amount of official involvement in delinquency, indicating that these samples are not composed of boys who are unusually good. The mean number of offenses per boy known to the police was 0.33 for Negroes and 0.22 for whites.

Middle class.—Non-gang middle class boys were reached through two YMCA's known to serve a middle class clientele and located in areas of Chicago judged to be middle class according to conventional demographic criteria. A total of twenty-four Negro and forty-one white

[2] The police record search was conducted by John M. Wise, who furnished the data upon which these figures are based (see his "A Comparison of Sources of Data as Indexes of Delinquent Behavior," unpublished Master's thesis, University of Chicago, 1962).

boys—from two Negro and two white clubs—is included. Just one boy within each race was known to police for delinquent activity, for a combined total of three offenses, all minor; the corresponding means were 0.08 for Negroes and 0.03 for whites. No examples of a middle class gang could be found locally.

The sample as a whole.—Mean ages and standard deviations for the six samples, in years, are shown in Table 3.1. The white gang sample includes the two oldest persons, one 24.4 and one 26 years old.

TABLE 3.1

MEAN AGES AND STANDARD DEVIATIONS
FOR SIX SAMPLES

Group	Mean Age	Standard Deviation
Negro		
Gang.	17.2	1.9
Lower class.	16.5	1.4
Middle class.	17.3	0.9
White		
Gang.	18.2	2.1
Lower class.	16.8	1.1
Middle class.	16.1	1.2

Although most of the age differences between samples were statistically significant, an examination of the correlations between the main data and age indicated that none of the interpretations to be presented could be accounted for by differences in age.[3] Although all the gang boys are definitely lower class, for convenience this report will dis-

[3] Some selected 1960 Census statistics for the Chicago community areas and tracts from which these samples were drawn are presented in a table (Table A), which is one of three tables (indicated by alphabetic references in this chapter) that, along with certain methodological notes, have been deposited with the American Documentation Institute. For a discussion of the examination of relations with age, see Note A. Order Document No. 7468 from ADI Auxiliary Publications Project, Photoduplication Service, Library of Congress, Washington 25, D.C., remitting in advance $1.25 for 35-mm. microfilm or $1.25 for 6 × 8-inch photocopies. Make checks payable to Chief, Photoduplication Service, Library of Congress.

tinguish the gang from non-gang lower class samples by the use of the terms "gang" and "lower class," respectively.

The Instrument and Procedures

The data were gathered by means of a semantic differential, which consists of a number of seven-point, bipolar, adjectival scales against which any set of concepts or descriptive images may be rated.[4] This instrument measures what Osgood terms "connotative meaning" which, for 'a variety of populations, has been found to have two main orthogonal dimensions when a large number of scales and concepts are administered and the scales then intercorrelated and factor-analyzed. To obtain adequate measures of these dimensions, only a small number of scales, found to have high correlations with the appropriate dimensions, are required.

A score for a dimension is obtained by averaging the appropriate scale values, which ranged from one to seven. These dimensions and the corresponding scales used in this study are:

Evaluation	Potency
clean-dirty	hard-soft
good-bad	large-small
kind-cruel	strong-weak
fair-unfair	brave-cowardly
pleasant-unpleasant	rugged-delicate

Three additional scales, derived from Miller's "focal concerns" of lower class culture, were also included. These were "smart-sucker," "lucky-unlucky," and "exciting life-boring life."[5]

The images (see Table 3.2) to be rated were chosen to represent salient examples of instrumental or dominant goal activity, leisure-time activity, and ethical orientation for each of five theoretically significant subcultures—middle class, lower class, conflict, criminal, and retreatist.[6] Leisure activity appeared to be essentially the same for three of the subcultures, and is therefore represented for all three by a single image.

Although they do not figure prominently in this analysis, the three aspects of subcultural roles did provide a basis for sampling widely

[4] See Charles E. Osgood, George J. Suci, and Percy H. Tannenbaum, *The Measurement of Meaning* (Urbana: University of Illinois Press, 1957).

[5] Miller, *op. cit.*, p. 6.

[6] The last three subcultures refer to types of delinquent gangs postulated by Cohen and Short, *op. cit.*, and by Cloward and Ohlin, *op. cit.*

within each domain. Of four additional images included because of their theoretical interest, only the one identified by the label "GIRL" requires comment. This image was included to furnish responses relevant to sexual demonstrations of masculinity. Hopefully, images were phrased so as to be as concrete as possible and yet personify the values hypothesized to distinguish the subcultures.

TABLE 3.2

SEMANTIC-DIFFERENTIAL IMAGES

Subculture	Label	Images: "Someone who . . ."
Middle class:		
Dominant goal activity..	GRAD	works for good grades at school
Leisure activity........	READ	likes to read good books
Ethical orientation.....	SAVE	saves his money
Lower class:		
Dominant goal activity..	SJOB	has a steady job washing and greasing cars
Leisure activity........	HANG	likes to spend his spare time hanging on the corner with his friends
Ethical orientation......	SHAR	shares his money with his friends
Conflict:		
Dominant goal activity	TUFF	is a good fighter with a tough reputation
Leisure activity........	HANG	(see lower class)
Ethical orientation.....	STIK	sticks by his friends in a fight
Criminal:		
Dominant goal activity..	FENC	knows where to sell what he steals
Leisure activity........	HANG	(see lower class)
Ethical orientation......	CONN	has good connections to avoid trouble with the law
Retreatist:		
Dominant goal activity..	PIMP	makes easy money by pimping and other illegal hustles
Leisure activity........	DRUG	gets his kicks by using drugs
Ethical orientation.....	COOL	stays cool and keeps to himself
Additional images	GIRL	makes out with every girl he wants
	SELF	Myself as I usually am
	IEGO	Myself as I would like to be
	GANG	is a member of (enter group name or if none, "your friendship group")

Administration of the semantic differential to small numbers of subjects at a time took place in an old, rather shabby one-time apartment building, where the subjects were fed hot dogs and soft drinks. The tester was quite permissive toward all departures from normally decorous behavior that did not jeopardize the validity of measures. Considerable care was taken to explain directions and check the boys' responses. A few boys, unable to read, had the semantic differential read to them as they responded.

Seventeen factor analyses of the evaluation and potency scales, performed for seventeen of the gangs and clubs studied, revealed evaluation and potency factors for all six populations matching those previously found by Osgood.[7] This rules out all but the most ingenious and most coincidentally patterned types of deliberately meaningless, falsified responding. It also justifies the scoring procedure.

Statistical Treatment

The data consist of the mean scores for both evaluation (Table 3.3 below) and the "smart-sucker" scale (Table 3.5 below) accorded to each of the seventeen images by each of the six populations. Three-way (image by race by social category) analyses of variance (Tables B and C) have indicated high levels of over-all significance for these data.[8] The sources of this significance are investigated further by comparing all six of the individual sample means for an image with each other, using two-tailed t-tests. Although this procedure carries a high risk of a Type I error[9]—because it inevitably compares the most extreme values in any set of six—it was felt that, because differences are theoretically more interesting here than similarities, this method is preferable to alternative tests having high risk of a Type II error. Important additional constraints upon interpretation are exerted, however, by (1) the fact that the three social categories are ordered with respect to presumed similarity (gang, lower class, middle class); (2) the presence of data for two races. Thus, any ordering of the data which is similar to that of the three categories, and which appears in both races, will strongly supplement the presence of statistical significance. This organization of the data has the advantage of possibly suggesting attitudinal trends in American society that may prove to be more useful in understanding delinquency than single comparisons holding constant race or class.

[7] See Robert A. Gordon, "The Generality of Semantic Differential Factors and Scales in Six American Subcultures," unpublished Master's thesis, University of Chicago, 1962.

[8] American Documentation Institute, *op. cit.* For a justification of the use of parametric statistics with semantic-differential data, see either Note B, *ibid.*, or Robert A. Gordon, "Values and Gang Delinquency," unpublished Ph.D. dissertation, University of Chicago, 1963.

[9] See Thomas A. Ryan, "Multiple Comparisons in Psychological Research," *Psychological Bulletin*, LVI (1959), 26–47.

Inferences from Theories

Cohen.—As an explanation of juvenile-gang delinquency, the hypothesis of a reaction formation against the standards of middle class society has been proposed by Albert K. Cohen. According to Cohen, reaction formation serves as a defense against the anxiety of status frustration, common to lower class youth and especially severe for those who join gangs. Although Cohen's theory holds that the wholesale repudiation of middle class values "does its job of problem-solving most effectively when it is adopted as a group solution,"[10] and that "group interaction is a sort of catalyst which releases potentialities not otherwise visible,"[11] thus seeming at times to leave unsettled the question of whether private values are similarly affected, the logic of the mechanism of reaction formation requires that middle class values be submerged in the consciousness of individuals as well as in the culture of the group. His point seems to be that the group experience, in which individuals come together with the common problem of status frustration, is necessary for the full unfolding and elaboration of a latent common solution, namely, total repudiation of middle class standards. Once exposed to the mutual self-recognitions and reinforcements of collective acting out, negative attitudes that were only latent in the individual's value processes become manifest. It is reasonable to expect that the resulting modification in values, while undoubtedly subject to intensification during group interaction, remains as a relatively enduring feature of an individual's personality, even when he is apart from the group. This interpretation is consistent with Cohen's emphasis upon the over-reactive quality of much delinquent behavior. Thus, although Cohen's theory asserts that middle class values are in fact internalized by gang boys, he clearly implies that they persist only as a repressed and unacknowledged source of anxiety.[12]

An instrument as baldly direct as the semantic differential would not be expected to bypass such a firmly established system of neurotic defenses. Accordingly, the explicit and highly developed negativism described by Cohen should characterize the conscious private values of the gang boy and be reflected in his evaluation of middle class images. As it was constructed, the instrument afforded subjects an opportunity to express bitterness and contempt toward rather tempt-

---

[10] Cohen, *op. cit.*, pp. 134–35.
[11] *Ibid.*, p. 136.   [12] *Ibid.*, p. 132.

ing middle class figures (see GRAD, READ, and SAVE in Table 3.2); they had only to avail themselves of the negativistic ends of the evaluative scales. Hence, if the hypothesis of reaction formation is correct, these evaluation scores for gang boys should be low.

In contrast, gang boys should evaluate images that are antithetical to middle class morality higher than the middle class images. This follows from Cohen's statement: "The hall-mark of the delinquent subculture is the explicit and wholesale repudiation of middle class standards and the adoption of their very antithesis."[13] Strictly speaking, only TUFF meets Cohen's specification that the negativism of the reaction formation is also non-utilitarian. Yet, it would seem that FENC, CONN, PIMP, and GIRL are sufficiently violative of middle class expectations to serve also as vehicles for the expression of negativism so presumably global (DRUG is perhaps too special a case to merit consideration). Whereas Cohen asserts that utility does not constitute the chief motivation of delinquent-gang boys, there is nevertheless nothing in his theory to suggest that such negativism would be inhibited if it happened to lead to a utilitarian end. For these reasons all of these images should be evaluated higher than the middle class images, but special attention should be paid to TUFF. The gang boys should also evaluate those images higher than do middle class boys.

Although not directly connected with the reaction-formation hypothesis, at least two of the lower class images, SHAR and HANG, according to Cohen should be acceptable to the gang boys; the first, because it represents the lower class ethic of reciprocity, and the second, because it is an activity favored by both stable lower class and delinquent boys. Whether gang boys would perceive the third lower class image, SJOB, as but another form of subservience to middle class standards rather than as an admissible lower class occupation is not indicated in Cohen's theory.

Miller.—The proposition that the lower class possesses a relatively distinct and autonomous value system is suggested, although not stated explicitly, by Walter B. Miller.[14] He does, however, clearly assert that the delinquent acts of lower class gang members have as their "dominant component of motivation" the "directed attempt by the actor to adhere to forms of behavior, and to achieve standards of value as they are defined by that community,"[15] the reference being to the lower class community. He characterizes these standards as "focal concerns," and it is clear that, although they may be present

---

[13] *Ibid.*, p. 129.   [14] *Op. cit.*   [15] *Ibid.*, p. 5.

to some degree in other strata, they receive radically different emphasis in the lower class than they might in the middle class. While it follows from this that lower class and gang values emphasize elements not emphasized in middle class values, Miller leaves unclear the weighting that lower class and gang values would accord to elements that do receive great emphasis in the middle class (unless one is willing to conclude that Miller intends his description of lower class values to be practically exhaustive, in which case elements emphasized in the middle class would be absent entirely from lower class culture). Despite this ambiguity, it seems reasonable to infer the following expectations from Miller's statement: lower class and gang boys should (1) not evaluate the middle class images as high as do middle class boys, (2) evaluate lower class images higher than middle class images, (3) evaluate the lower class images higher than do the middle class boys, (4) evaluate images that accord with lower class focal concerns, such as the retreatist, conflict, and criminal images, higher than do middle class boys.

Miller and others[16] also postulate the existence of a sex-identity problem for lower class males growing out of early socialization experiences in households in which adult male figures are not consistently present. According to this "female-based household" hypothesis, attempts by lower class males to achieve masculine identity are characterized by an exaggerated emphasis on sexual and aggressive exploits. Three images offer possibilities for testing this hypothesis: TUFF, GIRL, and PIMP, the last because it emphasizes a relationship with women in which the woman is controlled, exploited, and degraded. It was hypothesized that the order of evaluation of these images would run Gang>Lower Class>Middle Class and Negro> White within each of the three social levels. These orderings simply reflect the extent to which female-based households were assumed to occur in the family histories of members of each social category.

Because the focal concerns have themselves a dimensional character—consider, for example, *toughness, smartness,* and *excitement*—along which behaviors may be implicitly ordered, it might be questioned whether the evaluative responses of lower class respondents should reflect the same ordering. Miller, however, makes it quite clear that he expects evaluation and desirability to be linear functions of the focal concerns, rather than orthogonal to them, giving as one rea-

---

[16] E.g., Roger V. Burton and John W. M. Whiting, "The Absent Father and Cross-Sex Identity," *Merrill-Palmer Quarterly*, VII (1961), 85–95.

son for preferring to speak of "focal concerns" rather than "values" his feeling that the former is neutral with respect to the implied direction of positive evaluation.[17] This indicates that the two run generally parallel to each other in his thinking.

Cloward and Ohlin.—Two fundamental orientations of lower class youth have been distinguished by Richard A. Cloward and Lloyd E. Ohlin.[18] One is based upon attitude toward membership in the middle class, the other upon attitude toward improvement in one's economic position; a person may desire either, both, or none of these two objectives. The possible combinations of indifference or aspiration toward these objectives yield a typology—inspired by Merton's typology[19] of individual adaptation—of four kinds of lower class youth. Cloward and Ohlin hold that it is from Type III of their typology, those indifferent toward membership in the middle class but eager for improvement in their economic position, that the "principal constituents of delinquent subcultures" are drawn.[20] When legitimate avenues of opportunity are blocked for such boys, delinquent subcultures of different types emerge according to the pattern of illegitimate opportunities locally available.

It will be noted, however, that the middle class images used in the semantic differential appear to stand for striving, self-improvement, and sacrifice far more than for the "big cars," "flashy clothes," and "swell dames," that Cloward and Ohlin suggest epitomize the goals of Type III youth.[21] Therefore, insofar as the middle class images represent the style of life characteristic of actual membership rather than simply middle class economic position, it may be inferred that delinquents would be relatively cool toward them. Accordingly, they should evaluate GRAD, READ, and SAVE lower than does the middle class sample. But if they do evaluate the middle class images high it can be argued on a fortiori grounds that they would also evaluate images standing for middle class consumption patterns high. Indeed, despite the typology, it would be surprising if anyone did not. Thus, if gang boys evaluate the images GRAD, READ, and SAVE high it would constitute a conservative test in favor of Cloward and Ohlin's hypothesis concerning their attitudes toward economic position. But simul-

---

[17] *Op. cit.*, p. 7.

[18] *Op. cit.*, pp. 90–97.

[19] Robert K. Merton, "Social Structure and Anomie," *Social Theory and Social Structure* (Glencoe: The Free Press, 1957).

[20] *Op. cit.*, p. 96.   [21] *Ibid.*

taneously this would bring into question either the separate existence of the two orientations on which the typology is founded or the supposition that gang delinquents emerge mainly from Type III. (It may be that if presented with them, gang members would evaluate images representing middle class consumption patterns extremely high, higher even than GRAD, READ, and SAVE, and higher also than would middle class boys. If so, there would then be reason to continue to regard the two orientations as relatively independent and distinct.) In either case it would then seem that the emphasis which Cloward and Ohlin give to exclusively economic motivation may require qualification.

Hypotheses concerning the deviant subcultural images are complicated by the fact that, according to Cloward and Ohlin, members of gangs would be expected to endorse highly the images standing for the subcultural adaptation into which their own gang best fits. There is thus no reason to believe that a gang boy would evaluate all deviant subcultural adaptations high. Since this chapter makes no attempt to distinguish gangs according to this subcultural typology, any hypothesis dealing with the evaluation of illegitimate images by gang boys must be regarded as tentative. In general, it might be hypothesized that gang boys would evaluate illegitimate images higher than non-gang boys.

Types of Comparison and Summary of Hypotheses

Types of comparisons.—Implicit in the inferences from theory are two types of comparisons concerning the image means in Tables 3.3 and 3.5 below. One compares the six populations for a single image to detect *differentials between populations for the same image;* this comparison focuses on one *row* of a table. The other type of comparison examines different images for the same population to detect *differences in relative level of the images;* it focuses on one *column.* All of the comparisons for rows have been made, and the results are presented in Tables 3.4 and 3.6 below. Each image affords 15 possible comparisons between the 6 populations, for a total of 255 comparisons for all 17 images in each table. Of the 255 for evaluation, for example, 103 (over 40 per cent) were statistically significant, many at a very high level. The greater attention will be paid to these row comparisons. However, some reference will be made to column comparisons, which, when especially relevant, have been calculated.[22] As an

---

[22] Such tests, which apply to several observations on the same sample, take into account the correlation between observations.

aid to interpretation, the range of potential significance for column comparisons has been given in Tables 3.3 and 3.5 (below), with figures below each column showing the magnitude of the smallest difference possibly significant at the .05 level, as well as the smallest difference definitely significant at the .05 and .01 levels. All differences less than the former are not significant; all equal to or greater than the latter are. These boundaries tend to be extreme. On the average, a difference intermediate between these limits would probably mark the threshold of significance.

Summary of hypotheses.—On the basis of quite different assumptions, each of the theories leads to the expectation that gang boys will evaluate deviant or illegitimate images higher than do middle class boys (Cohen's theory because of reaction formation, Miller's because these images correspond to the focal concerns of lower class culture, and Cloward and Ohlin's because the images represent adaptations to the relative unavailability of legitimate opportunities for members of the lower class), but only Cohen's theory carries the stronger implication that gang boys will value deviant images even higher than the middle class images. All three theories imply that middle class values, as represented in the middle class images, are not endorsed as highly by gang boys as by middle class boys. A careful reading of these theories has led to the following explicit hypotheses:

1. Gang boys evaluate the middle class images lower than illegitimate images such as PIMP, FENC, CONN, GIRL, and TUFF (Cohen). A column comparison.
2. Gang boys evaluate the middle class images lower than do lower class and middle class boys (Cohen). A row comparison.
3. Gang and lower class boys evaluate the middle class images lower than do middle class boys (Miller). A row comparison.
4. Gang boys evaluate the middle class images lower than do middle class boys (Cloward and Ohlin). A row comparison.
5. Gang boys evaluate SHAR and HANG higher than the middle class images (Cohen). A column comparison.
6. Gang and lower class boys evaluate lower class images higher than middle class images (Miller). A column comparison.
7. Gang and lower class boys evaluate lower class images higher than do the middle class boys (Miller). A row comparison.
8. PIMP, GIRL, and TUFF are evaluated higher (a) by Negroes than whites, (b) by gang boys than lower class and middle class boys, and (c) by lower class boys than middle class boys (Miller and others). All row comparisons.

9. Gang boys evaluate illegitimate images higher than do non-gang boys (Cohen; Cloward and Ohlin). A row comparison.
10. Gang and lower class boys evaluate illegitimate images higher than do middle class boys (Miller). A row comparison.

Data and Interpretation

The images are discussed in the order in which they figure in the hypotheses. This leads first to a discussion of the middle class images (where the distinction between the moral validity and the legitimacy of norms is invoked in an effort to account for the findings). The remaining images are discussed in clusters bearing upon particular hypotheses and interpretations suggested by regularities in the data.

Middle class images.—Of forty-five differences between the six populations in evaluation of the middle class images, only two were significant (see Tables 3.3 and 3.4). Both Negro lower class and white lower class boys evaluated GRAD higher than did white gang boys, in both instances at the .05 level. This is almost precisely the number of significant findings out of forty-five totally independent tests (which these are not) to be expected at this level on the basis of chance alone. In view of the high risk of a Type I error in this statistical treatment, it is fair to describe the picture presented by these data as one of overwhelming homogeneity. *All six populations evaluated images representing salient features of a middle class style of life equally highly.*

Furthermore, no image representing the other four subcultures was evaluated significantly higher than the middle class images by any one of the six populations. Of the sixty means for non-middle class subcultural images, five were slightly higher than some of the means for middle class images. In every such instance the image involved was SHAR, standing for lower class reciprocity, an image that could not be characterized as illegitimate.

In fact, the middle class images were evaluated significantly higher by every one of the populations than nearly all other subcultural images, especially those that are unquestionably illegitimate.[23] None of the theories would have led one to expect these findings.

An explanation for the disparity between the theories and these particular data might be found in the distinction between moral validity and legitimacy. Cloward and Ohlin, for example, speak of "the legitimacy of social rules," which may be questioned by members of a

[23] As checked by means of the definitely significant difference (see Table 3.3).

socially disadvantaged population quite apart from their "moral validity." They assert that gang members no longer accord legitimacy to middle class norms because of social barriers obstructing their access to the opportunities implied by the norms.[24] Cohen, too, recognizes the importance of legitimacy when he states:

For the child who temporizes with middle class morality, overt aggression and even the conscious recognition of his own hostile impulses are inhibited, for he acknowledges the *legitimacy* of the rules in terms of which he is stigmatized. For the child who breaks clean with middle class morality,

[24] Cloward and Ohlin, *op. cit.*, pp. 16–20, 136–37.

TABLE 3.3

EVALUATION MEANS

IMAGES	NEGRO			WHITE		
	Gang	Lower Class	Middle Class	Gang	Lower Class	Middle Class
Middle class:						
GRAD......	5.58	5.72	5.68	5.35	5.79	5.61
READ.......	5.33	5.48	5.30	5.30	5.34	5.54
SAVE.......	5.30	5.33	5.18	5.12	5.17	5.15
Lower class:						
SJOB........	4.25	4.26	3.93	4.26	3.71	3.60
HANG......	4.05	4.29	3.52	4.23	4.02	2.98
SHAR.......	5.38	5.51	5.52	5.03	5.28	5.39
Conflict:						
TUFF.......	3.38	3.33	2.42	3.59	3.52	2.56
STIK........	4.65	4.75	4.58	4.61	4.92	4.41
Criminal:						
FENC.......	3.03	2.53	2.38	2.88	2.18	2.31
CONN.......	4.22	3.62	3.28	3.98	2.99	2.40
Retreatist:						
PIMP........	3.49	3.04	2.67	2.59	2.02	1.76
DRUG......	2.65	2.70	2.09	2.46	2.04	2.39
COOL.......	4.85	4.72	4.55	5.03	4.78	4.57
Additional:						
GIRL.......	5.32	5.09	4.96	4.32	4.24	3.52
IEGO.......	5.84	6.23	6.35	5.75	6.28	6.40
GANG......	4.63	5.24	5.92	4.56	5.00	5.81
SELF........	5.26	5.64	5.92	4.88	5.24	5.50
LSD:[a]						
p=.05.......	0.17	0.16	0.17	0.21	0.20	0.17
DSD:						
p=.05.......	0.38	0.55	0.99	0.58	0.86	0.60
p=.01.......	0.50	0.73	1.34	0.77	1.15	0.80

[a] For each column lowest significant differences (LSD) are such that any lower are not significant; definitely significant differences (DSD) are such that any equal or higher are significant at the given level.

TABLE 3.4

IMAGES EVALUATED SIGNIFICANTLY HIGHER BY ROW SAMPLE
THAN BY COLUMN SAMPLE
(.05 LEVEL OR BETTER)[a]

	NEGRO			WHITE		
	Gang	Lower Class	Middle Class	Gang	Lower Class	Middle Class
Negro						
Gang		FENC* CONN* PIMP	SJOB HANG* TUFF*** FENC* CONN* PIMP** DRUG	SHAR PIMP*** GIRL*** SELF	SJOB* FENC*** CONN*** PIMP*** DRUG* GIRL**	SJOB*** HANG*** TUFF*** FENC*** CONN*** PIMP*** GIRL***
Lower class	IEGO* GANG** SELF*		HANG** TUFF** DRUG	GRAD SHAR* PIMP GIRL** IEGO GANG* SELF***	SJOB* CONN PIMP*** DRUG* GIRL* SELF	SJOB** HANG*** TUFF** CONN*** PIMP*** GIRL***
Middle class	IEGO* GANG*** SELF**	GANG**		SHAR GIRL IEGO* GANG*** SELF***	PIMP GIRL GANG*** SELF*	HANG CONN* PIMP** GIRL*** SELF
White						
Gang			SJOB HANG* TUFF*** FENC CONN		SJOB* FENC* CONN*** PIMP	SJOB** HANG*** TUFF*** FENC* CONN*** PIMP*** COOL GIRL**
Lower class	IEGO*		TUFF**	GRAD IEGO		HANG*** TUFF** STIK CONN GIRL
Middle class	IEGO*** GANG***	GANG**		IEGO* GANG*** SELF**	GANG**	

[a] Italicized images are significant for evaluation, but not for smartness. Compare with Table 3.6
*p < .01.   **p < .001.   ***p < .0001.

on the other hand, there are no moral inhibitions on the free expression of aggression against the sources of his frustration.[25]

Even Miller may be responding to the legitimacy aspect of attitudes toward norms when he asserts that lower class culture is relatively autonomous. If it were true that the evaluation dimension reflects moral validity rather than legitimacy, these data would not constitute a proper test of the theories.

It seems reasonable to infer that anyone who complies with norms that lack legitimacy from the viewpoint of someone else faces the prospect of being branded a "sucker," that is, someone who is taken in and fooled by superficial appearances. This line of reasoning, coupled with Miller's assurances that "smartness," in exactly this sense, is a criterion of behavior to which lower class and gang members are sensitive, led to the "smart-sucker" scale as a measure of legitimacy.[26]

It might be argued that the "smart-sucker" scale is subject to being construed as an "intelligent-unintelligent" scale, and that since the three middle class images suggest rather cerebral types of performance, all the boys will rate these images high on smartness. On the other hand, the scale was always read aloud to the boys as part of an example of how to fill out the instrument: "Is he smart? Or is he a sucker?" Calling attention in this way to the presence of "sucker" at one end of the scale should be effective in defining its dimensionality, especially, according to Miller, for lower class and gang boys. Since these are the boys who presumably are motivated to withhold legitimacy from such images, the combination of this motivation with their sensitivity should be reflected in differential responses, even (or perhaps especially) if the middle class boys, lacking both the sensitivity and motivation, construe the scale as an intelligence measure.[27] Actually, there is no reason to suppose that middle class boys would not understand quite well a continuum delineated by "smart" and "sucker."

[25] Op. cit., p. 132.

[26] This interpretation is not without its problems, for while "sucker" is pejorative it does not necessarily connote illegitimacy. It may be smart (in a "conning" sense) to do something, but for other reasons a person might be considered a sucker to do it. Our use of the smartness scale as a measure of legitimacy provides an opportunity for additional theoretical assessment with the data on the basis of the argument that is developed. (J. F. S.)

[27] For a more thorough discussion of this point see American Documentation Institute, op. cit., Note C.

But the hypotheses placed in question by the evaluative findings enjoy only a brief respite. The smartness scores for all three middle class images for all populations are also virtually identical. Of forty-five comparisons, only one is significant; Negro middle class boys rated SAVE smarter than white lower class boys, at the .05 level (see Tables 3.5 and 3.6). The smartness ratings of middle class images by all populations are higher than those for any other subcultural image. Some readers may note that both gang samples rated READ noticeably lower on smartness than members of the other populations (the differences are not significant), and also that the three strata of both races were ordered for GRAD so that gang boys are lowest and middle

TABLE 3.5

SMARTNESS MEANS

IMAGES	NEGRO			WHITE		
	Gang	Lower Class	Middle Class	Gang	Lower Class	Middle Class
Middle class:						
GRAD......	6.35	6.61	6.58	6.43	6.54	6.66
READ......	6.03	6.22	6.21	6.07	6.27	6.22
SAVE.......	6.37	6.49	6.67	6.55	6.03	6.29
Lower class:						
SJOB........	4.99	4.70	4.17	4.69	4.30	4.10
HANG......	4.34	3.99	3.17	4.40	4.14	2.61
SHAR......	4.59	4.72	3.12	3.97	3.54	4.12
Conflict:						
TUFF.......	4.15	4.03	3.21	4.79	3.86	3.27
STIK.......	5.20	5.51	4.96	5.64	5.46	4.98
Criminal:						
FENC.......	4.99	4.38	3.75	4.98	3.24	3.15
CONN.......	5.75	5.33	4.96	5.71	3.70	3.80
Retreatist:						
PIMP........	4.39	3.57	3.62	3.69	2.08	1.61
DRUG......	2.37	2.04	1.17	1.93	1.19	1.15
COOL.......	5.63	5.26	4.12	5.90	4.54	3.76
Additional:						
GIRL.......	6.08	5.59	5.75	5.24	4.46	3.83
IEGO.......	6.21	6.45	6.33	6.64	6.43	6.76
GANG......	5.58	5.71	6.00	5.40	5.43	6.05
SELF.......	5.79	5.49	5.75	5.14	5.14	5.63
LSD:[a]						
p = .05.......	0.20	0.14	0.11	0.24	0.22	0.13
DSD:						
p = .05.......	0.54	0.84	1.69	0.93	1.27	1.08
p = .01.......	0.72	1.12	2.29	1.23	1.71	1.44

[a] For each column lowest significant differences (LSD) are such that any lower are not significant; definitely significant differences (DSD) are such that any equal or higher are significant at the given level.

TABLE 3.6

Images Rated Significantly Smarter by Row Sample than by Column Sample (.05 Level or Better)[a]

	Negro			White		
	Gang	Lower Class	Middle Class	Gang	Lower Class	Middle Class
Negro						
Gang...		PIMP* _GIRL_	SJOB* HANG** _SHAR_*** TUFF* FENC DRUG*** _COOL_**	SHAR PIMP GIRL* SELF*	SJOB* SHAR* FENC*** CONN*** PIMP*** DRUG*** _COOL_* GIRL*** SELF*	SJOB** HANG*** TUFF* FENC*** CONN*** PIMP*** _DRUG_*** _COOL_*** GIRL***
Lower class..			HANG _SHAR_*** TUFF DRUG*** _COOL_*	SHAR	_SHAR_* _FENC_ CONN** PIMP*** DRUG** GIRL*	SJOB HANG*** TUFF _FENC_* CONN PIMP*** _DRUG_*** _COOL_*** GIRL***
Middle class..				GANG SELF	_SAVE_ _CONN_ PIMP* GIRL* GANG SELF	CONN PIMP*** GIRL***
White						
Gang...	TUFF _IEGO_*	_TUFF_ _COOL_	HANG* _SHAR_ TUFF*** _STIK_ FENC _DRUG_* COOL***		_TUFF_* FENC** CONN*** PIMP*** _DRUG_* COOL**	SJOB HANG*** TUFF*** _STIK_ FENC*** CONN*** PIMP*** _DRUG_* COOL***
Lower class..			_HANG_			HANG***
Middle class..	IEGO*** GANG*	_IEGO_ GANG	_SHAR_	GANG* SELF	_IEGO_ GANG* _SELF_	

[a] Italicized images are significant for smartness, but not for evaluation. Compare with Table 3.4.
* p < .01.   ** p < .001.   *** p < .0001.

class boys highest. However, this ordering is offset by the fact that both gang samples rated the third image, SAVE, higher than the white middle class boys. While slightly suggestive, this evidence falls short of the dramatic differences that the Cloward-Ohlin theory would seem to require, especially in view of the absolutely high ratings of these images as compared to the deviant images for all six populations. On the basis of significance tests, one must conclude that there is evidence of neither differential nor low legitimation of the behaviors represented by the middle class images by any population.

A sharp difference is to be noted between the smartness ratings, for all populations, of SHAR and SAVE; this difference was *not* reflected in the evaluation scores. All populations feel that it is much smarter to save than to share, while five out of the six evaluated SHAR higher than SAVE. (All six smartness differences between SHAR and SAVE are significant at the .0001 level.) Smartness is thus a more sensitive indicator than evaluation of behavior that a person would actually en dorse after a realistic appraisal of its material consequences and the justice of its attendant social expectations. Hence its use as a measure of legitimacy in the sense intended by Cloward and Ohlin appears to be justified. Intuitively, it would seem that if the smartness score registers the difference in utility of the behaviors represented by SAVE and SHAR, it should also reflect any tendency by gang boys to view the middle class behaviors as deficient in utility.

Hypotheses 1 through 4 are not supported by these data. And even when "legitimate" is substituted for "evaluate" in these hypotheses, they are still not supported by data based on "smartness" as a measure of legitimacy.

Lower class images.—Hypotheses 5, 6, and 7 all deal with lower class images. Contrary to hypothesis 5, neither white nor Negro gang boys evaluated SHAR and HANG higher than middle class images. Contrary to hypothesis 6, neither gang nor lower class boys evaluated any of the lower class images significantly higher than any of the middle class images.

Before interpreting these results, the relevant row comparisons for hypothesis 7, involving SHAR, SJOB, and HANG, must be considered. The evaluation means for SHAR show no interpretable pattern (although all Negro samples evaluated sharing significantly higher than white gang boys). However, both gang samples evaluated SJOB and HANG significantly higher than both middle class samples; both lower class samples evaluated HANG significantly higher than their racially matched middle class sample; and the Negro lower class evaluated both SJOB and HANG significantly higher than the white middle class.

Joined with the patterns of these data, these significant findings strongly support hypothesis 7, derived from Miller. In effect, this supports Miller's general contention that the values of the lower class are distinguishable from those of the middle class. The failure of hypotheses 5 and 6 suggests that these differences are based more heavily on attitudes toward lower class norms than on those toward middle class norms.

These findings suggest that the idea of sharing money with friends taps a set of normative expectations that is more nearly universal than those associated with work and leisure, so that SHAR differentiates the samples only when the smartness scores, raising considerations of legitimacy or practicality, are inspected. As a matter of general interest, attention is called to the fact that gang boys of both races —together with Negro lower class boys—evaluated and legitimated higher than anyone else the idea of having a humble job in a gasoline station.

The nature of the remaining images.—The remaining subcultural images (plus GIRL) were chosen to represent behaviors that the theories hypothesize as deviant alternatives to a respectable style of life, either middle class or lower class. Not all of these behaviors are technically illegal or necessarily indicative of antisocial intent. The behavior described by COOL and STIK is intrinsically innocuous, and in the latter case even commendable. TUFF and GIRL, if perhaps more clearly at variance with middle class codes, nevertheless entail no necessary legal violation. And DRUG suggests behavior that, although illegal, is often more self-injurious than harmful to others. As a result, although the images were employed principally to aid in the identification of delinquent subcultures among gangs, they also represent points in what might be regarded—from a middle class standpoint— as the middle and lower ranges of an evaluative continuum. It is in this range of such a continuum that the most striking differences between samples appear.

Some consistent racial differences and masculinity.—Inspection of the main diagonal of the upper right quadrant (which compares the races holding social level relatively constant) of Table 3.4 discloses three images that Negro boys evaluated significantly higher than white boys within each one of the three social levels. These images are PIMP, GIRL, and SELF. The consistent reappearance of this constellation is slightly suggestive of a narcistic syndrome among Negro adolescent males. That two of these images figure in the sex-identity hypothesis supplements rather than precludes this possible interpretation. However, the higher evaluation of SELF by Negroes (GANG follows the same pattern) could also be a defense against low racial self-esteem, such as was recently suggested by James W. Vander Zanden.[28] Sexual self-indulgence, narcism, and defensive self-esteem all tend to shade into one another, and to disentangle these concepts would require more discriminating measures. Although tentative, such interpretations are of interest, however, in view of E. Franklin Frazier's description of Negro middle class males as tending to "cultivate their 'personalities,' " a phrase suggestive of narcistic concern, and evidence that Negroes spend more for food, clothing, and automobiles than whites at the same income level.[29] Negro consumer habits are apt to be attributed to their lack of other economic outlets and status-seeking, but it may be that such behavior reflects a deeper and more pervasive kind of self-indulgence (perhaps also compensatory) that manifests itself also in non-economic behavior.

Frazier's observations are especially reassuring concerning findings, for example, for PIMP and GIRL, that show the Negro middle class to be deviant in some respects from the white middle class and perhaps even from white gang boys. Although hypothesis 8 predicted such results between the two middle class samples, the magnitude of the differences at first aroused strong misgivings as to the representativeness of the Negro middle class sample.

Nevertheless, the data are consistent with other information indicating that these Negro middle class boys were definitely active sexually. Their sexual success is easy to account for in view of their strong competitive position, based on polish, money, and cars, and the sexual permissiveness of Negro lower class girls. Probably, it is difficult for Negro middle class girls to compete under these conditions without becoming themselves sexually accessible.

An impression of the sexual activity of these boys can be gained from an incident which occurred after one of the testing sessions. One boy raised his hand politely to inquire whether they could now ask

[28] See his "The Non-violent Resistance Movement against Segregation," *American Journal of Sociology*, LXVIII (1963), 544–50, and the literature cited there.

[29] See *Black Bourgeoisie* (Glencoe: The Free Press, 1957), p. 220. On the Negro consumer see, e.g., "The Negro Market," *Time*, February 9, 1962, pp. 80–81.

the tester some questions. Anticipating curiosity about the tests, the tester invited any questions the boys might wish to pose. The first question, put with sincere concern, was "If you do it (sexual intercourse) too much, is it true that you give out young?" The question drew little laughter.

Final doubts concerning the possible representativeness of this sample were then erased by Frazier, whose description of the Negro middle class emphasizes mediocre aspirations (the boys spoke of being physical education teachers, not doctors or lawyers), overcommitment to material satisfactions (they dressed extremely well, and arrived driving their own family cars), sexual promiscuity (already indicated), and involvement in recreation (one admitted, "all *we* do is party").[30] Everything pictured by Frazier seems to fit, even down to the fact that the two clubs to which these boys belonged were the only groups to refer to themselves by Greek-letter names and to order "pledges" around in a semiautocratic manner.

In interpreting the racial differences, however, it must be kept in mind that the Negroes in each social category really are socioeconomically lower than the whites in the corresponding category (see Table 3.5).

Turning to the sex-identity hypothesis proper, all the various predictions from that compound hypothesis hold for the evaluative patterns of PIMP and GIRL; most of them are statistically significant as well. Furthermore, the mean scores for these two images display similar gradients, running from left to right across all six populations in Table 3.3. In each case Negro gang boys are highest, each succeeding sample being lower until white middle class boys appear as the lowest. Both race and social level thus produce differences in the evaluation of PIMP and GIRL that accord with the sex-identity hypothesis; quite unexpected, however, is the finding that at every social level the Negro boys evaluated these two images higher than *any* sample of white boys.

With slight exceptions, the pattern for smartness of these two images is much the same. One noteworthy change is that non-gang Negro boys drop slightly below white gang boys in the legitimation of PIMP; since this places all non-gang boys now lower than all gang boys it suggests that the non-gang Negroes have reservations about pimping and illegal "hustling" that are not reflected in their evaluation of PIMP.

[30] *Op. cit.*

The third image included in the masculinity hypothesis was TUFF. This image was evaluated significantly higher by gang and lower class boys of both races than by either of the middle class samples. Within each stratum, the whites were higher, although not significantly so. This is contrary to the expectation stated in hypothesis 8 that the Negroes would evaluate TUFF higher at each social level, as they did PIMP and GIRL. However, since both gang samples also evaluated TUFF higher than did their racially matched lower class samples—although not significantly—the strata are ordered in accordance with the hypothesis. The smartness ratings produced a similar ordering of strata, but no sign of consistently higher ratings by Negroes. In fact, white gang boys legitimated TUFF significantly higher than Negro gang boys; this is the only instance in which a deviant image received a significantly higher rating from white gang boys than from Negro gang boys.

While it is felt that the preponderance of this evidence is consistent with the hypothesis dealing with problems of sex identity (though by no means proving it), the failure of TUFF to parallel the differences for race exhibited by PIMP and GIRL is puzzling. Whether sex identity or simply subcultural norms are responsible, these results suggest a degree of independence between attitudes toward the sexual and the aggressive expression of masculinity.[31] (It is interesting to note that between PIMP and TUFF, Negro gang boys favor PIMP, whereas white gang boys significantly favor TUFF at the .0001 level for evaluation and the .01 level for smartness.) Vander Zanden has also called attention to the historical necessity for Negroes to suppress aggression; possibly this accounts for the fact that for TUFF five out of six comparisons of evaluation and smartness means, within stratum, show Negroes lower than whites, despite the tendency for Negroes to be generally more tolerant than whites toward the other deviant images.[32]

The narcotics image.—Of all images, DRUG received the lowest evaluation from both gang samples, and the lowest legitimation from ev-

---

[31] A plausible case for race differences in sexual permissiveness may be derived from the comparison of sex norms as described for Negro gang boys and the Negro middle class, on the one hand, and the white lower class, on the other. For Negro gang boys see Chapter 2. For the Negro middle class see Frazier, *op. cit.* For somewhat dated accounts of the white lower class as contrasted with the white middle class see William Foote Whyte, "A Slum Sex Code," *American Journal of Sociology,* XLIX (1943), 24–31, and Arnold W. Green, "The 'Cult of Personality' and Sexual Relations," *Psychiatry,* IV (1941), 343–48.

[32] *Op. cit.*, pp. 545–46.

eryone. (Both lower strata Negro samples evaluated DRUG significantly higher than Negro middle class and white lower class boys,
and both gang samples and the Negro lower class legitimated it significantly higher than all three remaining populations.)

In view of the consistently low tolerance shown toward most other
deviant images by the white middle class, their evaluation of DRUG
seems rather high compared to the Negro middle class and the white
lower class. However, these three samples are virtually identical in
rejecting DRUG's legitimacy; here, the white middle class accords it
the lowest smartness score in the entire table. Personal knowledge
gained in working with the white middle class boys suggests that
their relatively higher evaluation score may be a reflection of sophisticated compassion. If so, this provides another indication of meaningful independence between the two scores.

Criminal images, utility, and legitimacy.—The two images representing the criminal subculture were FENC and CONN. With minor im-
perfections, both of these images manifest a gradient that appears
repeatedly among the deviant images for both evaluation and smartness: Gang > Lower Class > Middle Class. (Perfect examples of this
gradient may be noted for PIMP, GIRL, and COOL.) Negro gang boys
evaluated FENC and CONN significantly higher than all four non-gang
samples; white gang boys evaluated them higher than all non-gang
boys except those in the Negro lower class. Both gang samples, and
the Negro lower class, legitimated FENC and CONN significantly higher
than the non-gang whites. The Negro middle class evaluated and legitimated CONN significantly higher than the white middle class.

The two criminal images are among those that differentiate gang
boys from lower class boys: PIMP, FENC, and CONN for both races and,
in addition, SJOB for whites. The gang and lower class Negroes both
evaluated SJOB at virtually the same high level. These four images
have in common a utilitarian emphasis, indicating that the role of
material gain in the values of gang boys is by no means negligible.
That gang members do not repudiate the possibility of legitimate gain
is indicated by the presence of SJOB. The prominence of the illegitimately gainful images suggests, however, that a choice between legal
and illegal means is determined to a lesser degree in favor of legal
means for gang boys than for lower class boys.

It can be shown, too, that the consideration of legitimacy or practicality appears even more conducive than that of evaluation to a
choice of illegal means, especially for gang boys. For example, all six

samples *evaluated* SJOB significantly higher than FENC (each at the .0001 level). However, only the non-gang whites *legitimated* SJOB significantly higher than FENC (white lower class, .01; white middle class, .02), while Negro gang boys now tied the two images, and white gang boys legitimated FENC higher than SJOB.

A similarly revealing comparison concerns SJOB and CONN. SJOB was evaluated significantly higher than CONN by all four non-gang samples (Negro and white lower class, .01; Negro middle class, .05; white middle class, .001), and the gang samples showed the same tendency. However, except for the non-gang whites, all samples legitimated SJOB and CONN in reverse order, with both gang samples now rating CONN significantly higher than SJOB (Negro gang, .0001; white gang, .001; and Negro lower class, .10).

Not only the respectable image, SJOB, declines relative to criminal images when the basis of comparison is shifted to smartness. The conflict image, TUFF, follows the same pattern, thus indicating that it is not respectability per se that is the determinant, but rather differential practicality or utility. All samples evaluated TUFF higher than FENC; for the four lower strata these differences are significant (Negro and white lower class and white gang, .0001; Negro gang, .01). This order of the images is reversed for smartness by all but the non-gang whites, with the Negro gang sample now attaining significance (.001) in the new direction.

These last findings corroborate the importance that Miller attaches to smartness and Cloward and Ohlin to legitimacy. In some respects, however, they are not fully congruent with the expectations generated by these theorists. The tendency for smartness to rearrange the orderings of images for the Negro middle class, but not for the white lower class—in the examples given above—is not consistent with Miller's locating the salience of this dimension chiefly in the lower class. And the finding that gang boys grant greater legitimacy to deviant images, while not withdrawing legitimacy from middle class images, does not accord with Cloward and Ohlin's emphasis on middle class norms as sensitive to considerations of legitimacy. Their contention would now seem to apply to middle class proscriptive norms, but not to middle class prescriptive norms.

A quick review of the statistical findings and patterns for deviant images will indicate that hypotheses 9 and 10 are supported, and in this respect all three theories are correct. However, where none of the theories specified differences between each possible pairing of the three social levels, these data strongly indicate a gradient for attitudes toward deviant behaviors, such that the acceptability of these behaviors is inversely related to social level.

Another gradient.—The images GANG, SELF, and IEGO display a social level gradient opposite to that for deviant images; the higher the level, the more highly these three images are evaluated (see Tables 3.4 and 3.6 for significance levels). For the image GANG, this trend suggests that the gang is not the close-knit, highly cohesive entity which some might expect.[33] Conceivably, the trend for IEGO reflects superego strength.

The images SELF and IEGO serve to indicate the direction of preference for these scores, thus ruling out the possibility that gang boys completely invert the evaluative dimension while continuing to describe behavior verbally much as middle class people might. All six samples wanted to be significantly better (Negro middle class, .001; all others, .0001) and smarter (Negro gang, .01; Negro middle class, .10; all others, .001) than they usually are. An analysis of the five individual evaluative scales for seventeen of the groups making up the total sample showed this directionality for SELF and IEGO to prevail throughout, with the scale "good-bad" always contributing its proportionate share of the gain within each of the six samples.

Discussion

The finding that delinquent boys order behaviors as to their goodness much the same as do non-delinquents is not new, having been demonstrated as early as 1940 by Ruth Bishop.[34] Although Bishop was able to show that both delinquent and non-delinquent populations divide good from bad behaviors at the same neutral point, her technique leaves one in doubt as to whether her data reflect the affective preferences of her populations or merely their equal ability to perform a cognitive judgment task.[35]

Osgood, however, has come to the conclusion after years of experience that semantic differential responses have an affective character,

[33] Yablonsky has also called into question the cohesiveness of gangs (see Lewis Yablonsky, "The Delinquent Gang as a Near-Group," *Social Problems,* VII [Fall, 1959], 108–17).

[34] "Points of Neutrality in Social Attitudes of Delinquents and Non-Delinquents," *Psychometrika,* V (1940), 35–45.

[35] The ambiguities involved in making this determination are discussed by Warren S. Torgerson, *Theory and Methods of Scaling* (New York: John Wiley & Sons, 1958), pp. 48–49..

apparently coinciding in dimensionality with universal dimensions of affective meaning applicable to all sensory modalities. He also feels that these dimensions typify ways in which people respond or react to their environment, rather than ways in which they receive and organize incoming stimuli.[36] This would seem to imply a greater relevance for behavior than if semantic differential responses merely recorded the passive categorizing of external stimuli. In addition, the global connotative richness of the five evaluative scales, the direction of the differences between IEGO and SELF, and the fact that for college students rating Morris' "ways to live" on a semantic differential, the correlation between a heavily evaluative factor and preference was .66 for individual scores and .93 for group means[37]—all indicate strongly that evaluation and preference are closely related.

Although such considerations do much to clarify the meaning of the observed responses, it is nevertheless difficult to comprehend their full significance until the data are tied into a complex net of additional evidence. For despite the specificity of the images, the behaviors they represent were necessarily judged entirely apart from the contexts in which they are normally encountered by members of the six populations. The responses, therefore, must be viewed as having an "in principle" quality,[38] which, from the standpoint of assessing values, is not at all inappropriate, although it does imply that the information so obtained may be seriously incomplete for the purpose of explaining behavior. For example, some of the populations may view their own *real* school experiences in a highly unfavorable light, for a variety of both objective and subjective reasons, and yet maintain an essentially positive attitude toward the idea of education in general. This does not imply that it is any less important to know what these more abstract attitudes are.

The data imply that acceptance of middle class prescriptive norms (the middle class images) is quite general, while middle class pro-

[36] Charles E. Osgood, "Studies on the Generality of Affective Meaning Systems," *American Psychologist,* XVII (January, 1962), 10–28.

[37] Charles E. Osgood, Edward E. Ware, and Charles Morris, "Analysis of the Connotative Meanings of a Variety of Human Values as Expressed by American College Students," *Journal of Abnormal and Social Psychology,* LXII (1961), 62–73.

[38] This "in principle" quality corresponds to the idea of "potential demand" in values as used by Cyril S. Belshaw, who elaborates further its implications for behavior ("The Identification of Values in Anthropology," *American Journal of Sociology,* LXIV [1959], 555–62).

scriptive norms (the deviant images) either decline in force or are rejected more strongly as social level goes down. The former alternative suggests a weakening of inhibitory mechanisms as social level declines, perhaps ultimately traceable to a superego construct, such as was suggested by the IEGO gradient for evaluation. The latter alternative, of rejection, raises somewhat more strongly the possibility of a "rationally" motivated choice, as indicated by the sensitivity of the images CONN and FENC to the practical emphasis of smartness for gang boys. The two alternatives need not be mutually exclusive.

In any case, the delicacy of the prescriptive-proscriptive balance achieved in their evaluations by gang boys raises the question of whether it indicates ambivalence toward middle class culture as a whole of the sort claimed by Cohen. Certainly, that would be a plausible interpretation. However, given that the hypothesis of reaction formation does not seem to be supported,[39] and that ambivalence can be said to exist whenever competing alternatives are present, the concept of ambivalence by itself lacks explanatory force.

In addition, it remains to be demonstrated that gang boys perceive legitimate and illegitimate behaviors as being in some sense mutually exclusive, so that a choice of one has strong implications for their realization of the other. Without such a demonstration, even equal evaluation of both kinds of behavior would not constitute sufficient evidence for ambivalence.

The implication in these data that gang boys evaluate highest behavior that appears as remote from their actual conduct as that depicted by GRAD, READ, and SAVE will undoubtedly strike many persons as an absurdity. Certainly, if the finding is valid, three separate theoretical formulations failed to make sufficient allowance for the meaningfulness of middle class values to members of gangs. To others, the apparent pervasiveness of middle class values in American life may come as no surprise; Cloward and Ohlin, it will be recalled, actually postulated that gang boys share middle class consumption values, although, contrary to this chapter's indications, they also held that middle class norms are not legitimated by gang boys. Miller has given reason to believe that he would dismiss these findings as indicative merely of "official" ideals.[40]

---

[39] For other evidence against the reaction formation hypothesis see Albert J. Reiss, Jr., and Albert Lewis Rhodes, "Delinquency and Social Class Structure," *American Sociological Review,* XXVI (1961), p. 729.

[40] *Op. cit.,* p. 7.

A number of points, bearing also on the more general problem of accounting for the disparity between theories and these findings, can be made in response to such a criticism. For one thing, the allegation that gang boys mirror official ideals in their responses is consistent neither with the finding that they rated images which are highly deviant, such as PIMP, significantly higher than non-gang boys, nor with the social-level gradients for deviant images.

A second point concerns both the role of values in social theory and the methodology by means of which values are identified. Unless it is to be seriously maintained that values strictly determine behavior, or vice versa, one must be prepared for findings such as these. The discrepancy between these findings and the values reported for lower class culture (with respect to middle class values) by Miller may be related to his anthropological methodology. The anthropologist often assesses values by inferring them from extended observation of a population's spontaneous behavior, including verbal behavior. Since Miller has described the focal concerns as more readily derivable from direct observation than values, and also reflecting "actual behavior," it follows that this was also his method.[41]

When studying an entire primitive society in this way one can be fairly certain of having witnessed the full range of behavior that members of that society hold in high regard, given the relatively constant constraints of the physical environment. However, when this method is applied to subcultures contained within a single society, it is apt to lead to fallacious results; for, in such an instance, the values of the populations studied can never be reported as other than those implied by their behavior.

Within a complex society, the existence of a differentiated segment of population may result from the operation of processes that constrain behavior in ways independent of, and in addition to, the constraints imposed by the values of that particular segment's members. To deny this is to favor an overly simple model of society. Such constraining processes can be either external or internal to a subculture. The limitation on opportunity that the larger society imposes on certain minority groups would be an example, from the Merton tradition, of an external constraint. The hypothesized female-dominated household would be an internal constraint. This hypothesis asserts that within lower class culture there exists a self-maintaining process that leads males to behave in self-defeating ways; this, in turn implies the

[41] *Ibid.*

frustration of tendencies to behave in ways that may actually be held in high regard.

Not even the anthropologist's use of verbal behavior, especially public or spontaneous verbal behavior, is free from this criticism if it is granted that what members of a subculture verbalize may itself reflect or even constitute a basis for their being differentiated from the larger population, despite their own deepest preferences. This criticism gains plausibility when it is noted that behaviors readily available to gang and lower class members and hence visible to the anthropologist, such as criminality, promiscuity, and pimping, are ones upon which Miller and the semantic differential are in accord; behaviors whose realization may be limited for lower class persons—as represented by the middle class images—are ones over which Miller and the semantic differential disagree.

In view of the unexpected nature of some of these findings, additional efforts to test their validity are being undertaken. If they are valid, the interpretations that may prove most important to the refinement of delinquency theory are the following: (1) For all six populations, the endorsement "in principle" of middle class prescriptive norms is uniformly high. (2) Gang, lower class, and middle class boys differ most in their attitudes toward behaviors proscribed by the middle class, and they tend to be ordered as listed with respect to their tolerance toward these behaviors. (3) Legitimacy or practicality, as measured by a "smart-sucker" scale, seems to be a meaningful basis for distinguishing behavior. There is some evidence that gang boys, more than other boys, may be led by this distinction to a choice of criminal behavior over legitimately gainful behavior. (4) The hypothesis of a sex-identity problem for lower class and gang boys appears worth pursuing further.

Since these interpretations are not derived from true probability samples, it will be necessary for readers to employ discretion in applying them to other universes. A consideration of the degree to which other universes might reasonably be expected to differ in these respects from this chapter's samples should be of some guidance.

It is anticipated that the implications of these findings will be better understood if their further development is deferred until other relevant data have been analyzed.

CHAPTER 4

Behavior Dimensions of Gang Delinquency

Apparently the gang of today is not the gang of yester-
day. The rich "natural histories" compiled by the "old Chicago
school"—Shaw, McKay, Thrasher,[1] *et al.*—give accounts of gang behavior that differ in important respects from delinquency as it is hypothesized to exist today. For example, *specialization* of delinquency
pattern has received considerable emphasis in current literature as
compared with the past. Weapons and the intent of gang conflict are
more lethal, and "kicks" more addicting. Theoretically, delinquency
is seen as rooted less in community tradition and "fun," and more in
frustration and protest or in the serious business of preparing for manhood, whether in the female-based households of an autonomous lower class or in the mysterious and powerful underworld of organized
crime.[2]

This is an expanded version of a paper read at the annual meetings of the
American Statistical Association, 1962. See *Proceedings of the Social Statistics
Section*, pp. 62–67. The paper was published in the *American Sociological Review,*
XXVIII (June, 1963), 411–28. Co-authors were James F. Short, Jr., Ray A.
Tennyson, and Kenneth I. Howard. The authors wish to express their gratitude
to Robert A. Gordon, Hanan C. Selvin, and Stanton Wheeler for critical review
of earlier versions of the paper.

[1] See Clifford R. Shaw, *The Jack Roller* (Chicago: University of Chicago
Press, 1930); Clifford R. Shaw and Maurice E. Morre, *The Natural History of a
Delinquent Career* (Chicago: University of Chicago Press, 1931); and F. M.
Thrasher, *The Gang* (Chicago: University of Chicago Press, 1936). More recent
but unsystematically gathered and analyzed data are reported in many sources,
e.g., Donald J. Merwin (ed.), *Reaching the Fighting Gang* (New York: New
York City Youth Board, 1960). Discussion of the extensive clinical literature on
juvenile delinquency is omitted in this paper.

[2] Cf., in comparison with the references in footnote 1, the theoretical points
of view set forth in Albert K. Cohen, *Delinquent Boys: The Culture of the
Gang* (Glencoe: The Free Press, 1955); Albert K. Cohen and James F. Short, Jr.,
"Research in Delinquent Subcultures," *The Journal of Social Issues,* XIV (1958),
20–37; Richard A. Cloward and Lloyd E. Ohlin, *Delinquency and Opportunity:
A Theory of Delinquent Gangs* (Glencoe: The Free Press, 1960); Walter B.
Miller, "Lower Class Culture as a Generating Milieu of Gang Delinquency,"

Resolution of theoretical differences, between the past and the present and among currently competing theories, requires greater precision, theoretically and empirically, in the delineation of the dependent variables. We shall group these under the term "gang delinquency," avoiding for the moment the knotty problem of specifying the nature of "subcultural delinquency" or the even greater problem of defining delinquent subcultures. In this chapter discussion is limited largely to the measurement of individual *behavior*, rather than individual or group norms, values, or self-concepts. We shall review first of all the setting of the research and methods of gathering data. This will be followed by discussion of the statistical model chosen for analysis of the data, its application in the present instance, and interpretations of the behavior patterns isolated by this procedure. Finally, individual gangs will be described in terms of the patterns found among all gang boys studied, and an assessment undertaken of the implications of findings for subcultural theory.

The Research Setting

To review from Chapter 1, data were collected from 598 members of 16 "delinquent gangs" assigned detached workers by the Program for Detached Workers of the YMCA of Metropolitan Chicago. The gangs ranged in size from 16 to 68 members, on the basis of workers' judgments concerning who should and who should not be considered members. Initially, gangs were selected by the YMCA on the basis of their generally troublesome character to the community, as judged by police complaints and the reports of welfare agencies, and by field investigations of the detached-worker staff. Later, in collaboration with the research program, gangs were selected to fulfil requirements of a research design which sought to study gangs representative of major "delinquent subcultures."

Our gangs were deliberately chosen from the *delinquent* end of a delinquent–non-delinquent continuum, the primary effort being di-

---

The Journal of Social Issues, XIV (1958), 5–19; H. A. Bloch and Arthur Neiderhoffer, *The Gang: A Study in Adolescent Behavior* (New York: Philosophical Library, 1958). Bordua recently has remarked on the differences between past and present notions concerning the structural motivations of delinquency, and particularly on the greater strain. See David J. Bordua, "Some Comments on Theories of Group Delinquency," *Sociological Inquiry,* XXXII (Spring, 1962), 245–60, and "Delinquent Subcultures: Sociological Interpretations of Gang Delinquency," *Annals of the American Academy of Political and Social Science,* CCCXXXVIII (November, 1961), 119–36.

rected toward locating carriers of conflict, criminal, and retreatist subcultures.[3] In the end, the search for gangs concentrated on the "criminal" and "drug-use" types, principally because conflict-oriented gangs, particularly among Negroes, were abundant.

The Data

Dissatisfaction with official statistics as a basis for measuring delinquent behavior has led in recent years to experimentation with a variety of methods for obtaining better measures of such behavior. Combinations of a variety of public and private agency records,[4] anonymously completed self-reports,[5] survey-type interviews,[6] detailed clinical investigations,[7] and reports of field observers[8] confirm the suspicions of those who claim that official records are unreliable as a basis for determining either the extent or the nature of delinquent behavior.[9]

[3] Rather than concentrating wholly on one type or on the more amorphous "parent-delinquent subculture" which has been hypothesized as a general subculture from which specialized variants emerge. See Cohen and Short, *op. cit.*

[4] Edward E. Schwartz, "A Community Experiment in the Measurement of Juvenile Delinquency," *Yearbook of the National Probation Association*, 1945, pp. 157–82; Alfred J. Kahn, *Police and Children*, New York Citizens' Committee on Children of New York City, 1951.

[5] Austin L. Porterfield, *Youth in Trouble* (Fort Worth: Leo Potisham Foundation, 1946); James F. Short, Jr., and F. Ivan Nye, "Reported Behavior as a Criterion of Deviant Behavior," *Social Problems*, V (Winter, 1957), 207–13.

[6] Albert J. Reiss, Jr., and Albert Lewis Rhodes, "The Distribution of Juvenile Delinquency in the Social Class Structure," *American Sociological Review*, XXVI (October, 1961), 720–33; and Maynard L. Erickson and Lamar T. Empey, "Court Records, Undetected Delinquency, and Decision-Making," *Journal of Criminal Law, Criminology, and Police Science*, LIV (December, 1963), 456–69.

[7] The clinical literature is vast. Among the more research-oriented investigations are: Lester E. Hewitt and Richard L. Jenkins, *Fundamental Patterns of Maladjustment: The Dynamics of Their Origin* (Springfield: State of Illinois, 1947); and Fritz Redl and David Wineman, *Children Who Hate—The Disorganization and Breakdown of Behavior Controls* (Glencoe: The Free Press, 1951).

[8] Fred J. Murphy, Mary M. Shirley, and Helen L. Witmer, "The Incidence of Hidden Delinquency," *American Journal of Orthopsychiatry*, XVI (October, 1946), 686–96; Walter Miller's recent work and our own are the most extensive examples of the use of such methods of generating data.

[9] These same studies suggest that police and court data are likely to be more reliable and perhaps more valid, as a basis for studying certain types of behavior than others. Cf., particularly Schwartz, *op. cit.*; Murphy, Shirley, and Witmer, *ibid.*; James F. Short, Jr., and F. Ivan Nye, "The Extent of Delinquent Behavior: Tentative Conclusions," *Journal of Criminal Law, Criminology, and Police Science*, XLIX (December, 1958), 296–302; and from the present research program,

Consideration of alternative methods of generating data on the behavior of the gang boys under observation led to the rejection of most of the usual methods; instead, a system of ratings by the detached workers seemed the most feasible and reliable method of obtaining the needed data.

We required, first of all, a method of gathering data on a wide variety of behaviors, including many which were both illegal and regarded by society as definitely undesirable. This, plus the unfavorable exposure of many of these boys to law-enforcement agencies and the necessity of identifying the boys by name, led to the rejection of self-reporting by the boys as a primary method of data collection. Resources for extensive clinical investigation of individual boys were not available to us and the widely scattered location of the gangs throughout the inner-city area made the inter-agency "clearing house" method impractical for our purposes.

The availability of detached workers as intimate observers of the boys, particularly in the gang setting, offered a rare opportunity to gain more complete and objective insights into the behavior of these boys than could be provided by any other method. Weekly interviews with the workers convinced us that they shared intimately in the on-going life of the gang.[10] Such behavioral information as was not known by direct contact with a boy could usually be inferred from conversations among the boys or directly with the worker in the endless "bull sessions" on the street corner. The nature of these contacts seemed particularly conducive to objective reporting of the type of behavior we were interested in measuring, i.e., street-corner behavior.[11] This behavior could be described in concrete terms and it did not require abstract conceptualization by our informants.

John M. Wise, "A Comparison of Sources of Data as Indexes of Delinquent Behavior," Master's thesis, University of Chicago, 1962, unpublished. This matter is of the greatest significance for the large-scale and long-term measurement of delinquent behavior because only official sources of data have the potential for objective, continuous collection of data from very large populations and subpopulations. For the most recent and sophisticated attempt to utilize police data for delinquency measurement, see Thorsten Sellin and Marvin E. Wolfgang, *The Measurement of Delinquency* (New York: John Wiley & Sons, Inc., 1964).

[10] See Ray A. Tennyson, "Detached Workers as Sources of Data," paper read at the annual meetings of the Society for the Study of Social Problems, August, 1960 (dittoed).

[11] In contrast to information concerning the behavior of the boys within the context of family, school, employment, and other more conventional institutions. For the latter we have relied particularly upon survey methods.

What we needed was a "baseline" of information on the behavior of our population, information which could be statistically manipulated and related to other variables we were studying. Toward this end a list of sixty-nine behavioral categories was drawn up.[12] Because we were interested more in incidence of behaviors and their relative frequency, rather than absolute frequencies, and because workers' observations could not extend to actual counts of behavior, we asked only that each boy be rated in terms of whether he had *engaged* in a particular type of behavior only a few times or many times. Workers were asked to report only after they had been in contact with a group for at least six months, to restrict their reporting to boys whom they and the group recognized as group members, and to limit their reports to information in which they were confident. An item-by-item review of their reports was undertaken by the research staff to insure the most accurate reporting possible. Most gang members were rated by only one rater, though two gangs had more than one worker over the rating period, and members of these were rated by each worker having at least six months' contact. A high degree of consensus was noted in these ratings. Comparison of worker reports with police records reveals no marked tendency for workers to "underreport" or "overreport."[13] Length of contact with the gang, beyond the six-month minimum requirement, is unrelated to behavior ratings so far as "reliability" is concerned.[14] Our assumption is that obtained differences between gangs were due to differences in behavior rather than differences in rater characteristics.

The sixty-nine behaviors, together with their reported incidence by Negro and white gang boys, are listed in Table 4.1.

There are great differences in the incidence of these behaviors among our gang boys, and apparently some of these are related to racial composition of the population. In this form, however, the data

[12] We are indebted to Walter B. Miller for allowing us to utilize the Special Youth Program Coding Manual (March, 1958) in drawing up the list of behaviors to be studied.

[13] See Wise, *op. cit.*

[14] See footnote 23. The point here is that groups with which the program has had the longest contact are not necessarily the most delinquent. Our interpretation is that workers come to know a great deal about the boys in a relatively short period of time and that reported differences between groups outweigh any tendency for boys to become "more delinquent" (in a cumulative sense) with the passage of time.

TABLE 4.1

INCIDENCE OF SIXTY-NINE BEHAVIORS AMONG NEGRO AND WHITE GANG BOYS, RANKED BY PERCENTAGE OF REPORTED INVOLVEMENT

	Negro N = 464	White N = 134	Total N = 598
Hanging on the street................	89.2	95.5	90.6
Alcohol (drinking)....................	85.6	89.6	86.5
Dancing............................	85.1	63.4	80.3
Loitering...........................	72.0	84.3	74.7
Smooch, neck, petting...............	72.8	78.4	74.1
Sexual intercourse...................	78.9	57.5	74.1
Signifying (playing the dozens)*......	79.1	53.7	73.4
Joy riding..........................	67.5	93.3	73.2
Softball............................	71.1	67.9	70.4
Statutory rape......................	73.1	50.7	68.1
Playing cards (for money)............	62.7	85.8	67.9
Playing cards (for fun)..............	66.6	70.1	67.4
Drunk.............................	62.5	82.1	66.7
Working (on a job)..................	59.1	79.9	64.2
Individual fighting—without weapons.	67.5	52.2	64.0
Pool...............................	60.1	69.4	62.2
Basketball.........................	61.6	51.5	59.4
Shooting dice......................	64.4	35.1	57.9
Gang fighting—without weapons.....	61.4	44.8	57.7
Boxing............................	59.5	38.8	54.8
Penny pitching.....................	58.8	33.6	53.2
Buy and sell alcohol................	52.8	70.9	53.0
Theft..............................	50.9	58.2	52.5
Carry concealed weapons............	55.8	40.3	52.3
Swimming..........................	51.1	56.0	52.2
Gang fighting—with weapons........	53.2	40.3	50.3
Truancy...........................	48.3	53.7	49.5
Create public disturbance...........	44.6	64.9	49.2
Shoplifting.........................	47.2	47.0	47.2
Vandalism.........................	40.9	64.9	46.3
Assault............................	48.7	35.1	45.7
Being "shook down".................	44.2	36.6	42.5
Smoke pot.........................	42.5	33.6	40.5
Individual fighting—with weapons....	45.0	23.9	40.3
Auto theft.........................	35.1	57.5	40.0

* Signifying is a form of systematic exchange of insults, ordinarily carried out in the presence of an audience. It serves as a social control mechanism and a device for displaying verbal virtuosity. "Playing the dozens" is a special form of signifying, concentrating in pornographic insults concerning family members of opponents. See Ralph F. Berdie, "Playing the Dozens," *The Journal of Abnormal and Social Psychology*, XLII (January, 1947), 120–21.

TABLE 4.1—*Continued*

	Negro N = 464	White N = 134	Total N = 598
Strong-arm	45.6	12.7	38.3
Burglary	30.0	53.7	35.3
Running errands (for parents)	37.7	23.1	34.4
Ping Pong	26.5	48.5	31.4
Football	28.7	35.8	30.3
Driving without a license	24.4	44.0	28.8
Wrestling	30.6	19.4	28.1
Baby sitting	27.2	20.1	25.6
Baseball	23.7	28.4	24.7
Drunk driving	18.5	31.3	21.4
Runaway	17.7	29.1	20.2
Track and field	24.6	4.5	20.1
Buy and sell marihuana	19.8	19.4	19.7
Shakedown	22.4	6.0	18.7
Gang bang	18.3	17.2	18.1
Skating	20.3	9.0	17.7
Robbery	18.7	11.9	17.2
Bowling	5.8	32.1	11.7
Use hard narcotics	7.3	23.1	10.9
Fathering an illegitimate child	17.0	3.7	10.7
Child or wife abandonment	11.9	6.0	10.5
Homosexuality	6.5	14.2	8.2
Offering "protection"	9.5	3.0	8.0
Buy and sell narcotics	6.0	14.9	7.9
Forgery	7.3	6.7	7.2
Bribery	2.6	18.7	6.2
Rape	5.0	5.2	5.0
Lottery	1.7	15.7	4.8
Common-law marriage	4.7	3.7	4.5
Pimping	5.6	.7	4.5
Playing horses (betting)	1.3	4.5	2.0
Homicide	1.7	.7	1.5
Arson	.2	2.2	.7
Suicide (attempt)	.2	1.5	.5

are not interpretable as behavior patterns. We turn next, therefore, to the reduction of these data.

The Dimensionality of Delinquent Behavior

Empirically, our problem was to determine the nature of behavioral patterns characterizing the boys and gangs studied. Theoretically, we wanted to relate observed to hypothesized patterns and to assess their significance for subcultural theory.

The dimensionality of delinquent and criminal behavior has been approached by a variety of clinical and statistical techniques, and occasionally by a combination of these.[15] Several investigators have found self-reported delinquency to scale acceptably when unidimensional scaling methods are employed.[16] These methods tend to be arbitrary in assigning items to particular scales, however, and to select for study dimensions which are not especially relevant to theories of delinquency causation. Unfortunately, the theories are not very helpful in this matter, for they lack specificity in describing the patterns of behavior they purport to explain. Hence the problem: the theories regard delinquency as multidimensional, but they do not tell us precisely the nature of these dimensions. Our delinquent population consisted of boys who were members of gangs and who thereby presumably met one of the principal criteria of subcultural delinquency. Furthermore, these gangs were selected on the basis of at least superficial similarity to the subcultural patterns we wanted to study. We therefore chose a model which would tell us how the behavior of these boys "hangs together"—whether in demonstrable packages which could be interpreted in the light of subcultural theory, or in a more or less undifferentiated way.

Because we wished not to have a large number of dichotomous "variables," the sixty-nine behaviors were combined into thirty-seven items on the basis of similarity of item content. These combinations are presented in Table 4.2.

Product-moment correlations were calculated for all thirty-seven items (Table 4.3). The generally positive character of the resulting correlation matrix suggested that involvement in delinquency is to some extent a global phenomenon, the dimensions of which might lie along a continuum of more or less delinquency involvement, regardless of the specific offenses committed. However, the considerable range in incidence of the several types of delinquency found in Table 4.1—together with variations in the seriousness with which these be-

---

[15] Hewitt and Jenkins, *op. cit.*; Albert J. Reiss, "Social Correlates of Psychological Types of Delinquency," *American Sociological Review*, XVII (December, 1952), 710–18.

[16] F. Ivan Nye and James F. Short, Jr., "Scaling Delinquent Behavior," *American Sociological Review*, XXII (June, 1957), 326–31; John F. Scott, "Two Dimensions of Delinquent Behavior," *American Sociological Review*, XXIV (April, 1959), 240–43; Robert A. Dentler and Lawrence J. Monroe, "Social Correlates of Early Adolescent Theft," *American Sociological Review*, XXVI (October, 1961), 733–43.

TABLE 4.2

Reclassification and Scoring of Behaviors for Statistical Purposes

New Classification	Old Classification	Range of Scores, New Classification
Domestic chores	Baby sitting; running errands	0–2
Team sports	Baseball; basketball; football; softball	0–4
Individual sports	Bowling; boxing; ping pong; pool; skating; swimming; track; wrestling	0–8
Signifying (playing the dozens)	No change	0–2
Hanging on the street	No change	0–2
Joy riding	No change	0–2
Social activities	Dancing; singing; playing cards for fun	0–3
Gambling	Playing horses; lottery (numbers, etc.); penny pitching; playing cards for money	0–4
Petting	No change	0–2
Working (on a job)	No change	0–2
Sexual intercourse	No change	0–2
Fathering an illegitimate child	Abandonment; fathering illegitimate child	0–2
Arson	No change	0–1
Auto theft	No change	0–2
Bribery	No change	0–1
Theft	Burglary; shoplifting; theft	0–6
Alcohol (drinking)	Use of alcohol; buying and selling alcohol; drunk; drunk driving	0–11
Narcotics	Use of narcotics; buying and selling narcotics	0–3
Marihuana (Pot)	Use of marihuana; buying and selling marihuana	0–3
Carry concealed weapon	No change	0–2
Common-law marriage	No change	0–1
Public nuisance	Loitering; creating a public disturbance; vandalism	0–4
Driving without a license	No change	0–2
Group fighting	Group fighting with weapons; group fighting without weapons	0–6
Individual fighting	Individual fighting with weapons; individual fighting without weapons	0–6
Forgery	No change	0–2
Gang bang	No change	0–2
Homicide	No change	0–1
Homosexuality	No change	0–2
Pimping	No change	0–1
Robbery	Armed robbery; strong-arming; offering protection; shakedown	0–7
Rape	No change	0–1
Statutory rape	No change	0–2
Run away from home	No change	0–2
Suicide (attempt)	No change	0–1
Truancy	No change	0–2
Assault	No change	0–2

TABLE 4.3

PRODUCT-MOMENT CORRELATIONS BETWEEN THIRTY-SEVEN BEHAVIORS, FOR ALL GANG BOYS

	Assault	Truancy	Suicide	Runaway	Statutory rape	Rape	Pimp	Homosexual	Homicide	Gang bang	Forgery	Driving without license	Common-law marriage	Concealed weapon	Bribery	Auto theft	Arson	Sex Intercourse	Work experience	Petting	Joy Ride	Hanging	Signifying	Robbery	Individual fighting	Group fighting	Public nuisance	Narcotics	Pot	Alcohol	Theft	Illegitimate children	Gambling	Social acts	Individual sports	Team sports	Domestic chores
Domestic chores	22	24	-04	06	21	-00	00	-06	04	16	18	09	-01	30	02	08	-05	19	11	24	22	26	26	12	30	34	25	-11	07	16	18	08	17	32	26	28	
Team sports	07	20	03	05	11	-23	-00	-08	02	06	05	16	01	00	01	07	07	09	17	19	21	25	21	05	09	10	18	-04	01	06	16	06	27	37	58		
Individual sports	19	26	03	14	13	06	01	-08	-04	11	-04	15	04	10	09	12	-04	16	21	24	35	30	28	20	14	16	29	07	24	21	29	13	44	45			
Social acts	27	28	-06	09	25	02	14	08	-02	16	16	10	05	16	10	07	-05	29	32	32	31	34	38	18	27	29	25	-14	09	18	20	09	44				
Gambling	25	35	-01	16	28	07	12	03	14	19	16	23	11	26	14	18	-01	24	13	28	23	33	28	33	22	29	36	02	24	33	35	09					
Illegitimate child	16	02	09	06	24	14	18	16	16	24	02	16	39	17	24	04	10	21	12	23	10	05	06	23	20	18	12	16	25	25	16						
Theft	58	43	06	46	30	15	20	28	08	33	23	50	14	47	24	62	05	42	21	25	38	31	25	56	47	48	60	27	44	06							
Alcohol	53	30	07	37	47	11	22	28	10	37	23	56	13	50	24	62	08	28	07	39	33	27	27	49	54	54	60	31	48								
Pot	39	15	12	20	29	20	17	39	11	30	09	25	21	36	01	51	-01	-00	21	18	16	18	18	49	35	30	35	48									
Narcotics	19	10	11	16	10	04	17	42	19	22	13	20	17	10	15	28	08	20	09	04	15	04	07	26	11	08	21										
Public nuisance	56	54	08	38	31	05	13	19	09	38	28	43	11	44	22	51	05	43	06	35	47	37	09	40	51	53											
Group fighting	60	28	04	27	53	13	17	10	11	35	26	32	11	64	14	37	01	40	11	35	24	22	37	45	77												
Individual fighting	65	26	01	31	47	17	20	18	17	36	27	28	09	50	12	44	01	25	09	18	23	16	29	47													
Robbery	51	24	09	31	34	20	04	30	12	36	27	36	20	55	-01	17	-04	34	-01	50	22	48	18														
Signifying	22	19	03	12	40	21	06	01	09	12	14	15	03	24	01	23	00	17	24	48	43	16															
Hanging	19	27	05	13	30	04	08	03	01	12	11	20	08	21	06	33	01	12	18	22	24																
Joy ride	32	38	-03	22	50	05	02	04	06	09	16	29	07	29	23	22	01	57	26	35																	
Petting	17	19	-00	12	08	04	16	-00	12	15	16	25	06	08	12	09	-01	28	18																		
Work experience	06	-00	-05	-00	50	-02	04	12	08	06	06	13	11	34	08	24																					
Sex intercourse	29	-03	-00	14	19	13	15	05	06	21	34	60	08	16	14	10																					
Arson	02	03	05	02	74	07	15	15	09	15	21	25	14	36	16																						
Auto theft	44	04	05	13	02	05	17	15	11	32	25	28	12	09																							
Bribery	10	23	04	11	26	09	22	13	02	17	07	29																									
Concealed weapon	54	01	23	25	13	12	16	16	-02	35	24																										
Common-law marriage	11	-00	10	-00	44	18	04	15		10																											
Driving without license	30	28	12	32	15	-05	18	11		33																											
Forgery	36	16	12	12	27	12	02	28		31																											
Gang bang	26	24	17	21	17	07	18	06																													
Homicide	13	02	-02	13	26	12	03																														
Homosexual	22	04	23	20	06	12	10																														
Pimp	17	09	16	06	10	10																															
Rape	14	15	-02	15	16																																
Statutory rape	34	29	06	20																																	
Runaway	37	01	06																																		
Suicide	05																																				
Truancy	29																																				
Assault																																					

haviors are regarded by the law and the wide variation in the size of correlations between behaviors—suggested that it might be possible to find clusters of related items which would prove to be theoretically interesting. A preliminary cluster analysis suggested that factor analysis was a promising model.[17]

The correlation matrix was factor analyzed, using the principal axis method and entering the highest column correlations in the main diagonal. Following a modification of Wrigley's criterion for when to stop factoring,[18] five factors were extracted and rotated using Varimax. The first unrotated factor accounted for much more of the common variance than did any succeeding factor, again pointing to the existence of a general delinquency trait; but there was ample evidence from the factor analysis that somewhat specialized adaptations also existed among our subjects. Communalities of the thirty-seven behavior items and their loadings on each of the factors are presented in Table 4.4.

Factor I is essentially a *conflict* factor, its highest loading items being individual fighting (.79), group fighting (.76), carrying concealed weapons (.67), and assault (.67). None of these behaviors loads highly on any other factor. Robbery, theft, public nuisance, and statutory rape also load fairly highly on this factor, ranging from .51 to .40, but these items have similarly high loadings on other factors. Factor I may be more precisely characterized as consisting of conflict offenses, both acquisitive and destructive. Note the negative (though low) loadings on this factor of work experience, team sports, attempted suicide, and narcotics involvement.

Factor II has highest loadings of individual sports (.71), team sports (.68), social activities (.60), and gambling (.48). Other loadings higher than .40 are obtained for joy riding, truancy, and hanging. The latter behaviors have similarly high loadings on other factors, however. This factor may be characterized as a configuration of

[17] Louis L. McQuitty, "Elementary Linkage Analysis for Isolating Orthogonal and Oblique Types and Typal Relevancies," *Educational and Psychological Measurement*, XVII (Summer, 1957), pp. 207–29; Louis L. McQuitty, "Hierarchical Syndrome Analysis," *Educational and Psychological Measurement*, XX (Summer, 1960), 293–304; Louis L. McQuitty, "A Method for Selecting Patterns to Differentiate Categories of People," *Educational and Psychological Measurement*, XXI (Spring, 1961), 85–94.

[18] Kenneth I. Howard and Robert A. Gordon, "Empirical Note on the 'Number of Factors' Problem in Factor Analysis," *Psychological Reports*, XII (February, 1963), 247–50.

TABLE 4.4

Item	Commu- nalities	Factor I	Factor II	Factor III	Factor IV	Factor V
Group fighting.........	73	76	13	−30	−06	−19
Individual fighting....	72	79	10	−22	−09	−19
Sex intercourse........	70	26	02	−77	−17	−08
Statutory rape........	66	40	01	−68	−18	−09
Public nuisance.......	65	43	34	−05	−10	−58
Theft...............	62	44	32	03	−22	−53
Assault.............	61	67	17	−03	18	32
Alcohol.............	60	36	06	−39	−26	−49
Auto theft...........	58	26	07	−10	−14	−69
Concealed weapon.....	56	67	05	−22	−13	−21
Individual sports......	56	01	71	−13	−17	−07
Petting..............	55	12	22	−67	−01	−18
Robbery.............	51	51	09	−04	−35	−33
Driving without license	50	13	11	−17	−14	−65
Social activities.......	48	22	60	−26	06	06
Team sports..........	48	−06	68	−11	−02	03
Pot.................	46	29	10	−11	−55	−23
Hanging.............	42	07	40	−44	03	−25
Narcotics............	42	−01	−08	04	−56	−32
Signifying...........	42	21	31	−53	04	−05
Truancy.............	41	26	43	04	09	−39
Joy riding...........	39	09	45	−10	−01	−41
Homosexuality........	37	05	−10	03	−53	−27
Gambling...........	35	19	48	−20	−10	−17
Gang bang..........	29	32	08	−08	−28	−32
Illegitimate child......	29	14	06	−15	−50	04
Runaway............	28	27	10	02	−06	−44
Domestic chores.......	27	31	36	−17	11	02
Common-law marriage.	25	06	06	−07	−48	05
Work experience......	18	−09	17	−36	−06	−10
Forgery.............	16	24	03	−09	−06	−30
Attempted suicide.....	14	−02	00	03	−36	−06
Bribery.............	11	03	−02	−10	−10	−29
Pimping.............	11	14	02	−07	−27	−11
Rape...............	10	18	−16	−05	−04	−19
Arson...............	04	00	−11	−01	−04	−15
Homicide...........	03	12	−03	−01	−11	−03

stable corner-activities. No seriously delinquent behavior loads highly, though several minor types of delinquency have moderate loadings.

Factor III is difficult to characterize. It has as its highest loading items sexual intercourse (.77), statutory rape (.68), petting (.67), signifying (.53), hanging on the corner (.44), and the use, buying, and selling of alcohol (.39). It also has the only moderately high loading of any factor for work experience (.36), accounting for nearly all of this item's common variance. We have chosen to call this a *stable sex* pattern and to regard the loading of work experience as a further indication of a type of relatively adaptive behavior which is represented by the factor.

Factor IV is characterized by high loadings for quite different sex behaviors, namely homosexuality (.53), fathering an illegitimate child (.50), and common-law marriage (.48). Additionally, it has as its highest loading the use, buying, and selling of narcotics (.56) and of marihuana (.55). This factor accounts for virtually all of the low communalities of suicide and pimping, with loadings of .36 and .27, respectively. In contrast with Factor III, work experience has a loading of only .06, sex intercourse .17, statutory rape .18, petting .01, hanging .00, and signifying .00 on Factor IV. The combination of narcotics involvement, the "deviant" sex behaviors, and attempted suicide, leads us to identify this factor as *retreatist*.

Factor V includes the highest loadings of auto theft (.69) driving without a license (.65), public nuisance (.58), theft (.53), use, buying, and selling of alcohol (.48),[19] and running away from home (.44). In addition, this factor includes moderately high loadings for joy riding (.41) and truancy (.39). The versatility of this combination of offenses within a variety of institutional contexts (e.g., the "institutions" of property, school, and family, and in general the maintenance of public order) leads us to characterize this factor as an *auto-theft–authority-protest* pattern. As an abbreviated description we shall refer to Factor V as representing *authority protest*.[20]

We note that no clearly "criminal subculture" factor was extracted by our procedures. The variance of criminal behaviors is spread over

[19] We note, parenthetically, that only about 7 per cent of alcohol's variance is accounted for by its interaction on Factor IV. It seems clear that only a small proportion of the buying, selling, and use of alcohol is related to the extreme emphasis placed on kicks which is represented by Factor IV. Alcohol is virtually ubiquitous, loading on all but the non-delinquent Factor II.

[20] We note the similarity of authority protest to the delinquent subculture hypothesized in Cohen, *op. cit.*

all of the factors to a greater extent than either conflict or retreatist behaviors. It is clear from an examination of the seven most "criminal" items in Table 4.5, however, that the five factors are not "equally criminal."

While there is much variation in the loadings of items on each factor as well as across factors, Factor V emerges as the most generally "criminal" ($\bar{x} = 15.4$), followed by Factors I ($\bar{x} = 9.1$), II ($\bar{x} = 4.9$), IV ($\bar{x} = 4.1$), and III ($\bar{x} = 0.7$). The means for these criminal items are deceiving, however, because they cover up variations which aid in the interpretation of the factors and of these specific criminal

TABLE 4.5

LOADINGS AND PROPORTION OF VARIANCE OF SEVEN CRIMINAL BEHAVIORS ACCOUNTED FOR BY EACH OF FIVE FACTORS*

Criminal Behaviors	Factor I	Factor II	Factor III	Factor IV	Factor V
Robbery........	51 (26.0)	09 (.8)	−04 (.2)	−35 (12.3)	−33 (10.9)
Theft..........	44 (19.4)	32 (10.2)	+03 (.1)	−22 (4.8)	−53 (28.1)
Auto theft.....	26 (6.8)	07 (.5)	−10 (1.0)	−14 (2.0)	−69 (47.6)
Forgery........	24 (5.8)	03 (.1)	−09 (.8)	−06 (.4)	−30 (9.0)
Pimping.......	14 (2.0)	02 (.0)	−07 (.5)	−27 (7.3)	−11 (1.2)
Bribery........	03 (.1)	−02 (.0)	−10 (1.0)	−10 (1.0)	−29 (8.4)
Gambling......	19 (3.6)	48 (23.0)	−10 (1.0)	−10 (1.0)	−17 (2.9)
$\bar{x}$..........	(9.1)	(4.9)	(0.7)	(4.1)	(15.4)

* Proportion of variance placed in parentheses.

behaviors. For example, auto theft and bribery are relatively specific to Factor V, pimping to Factor IV, and gambling to Factor II.

Except for the high loadings of non-criminal behaviors on Factor V, this might be considered an essentially criminal factor. Our characterization of this factor, however, suggests that such a designation is not appropriate; observation of gangs with the highest Factor V scores, below, confirms this decision. Thus, the criminal behaviors studied are associated with different configurations of offenses rather than as a factor themselves. No rationally directed effort to acquire money emerges in isolation from other factors. Instead, criminal activity is associated with conflict, retreatism, and general rebellious activity, and to some extent also with stable corner-boy activity. Only the stable-sex factor fails to share at least 10 per cent of the variance of at least one of these "criminal" behaviors. This factor accounts for no more than 1 per cent of the variance of any of these behaviors. The behaviors loading high on Factor IV, strong-arm robbery, pimping, and petty thefts, seem most appropriately characterized as "hustles" toward the acquisition of money to finance drugs, alcohol, and other kicks. The motivation for criminal activity is less clear in their association with other factors. Further interpretation of the relation of criminal and other types of behavior is undertaken in the "Discussion" section of the chapter.

To maximize the independence of factors for etiological inquiry, we decided to eliminate from factor scoring all items which were not relatively "pure" on a given factor, and to weight the contribution of each item to a factor score according to the proportion of the item's variance which was accounted for by interaction with other items on a given factor. Loadings of .40 or higher on more than one factor were considered sufficient to eliminate an item from scoring.[21] Table 4.6 lists the items utilized for factor scoring. Scoring involved summing of the standard score, weighted by the factor loading of each item, for each boy.

The list of items *eliminated* from scoring by our criteria is instructive theoretically as well as empirically. Table 4.7 lists the ten most common of these items, together with their loadings on each of the factors.

Robbery and theft, two of the previously considered "criminal" offenses, are the only two relatively serious "delinquencies" on this list. Slightly more than 10 per cent of robbery's variance in the original matrix is accounted for by Factors IV and V, and about 25 per cent by Factor I. Virtually no robbery variance is accounted for by the "non-delinquent" Factors II and III. The variance of theft, by contrast, is distributed more evenly over four of the five factors.

The behaviors listed in Table 4.7 are interesting from still another standpoint, i.e., their versatility and, with the exception of theft and robbery, what might be called their "low-delinquency valence" relative to the more seriously delinquent items. This is not to say that these items are non-delinquent in a legal sense. But they tend to be "non-

---

[21] Items with nearly equal (but smaller than .40) loadings on more than one factor were eliminated, as were several items which did not load highly on any factor. For the latter, very little of their variance could be accounted for by the factors extracted from the original matrix. In some instances these behaviors were so infrequently committed that the items had virtually no variance. Items eliminated by this criterion were homicide, arson, rape, bribery, and forgery. Fathering an illegitimate child was eliminated because it is an "outcome," rather than a behavior. See Chapter 2.

TABLE 4.6

Factor I
Individual fighting.....................	79
Group fighting	76
Concealed weapons....................	67
Assault..............................	67

Factor II
Individual sports.....................	71
Team sports.........................	68
Social activities......................	60
Gambling............................	48

Factor III
Sexual intercourse....................	−77
Petting..............................	−67
Signifying...........................	−53
Work experience......................	−36

Factor IV
Narcotics............................	−56
Pot.................................	−55
Homosexuality.......................	−53
Common-law marriage.................	−48
Attempted suicide....................	−36
Pimping.............................	−27

Factor V
Auto theft...........................	−69
Driving without license...............	−65
Runaway.............................	−44

TABLE 4.7

LOADINGS OF TEN NON-SCORED ITEMS ON EACH OF FIVE FACTORS

Behavior	Factor I	Factor II	Factor III	Factor IV	Factor V
Domestic chores..	31 (9.6)	36 (13.0)	−17 (2.9)	11 (1.2)	02 (.0)
Theft.............	44 (19.4)	32 (10.2)	03 (.1)	−22 (4.8)	−53 (28.1)
Alcohol..........	36 (13.0)	06 (.4)	−39 (15.2)	−26 (6.8)	−49 (24.0)
Public nuisance...	43 (18.5)	34 (11.6)	−05 (.3)	−10 (1.0)	−58 (33.6)
Robbery.........	51 (26.0)	09 (.8)	−04 (.2)	−35 (12.3)	−33 (10.9)
Hanging.........	07 (.5)	40 (16.0)	−44 (19.4)	03 (.1)	−25 (6.3)
Joy riding........	09 (.8)	45 (20.3)	−10 (1.0)	−01 (.0)	−41 (16.8)
Gang bang.......	32 (10.2)	08 (.6)	−08 (.6)	−28 (7.8)	−32 (10.2)
Statutory rape....	40 (16.0)	01 (.0)	−68 (46.2)	−18 (3.2)	−09 (.8)
Truancy.........	26 (6.8)	43 (18.5)	04 (.2)	09 (.8)	−39 (15.2)
$\bar{x}$.............	(12.1)	(9.1)	(8.6)	(3.8)	(14.6)

criminal" in character, in the sense that their commission by adults is not considered to be criminal, and the "norms" which they violate are of a predominantly moral character (as in the case of the sex offenses) or they are concerned specifically with upbringing of children (truancy and alcohol connected offenses) or with keeping the peace (hanging, public nuisance, and joy riding). Joy riding may in some instances be directed toward economically utilitarian goals, but the fact that its highest loading is on the essentially non-delinquent Factor II suggests that this rarely is the case. Joy riding, like most of the other behaviors in Table 4.7, is delinquent in the sense suggested by the term "parent-delinquent subculture," i.e., associated with the general problems of adolescence, accentuated in most cases for gang boys (e.g., problems of interpersonal relations and striving for status and recognition). Such problems involve adolescents' relations among themselves and with the institutions of adult authority—property and school—or adult-adolescent relations in the process of keeping the peace.[22]

Behavior Factor Profiles of 16 Gangs

We turn now to an examination of the mean factor scores of our sixteen gangs presented in Table 4.8. The data are presented in standard-score form and from the highest to the lowest ranking gang on each factor in order to facilitate comparison of gangs and examination of the total range of each type of behavior which is found within our population. In Table 4.9 the sixteen groups are *ranked* according to the size of their mean score on each of the factors.

Because of the method of sample selection we must be extremely cautious in "hypothesizing" relationships between variables within our population on the basis of competing theories of delinquent subcultures. In this section we limit ourselves to the relation of race to group mean factor scores. Following Cloward and Ohlin, we expected that Negro gangs would have higher conflict factor scores than would white gangs. That is, both legitimate and illegitimate economic opportunities seem objectively more limited for Negroes than for whites —hence, the expectation of greater conflict orientation among Negro

---

[22] This usage of the term "parent-delinquent subculture" does not imply rejection of adult or middle class values in the manner of "reaction-formation," as originally hypothesized by Cohen. It implies, rather, recognition of the moral validity and legitimacy of adult and middle class prescriptive norms. See Chapter 3.

TABLE 4.8

MEAN BEHAVIOR FACTOR SCORES FOR ELEVEN NEGRO AND FIVE WHITE GANGS, RANKED BY SIZE OF GROUP MEANS

Behavior	Group Identification Number and Race															
Factor I (conflict)	03 Negro 1.25	15 Negro 1.10	20 Negro .23	05 Negro .19	09 Negro .14	02 Negro .01	24 White −.03	18 White −.24	13 White −.25	23 Negro −.28	01 Negro −.38	22 White −.43	21 Negro −.55	10 Negro −.80	17 White −.95	11 Negro −1.08
Factor II (stable corner-boy activity)	23 Negro 1.20	20 Negro .76	09 Negro .71	21 Negro .63	13 White .43	15 Negro .32	17 White .19	10 Negro .08	03 Negro .07	02 Negro −.28	05 Negro −.40	22 White −.41	11 Negro −.52	18 White −.61	01 Negro −.65	24 White −.75
Factor III (stable sex-maturity)	09 Negro .74	15 Negro .72	03 Negro .61	05 Negro .47	10 Negro .45	13 White .02	24 White .01	20 Negro −.03	02 Negro −.15	22 Negro −.21	18 White −.22	11 Negro −.28	01 Negro −.72	23 Negro −.99	21 Negro −1.00	17 White −1.13
Factor IV (retreatist)	24 White 2.59	09 Negro .76	20 Negro .61	02 Negro .12	05 Negro .00	22 White −.04	23 Negro −.11	15 Negro −.12	03 Negro −.16	18 White −.27	01 Negro −.32	21 Negro −.37	13 White −.50	10 Negro −.54	11 Negro −.57	17 White −.59
Factor V (authority protest)	24 White .90	15 Negro .84	18 White .47	13 White .44	20 Negro .29	03 Negro .27	11 Negro .25	22 White .13	02 Negro −.12	09 Negro −.15	23 Negro −.21	17 White −.23	05 Negro −.39	01 Negro −.55	21 Negro −.55	10 Negro −.73

than among white gangs. No inference from the various theoretical positions under examination relative to the expected elevation on other factors among Negro and white gangs seemed clear enough to be included in this paper. Several findings emerge:[23]

TABLE 4.9

FACTOR SCORE RANKS OF SIXTEEN GANGS ON FIVE FACTORS

Gang Name and Code No.	Factor I	Factor II	Factor III	Factor IV	Factor V
Negro Gangs:					
Midget Knights......01......	11	15	13	11	14
Junior Knights......02......	6	10	9	4	9
Vice Kings..........03......	1	9	3	9	7
Rattlers............05......	4	11	4	5	13
Chiefs..............09.......	5	3	1	2	10
Garden Gang.......10.....	14	8	5	14	16
Mighty Peewees.....11......	16	13	12	15	5
Southside Rattlers...15......	2	6	2	8	2
Vandals............20......	3	2	8	3	6
Midget Vandals......21......	13	4	15	12	15
Navahoes..........23......	10	1	14	7	11
Mean rank..............	7.7	7.5	7.8	8.2	9.8
White Gangs:					
Amboys............13......	9	5	6	13	4
Aces...............17......	15	7	16	16	12
Ravens............18......	8	14	11	10	3
Pizza Grill.........22......	12	12	10	6	8
Pill Poppers........24......	7	16	7	1	1
Mean rank..............	10.2	10.8	10.0	9.2	5.6

[23] The reliability problem referred to earlier in the chapter may be assessed in part by examination of the mean months of contact with the groups, in terms of their mean factor scores. A crude measure is provided in the following table:

MEAN MONTHS OF WORKER CONTACT
WITH GROUPS RANKING

Factor	1–8	9–16
I......................	13.0	12.8
II.....................	12.5	13.5
III....................	13.8	12.0
IV....................	12.3	13.5
V.....................	11.5	14.3

The one factor which might be expected to show the greatest tendency for increased incidence with time does so—that is, Factor III—due primarily to the increase in work and heterosexual activity with age. The difference in mean

(1) The most conflict-oriented gangs are Negro. All six gangs with mean scores above the total population mean are Negro. The *mean rank* of Negro gangs on Factor I is 7.7 (out of 16) as compared with 10.2 for white gangs. (There is much variation in conflict orientation among Negro gangs, however. Three of the four least conflict-oriented gangs also are Negro.)

(2) The range of between-group variation within this population is greatest for Factor I (conflict) and least for Factor V (authority protest).

(3) The largest *difference* between contiguous groups in rankings occurs between the highest and next highest ranking groups on Factor IV (retreatism). This difference is 1.53 standard units, while the difference between the second highest group on retreatism and the lowest is only 1.12 standard units. The magnitude of these differences makes comparison of mean ranks of Negro and white groups relatively meaningless for this factor.

TABLE 4.10

RANK ORDER CORRELATIONS BETWEEN GANG MEAN
FACTOR SCORES, FOR SIXTEEN GANGS, BY FACTOR

	Factor II (Stable Corner-Boy Activity)	Factor III (Stable Sex-Maturity)	Factor IV (Retreatist)	Factor V (Authority Protest)
Factor I (conflict)	.16	.71	.68	.40
Factor II (stable corner-boy activity)		.09	.04	−.22
Factor III (stable sex-maturity)			.44	.29
Factor IV (retreatist)				.18

(4) Negro gangs are, on the average, higher on Factors II and III, with mean ranks of 7.5 and 7.8, respectively, compared with mean ranks of 10.8 and 10.0 for white gangs.

(5) Only on Factor V do white gangs clearly rank higher than Negro gangs. Four of the five white gangs have positive group means for this factor, and three of the four highest-ranking groups are white. Mean rank for white gangs is 5.6, compared to 9.8 for Negro gangs.

(6) With one exception, individual group profiles are positively correlated with one another, but vary greatly and inconsistently in the relative elevation of different factors. Rank order correlations between the ranks of the 16 gangs studied on each of the five factors are presented in Table 4.10.

months of contact between groups ranking 1–3 and 14–16 on Factor III is even more striking—14.7 months and 10.0 months, respectively. Age differentials in factor scores will receive further discussion in a later paper. Suffice it to say that for both Negroes and whites, Factor III is positively related to age.

Only Factor II rankings fail to correlate consistently in the positive direction with the rankings of other factors.[24] No positive correlation with Factor II rankings is high, and its highest correlation is negative, with Factor V. Groups high on conflict tend also to be high on stable sex, retreatism, and authority protest. The correlation between rankings on Factors III and IV is moderately high; other correlations are comparatively low but positive. Despite these generally positive correlations, however, much variation in the relative elevation of any group on any given factor remains unexplained by its elevation on any other factor.

Discussion

Data presented here are only indirectly relevant to the issue of the existence or the nature of delinquent subcultures. We have, after all, investigated the behavior of individuals rather than groups. To assess subcultural theory on the bases of these data, we must assume the relevance of the groups to which these individuals belong for understanding their behavior. Such an assumption seems warranted in view of the methods of selection of boys for study and the group context within which the raters (detached workers) know the boys.[25]

Conflict and retreatism emerge as fairly distinct emphases in terms of factor structure, but criminal behavior does not. Observational data clarify the relation between various types of "criminal" behavior and other types of delinquency which were found in Table 4.5. We know, for example, that tough, conflict-oriented boys sometimes display and utilize their neighborhood "rep" by charging small amounts from younger boys for "protection" or by "shaking down" paper boys. Members of such gangs are known to purse-snatch, shoplift, and burglarize. The norms of the gang regard these as acceptable ways of acquiring a little "bread" to buy a bottle of wine, a bite to eat, one's share of the cost of a game of pool, and the like.

By contrast, these criminal activities are directed toward the acqui-

---

[24] When factor scores are intercorrelated for individual boys, the resulting matrix also is positive, with product-moment correlations ranging from .06 to .47. Differences appear also between Negroes and whites in this matrix. These findings will be developed further in the next chapter.

[25] Selvin and Hagstrom have suggested factor analyzing grouped data as a means of empirically classifying groups. The small number of groups (sixteen) in our study is a problem, but an attempt will be made to look at our data in this way. See Hanan C. Selvin and Warren O. Hagstrom, "The Empirical Classification of Formal Groups," *American Sociological Review*, XXVIII (June, 1963), 399–411.

sition of larger sums of money when related to drug use. Even a "nickel bag" of marihuana costs five dollars. Pills are less expensive but the habit requires a continuous supply, and heroin is very expensive. In addition to robbery and theft, pimping emerges as a retreatist-related activity consistent with the joint emphasis on "kicks" and "hustles."[26]

Auto theft often is part of a complex which involves dressing up one's own auto, "souping up" the motor, etc. These things require money or appropriate auto parts. Groups highest on this factor are known also to sell parts of stripped autos. Forgery and bribery are also related to Factor V. Observational data suggest that both are relatively petty among our boys, involving attempts to cash forged checks in small denominations and bribing policemen who apprehend them in various delinquencies. Gambling and theft, which are the only criminal items with moderate loadings on Factor II, are part of a recreational rather than a criminal pattern. No criminal item has even a moderate loading on Factor III.

None of our gangs is properly characterized as a "criminal subculture," or a carrier of such a subculture. No clear separation between criminal and conflict emphases is apparent from the factor analysis or from observational data. The latter suggest, however, that various criminal activities may characterize *cliques* of *conflict* gangs. Data from a large, white street-corner group *without discernible delinquency specialization* (not included in this analysis because they were discovered too late) also suggest that "criminal cliques" may develop within such groups. In the observed case a clique of eight boys formed exclusively around rationally directed theft activities— auto stripping, burglary, shoplifting, etc. This clique did not hang together on the corner, but met in one another's homes. When on the corner they hung with other members of the larger group. They participated in the general hanging and drinking patterns, and in occasional altercations with various adults as part of this larger group, but not as a distinguishable clique. *Only in their pattern of theft activities were they a clique.* For at least two years they were reasonably successful in these activities, in terms of money and goods acquired, in fencing or selling directly to customers, and in avoiding arrest or "fixing" arrests when they were apprehended. Several members of the group eventually were arrested, however, and several

[26] Harold Finestone, "Cats, Kicks, and Color," *Social Problems,* V (July, 1957), 3–13.

thousands of dollars worth of stolen goods was found stored in one of their homes. Prior to this, the activities of the group had been considerably cramped by the "capture" of the leader by a detached worker from the YMCA.

On balance, the criminal data concerning our gangs, based on ratings and preliminary analysis of observational data, are consistent with descriptions of "semi-professional" theft as an emphasis of individuals and cliques developed within the context of a "parent delinquent subculture" rather than as a fully developed criminal subculture as described by Cloward and Ohlin.[27] The "criminal clique" referred to above has this character, as do other cases from our observational data. The absence of a clear-cut factor among our boys, or of a clearly criminal gang, in no way demonstrates the non-existence either of the criminal subculture or of criminal gangs such as those described in the Cloward-Ohlin typology. On the basis of our experience in Chicago, however, we are skeptical of the existence in this city of gangs of this type.

The evidence presented here argues for the existence of types of behavior which are common to all gangs. It has been suggested that these items may constitute a "parent-delinquent subculture," out of which the more specialized delinquent adaptations emerge. Neither the validity nor the utility of such a concept can be assessed on the basis of data presented in this paper, but the data are consistent with such a formulation. The extent to which specific delinquency emphases come to characterize a gang at any point in time—and if they do, just how such specialization comes about—is unclear from these data. Hopefully, answers to such questions will be provided from further study of such variables and processes as (1) the reaction of these lower class gang boys to a variety of institutional contexts (involving, for example, relations in the family and at school, and the values of private property and keeping the peace); (2) the study of interpersonal relations within the gang as well as between gangs, and relations between the gang and the external world; and (3) the study of other variables specified in competing theories attempting to account for subcultural delinquency.

---

[27] Cf. Cohen and Short, *op. cit.*; and Cloward and Ohlin, *op. cit.* Quay and Blumen also failed to discover a "delinquency for profit" factor in their factor analysis of data from juvenile court records of 191 male delinquents with repeated court contacts. See Herbert C. Quay and Lawrence Blumen, "Dimensions of Delinquent Behavior," *Journal of Social Psychology*, LXI (1963), 273 77.

From one point of view, the positive correlations between delinquency factor scores, both between individuals and groups, argues against the existence of specialized delinquent subcultures. Two considerations give us pause in following this line of argument. The first of these concerns evidence supportive of subcultural differentiation drawn from our own observational data. The second concerns the nature of the rating data employed in the analysis. In short, the positive association of factor scores found in our data may be due to the operation both of a theoretical characteristic of delinquent subcultures *and* to a methodological artifact. Concerning the first point, theories of delinquent subcultures hypothesize that groups may move from one adaptation to another. This is particularly true of discussions of the evolution of more specialized varieties of delinquent subcultures from a more amorphous parent-delinquent subculture, and of discussions of the development of retreatist adaptations as a consequence of failure in other adaptations such as conflict or crime.[28]

Observational data tell us that this is indeed what happens in some cases among our groups. The most retreatist group studied, it may be noted, also was the highest scoring *white* group on conflict and the highest of all groups on Factor V. We know, however, that this group has not been involved in conflict at least as long as we have observed them.[29] Their conflict score results from knowledge of *prior* conflict activities by this group. They had, at one time, been very much engaged in conflict, but during the past two years had turned completely from conflict to embrace drug use and other kicks. Although our documentation is incomplete, their sequence of delinquency adaptation could be characterized as beginning with parent-delinquent subcultural involvement to which were added, successively, conflict and then retreatism. Conflict was given up as an activity either participated in by the group or serving as a status-giving activity of the group. Conflict was no longer normatively prescribed by the group, if indeed it ever was, as kicks and other esoteric experiences became highly valued in terms of the individual and collective experiences of these boys. At the same time, the activities represented by Factor V (auto theft, driving without a license, runaway, etc.) were not given up, but continued in forms consistent with their other delinquency adaptations. The observational materials are rich and complete enough in this instance to encourage considerable confidence

[28] *Ibid.* See, also, Bloch and Neiderhoffer, *op. cit.*
[29] On this point, see Chapter 9.

in labelling the retreatist phase of the group's behavior as subcultural in nature. This is true, also, of the criminal clique described above. Our difficulty in locating groups such as these, however, suggests that they were rare in Chicago, at the time of our investigation, relative to conflict gangs and gangs without discernible specialization.

The methodological artifact which inhibits interpretation of these findings as contraindicative of the existence of delinquent subcultures is related also to the phasing hypotheses of subcultural adaptation. Recall that the raters were asked whether a boy ever had engaged in a particular type of behavior and how frequently. Thus, the data are cumulative and not sensitive to changing adaptations over time. A related consideration concerns the problem of the reliability of behavioral ratings based upon past as opposed to present behavior. Data on past activities are less reliable than reports of current activities.

Despite these limitations of the data, we believe that the data are useful in introducing greater precision in the measurement of the behavior of individuals and groups studied and that further analyses of data from the several phases of our research program will permit more complete documentation and modification of hypotheses concerning the subcultural nature of gang delinquency.

Conclusion

The full implications of our findings for subcultural theories of juvenile delinquency cannot be assessed until the data are viewed in combination with observational data from detached workers and our own staff, and in terms of analyses of their relation to etiological variables specified by the theories. The former add the richness and detail of situational and group-process determinants which the ratings employed in the factor analysis miss entirely. At the same time, without the more systematic and "objective" ratings, one can never be certain as to the representativeness of his observations or his own objectivity in recall and choice of behavior reported. Our tentative conclusion is that delinquent subcultures exist, but that they are not as "pure" as they have been pictured, and they become articulated in ways much more complex than existing theories specify. Further study is needed of within- as well as between-group variations in behavior. These, in turn, must be related to assumed causal variables within the group, community, and larger social system; and to variations in individual abilities, motivations, values, and personality characteristics.

CHAPTER 5

Racial Differentials in Gang Behavior: An Interpretation

As a first "next step" in deciphering the delinquency patterns of our gangs, in this chapter we will examine further the interrelations of behaviors measured in the last chapter, using race as a primary variable. Field observations by detached workers will supplement the statistical analysis.

We look first of all at the matrix of correlations between the factors described in Chapter 4, by the 464 Negro and 134 white gang boys. In Table 5.1 we see that these correlations tend to be moderate in size and positive in direction. For both races boys with high scores on one factor tend to be high on the other factors. Only in the case of conflict and authority protest (Factors I and V), however, do scores on one factor account for as much as 25 per cent of the variance of the other factor. For present purposes, the major point of interest in the table concerns the radically different relation between stable corner activities (Factor II) and the other factors for white, as compared with Negro, gang boys. For the latter, the pattern of correlations between all factors is consistent—greater involvement in corner-boys' activities means greater delinquency for Negro gang boys. For white boys, however, corner boys' activities are unrelated in any systematic way to conflict, stable sex-maturity, and authority protest, and their highest correlation is negative with retreatist behavior, indicating a degree of incompatibility of these behaviors. The only other significant difference between Negro and white correlations involves Factors III and V, and both of these correlations are positive and significant at the .01 level.

We had expected "retreatist" behaviors to be negatively correlated with corner-boy activities for both whites and Negroes, since they

We wish to thank Ray A. Tennyson for aid in preparation of tables and selection of case materials for this chapter.

represent an emphasis upon kicks, which in its extremity is even further removed from conventional behavior than are other types of delinquency. Such an expectation is consistent, also, with Cloward and Ohlin's hypothesis of retreatism as a reaction to double failure, in illegitimate as well as legitimate pursuits.

TABLE 5.1

INTERCORRELATIONS OF INDIVIDUAL SCORES ON FIVE
BEHAVIOR FACTORS BY RACE

	(STABLE CORNER-BOY) FACTOR II		(STABLE SEX-MATURITY) FACTOR III		(RETREATIST) FACTOR IV		(AUTHORITY PROTEST) FACTOR V	
	Negro	White	Negro	White	Negro	White	Negro	White
Factor I (conflict)								
Negro	.28*		.44*		.34*		.53*	
White	**	−.01		.45*		.38*		.53*
Factor II (stable corner-boy)								
Negro			.41*		.22*		.24*	
White			**	.12	**	−.32*		.14
Factor III (stable sex-maturity)								
Negro					.17*		.28*	
White						.27*	**	.49*
Factor IV (retreatist)								
Negro							.32	
White								.39

* $r > 0$, $p < .01$.
** Difference between Negro and white correlations significant, $p < .01$.

In Chapter 4 we noted that 42.5 per cent of our Negro as compared with 33.6 per cent of our white gang boys "smoked pot." By contrast, only 7.3 per cent of the Negro boys had used hard narcotics, as compared with 23.1 per cent of the white boys. We noted also that all of our evidence pointed to the fact that we had only one clearly defined retreatist-oriented gang, and this was a group of white boys. Observational data suggest that marihuana use was more matter-of-fact among Negro gangs, while it represented a much sought after and more esoteric kick among the somewhat fewer white boys who practiced it. Even the use of hard narcotics was viewed more casually and as experimental in nature among the Negro boys, with the one exception who became an addict (as noted in Chapter 2). Reactions to his addiction by fellow members of the Chiefs (group 09 in the previous chapter) confirms the non-retreatist nature of drug use among those boys, the highest scoring Negro gang on Factor IV. By contrast, the Pill Poppers (group 24) actively sought new "highs"; these experiences formed a major part of their conversation with each other and the principal activity in which they had a joint interest.[1] Evidence concerning the community setting as it bears on these differences will be deferred until later in the chapter.

TABLE 5.2

CORRELATIONS BETWEEN STABLE CORNER-BOY FACTOR
SCORES AND TEN BEHAVIORS BY RACE

Behaviors	Negro Gang Boys	White Gang Boys
Domestic chores.......	.36**	.24**
Theft...............	.36**	.21*
Alcohol.............	.30** a	−.02
Public nuisance.......	.40**	.25**
Robbery.............	.27** a	−.14
Hanging.............	.46** a	.05
Joy ride.............	.46** a	.09
Gang bang...........	.21** a	−.14
Statutory rape........	.25**	.06
Truancy.............	.37**	.27**

* r > 0, p < .05.
** r > 0, p < .01.
a Difference between correlations for Negro and white boys significant, p < .01.

The relation between corner-boy behaviors and delinquency among our gang boys is further informed by correlations in Table 5.2 between Factor II scores and scores on the ten behaviors which were too generally associated with the factors to be included in factor scoring.

Here again stable corner-boy activities are positively related to delinquent as well as non-delinquent behaviors for Negro gang boys. For whites, four of the ten correlations also are positive and significant. The other six correlations for white boys do not reach satisfactory levels of significance (with N = 134, p < .05 for r = .17), but the most seriously delinquent behavior in the list (robbery) tends to be negatively related to corner-boy activities, as does gang bang. Use of alcohol, robbery, hanging, joy ride, and gang bang all are clearly

[1] For further discussion of this group, see Chapters 8 and 9.

more closely involved with sports, singing and dancing, and gambling among Negro boys than is the case for white boys. The closer correlation of peer-related delinquent and non-delinquent activities among Negro gang boys is confirmed.

With this confirmation in mind, we turn to an examination of involvement in delinquency and in the family-related behaviors represented by domestic chores (baby sitting and running errands). In Table 5.2 domestic chores are positively correlated with corner-boy activities among both Negro and white boys. In Table 5.3, however, we see a dramatic reversal of the relation between domestic chores and the more delinquent behaviors by race.

TABLE 5.3

CORRELATIONS BETWEEN DOMESTIC CHORES AND
DELINQUENCY FACTORS BY RACE

	Negro Gang Boys	White Gang Boys
Factor I (conflict)............	.42** [a]	−.14
Factor III (stable sex-maturity)..	.38** [a]	−.21*
Factor IV (retreatism).........	.04[b]	−.18*
Factor V (authority protest)....	.19** [a]	−.07

* $r > 0$, $p < .05$.
** $r > 0$, $p < .01$.
[a] Difference between correlations for Negro and white boys significant, $p < .01$.
[b] Difference between correlations for Negro and white boys significant, $p < .05$.

Performance of domestic chores is compatible with delinquency involvement as represented by three of the four delinquency factors among Negro gang boys. By contrast, the trend is clearly toward incompatibility of domestic chores and delinquency among the white gangs.

Two points of special interest emerge from these findings. They suggest first of all that the delinquency of these white gang boys involves *protest against conventional family obligations* to a greater extent than is the case for the Negro boys. And the low but positive association of domestic chores and Factor V, specifically, suggests that the interpretation of this factor as representing authority protest may be inappropriate for Negro boys. This reservation is weakened somewhat by the positive correlation of Factor V with still another institutional context, the school; correlations with truancy are positive and significant for both Negro (.37) and white gang boys (.27).

The picture which emerges from these tables is that Negro gang delinquency tends *not to be clearly differentiated from non-delinquent behavior*—that participation in the "good" aspects of lower class Negro life (responsibility in domestic chores and organized sports activities) is closely interwoven with "bad" aspects (conflict, illicit sex, drug use, and auto theft).

The literature on lower class Negro life is rich in detail which supports such a conclusion among adults as well as children and adolescents.[2] As compared with lower class white communities, delinquency among lower class Negroes is more a part of a total life pattern in which delinquent behaviors are not as likely to create disjunctures with other types of behavior. Differences in life styles between white and Negro communities are economic as well as ethnic, historical as well as current.[3]

It is clear, for example, that Negro gang boys in our study are more firmly imbedded than the white boys in the lower regions of the lower class, although there are variations in this respect among the communities in which the boys lived and hung out. Demographic data make the point very clearly, as in Table 1.1 in Chapter 1. It will be recalled that there was a complete lack of overlap between white and Negro lower class areas in median income. Very little overlap was found in any of the columns except median rent, where the disadvantage of Negroes is even more apparent by the comparison with income levels. Three other comparisons between our Negro and white lower class study areas are just as striking. The percentage of males aged fourteen and above who are unemployed averages 4.8 for white areas and 10.6 for Negro; percentage of families with incomes under $3,000 stands at 13.7 for whites and 34.1 for Negroes; and a measure of overcrowding (percentage of dwelling units with 1.01 or more persons per room) finds 39.7 per cent of the homes in Negro areas overcrowded in contrast with 14.3 per cent in white areas.[4] No white area is as disadvantaged as the least disadvantaged Negro area with respect to these measures.

Occupational prestige data also are relevant to this point. As part of an extended interview, boys were asked to specify the occupation of the main earner in their families. By scoring these on the Duncan

---

[2] See especially St. Clair Drake and Horace R. Cayton, *Black Metropolis: A Study of Negro Life in a Northern City* (revised and enlarged edition, New York: Harper and Row, 1962), Chapters 20 and 21.

[3] *Ibid.*

[4] Daniel S. Parrish compiled census tract figures for these comparisons.

transformation to the NORC–North-Hatt scale, an index of the relative social position of each boy's family was obtained.[5] The mean decile rank of main earner's occupations for 196 Negro gang boys interviewed was 3.6, corresponding to laborer in metal industry, cook, or waiter, while 88 white gang boys reported occupations averaging 5.0, comparable in status to an auto mechanic or bartender. The difference is significant statistically and in terms of our argument. These same figures for lower class non-gang boys were for Negro 4.2 and for white 5.1. Data on family stability suggest further that Negro gang boys were most likely to come from that segment of the lower class which S. M. Miller has referred to as the "unstable poor," while white gang boys and lower class non-gang boys in both races were more likely to belong to the "stable poor."[6]

Finally, interviews with detached workers suggest that in contrast with lower class white areas, life in the lower class Negro areas was oriented around such "institutions" as "quarter parties," informal neighboring from the vantage of one's front steps, and neighborhood pool halls and taverns, to a greater extent than in otherwise comparable white areas. In short, "community" life, for adults as well as children and adolescents, was largely informal and quasi-public in the Negro areas.[7] White areas had their neighborhood taverns—sometimes with a distinct ethnic flavor—but these tended to be the exclusive domain of adults. Indeed, at times they became the focus of

[5] See O. D. Duncan, "A Socioeconomic Index for All Occupations," and "Properties and Characteristics of the Socioeconomic Index," in Albert J. Reiss, Jr., *Occupations and Social Status* (New York: The Free Press of Glencoe, Inc., 1961). See also Appendix B-1.

[6] Miller constructs a four-fold typology involving economic security or insecurity and family stability or instability. Economic stability plus family stability is labeled the "stable poor," while economic insecurity and family instability is called the "unstable poor." Economic stability plus family instability is referred to as the "strained"; economic insecurity plus family stability, the "copers." See S. M. Miller, "The American Lower Class: A Typological Approach," *Social Research* (Spring, 1964). Republished in the Syracuse University Youth Development Reprint Series, pp. 1–22. For additional data on these points for the boys we have studied, see Ramon J. Rivera and James F. Short, Jr., "Occupational Goals: A Comparative Analysis," and Ray A. Tennyson, "Family Structure and Delinquent Behavior," *Juvenile Gangs in Context: Theory, Research, and Action,* Malcolm W. Klein and Barbara G. Myerhoff, eds. (Conference Report, Youth Studies Center, University of Southern California, 1964, mimeographed).

[7] Compare the following observations from our data with the description of "The Street" provided in Joseph S. Himes, "Negro Teen-Age Culture," *The Annals of the American Academy of Political and Social Science* (November, 1961), pp. 91–101.

tensions between adolescents and adults, as witness the account of conflict between a gang of white boys and adult men from a neighborhood tavern in Chapter 9.

In the white areas, life generally revolved around more conventional institutions—the Catholic church in particular, and local political and "improvement" associations (organized in large measure to keep the Negroes out), ethnicity and the extended kinship group, union and other job associations, and more formally organized recreational patterns, e.g., bowling leagues and the like.

Institutions in the lower class Negro community are illustrated by a detached-worker's descriptions of poolrooms and events in them, in the area where the Chiefs (group 09) hung out. Worker Bill G. was an expert pool player. One afternoon he accompanied two of his boys into the "rougher" of two poolrooms in the area:

> That poolroom down there is nothing but hustlers—the worst type of people in the area. These were known prostitutes . . . dressed in shorts and kind of flashy, and their pimps. . . . There was one guy, he is a dope addict, wears his shades. . . . He is one of the regulars in the other pool hall. He was shooting pool, and he recognized me and spoke to me and to the fellows. . . .
>
> The three of us started shooting a game of bank on the back table. . . . There was a conversation that the older fellows were having on one of the front tables about some kind of robbery that they had just pulled. . . . They had been busted. It was funny, because they were all teasing one of the guys that was shooting, about the fact that he was caught. The police had him chained with another guy around a lamp post. And some kind of way he got his hand out of one of the cuffs, but he still had one of the cuffs on. He couldn't get it off, and they were teasing him about this. . . . Everyone in the poolroom was well aware of what was going on.
>
> Another thing that was funny—all of them didn't get away. . . . They were laughing about this one guy that didn't get away—he wasn't supposed to go [on the robbery] anyway. He was just there. . . . The guy that had thought up the whole scheme was the guy with the handcuff on his hand. There were two games going on where they were shooting and talking back and forth to the man ringing the cash register. And these guys around the side were commenting, laughing![8]

The other pool hall in this neighborhood was a major center of drug traffic. An earlier report from worker Ben R. described the activities of one of the members of his gang, the Chiefs, in this regard:

[8] Interview, 11/7/60 (Gillmore).

Henry came in, and a few fringe members, and they were sitting around shooting pool. . . . I pointed out to [the research observer] that there was a dope transaction going on in front of him, and he couldn't see it. As I later related to him, Billy stopped shooting pool on four different occasions—in the middle of the game, to leave the poolroom. He would give his stick to someone else to shoot until he got back. Each time, a person came in and whispered to him, and then left. . . . Betty came in the last time—with a woman prostitute from 39th Street—and she took Billy's stick for him. . . . Betty is only 19 years old, but she is Billy's boss—a prostitute-pusher.[9]

Here we see the informal association of young and old, teachers and the taught—a type of "integration" of age grading and of conventional and criminal values not altogether encompassed by the "opportunity structure" notion.

These excerpts remind us again of the differential exposure of youngsters to crime and delinquency which is attributable to neighborhood influences. The area in question was especially noted as a center of drug traffic, and, although it may have been extreme in this respect, it was not unique among our lower class Negro communities. In another Negro gang area (the Garden Gang, 10) the worker reported that a local adult pusher, when she moved from the area, included with each bag of marihuana sold a note explaining that she would no longer be living in the area, and giving her new address. Patrons were thanked for past purchases and requested to come to the new location in the future! Such an occurrence is inconceivable in any of the communities where our white gang boys were located. Under circumstances such as these the positive association of drug use and stable corner activities, and the failure of drug use to correlate negatively with domestic chores (.04 for Negroes in contrast with a statistically significant $-.18$ for whites) is understandable. So, too, the positive association for Negroes between truancy and drug use (.23, $p < .01$), as contrasted with a negative correlation among whites ($-.25, p < .01$). Drug use among these Negro boys seems to be part of the "normal" pattern of street life and to have much in common in this respect with local adults. By contrast, the white drug users in our sample were beyond the "kid stuff" of skipping school and more committed to the search for kicks as a way of life.

As a final example, we attend a "quarter party" with members of the Rattlers (group 05), a tough Negro gang with a well-deserved

[9] Interview, 11/25/59 (Ross).

reputation for conflict and strong-arming persons who came into the commercial area adjacent to "their street," whether for legitimate or illegitimate (e.g., to patronize local prostitutes) purposes. "Quarter parties" do not follow any single format, but there are common objectives in all such gatherings. An adult will "throw" the party in his or her (usually her) home, for other adults, teens, or both. The objective of the host is to make money. (In some places such gatherings are called "rent parties.") There may be an entrance charge of a quarter, and refreshments will be sold—most commonly at a quarter per drink. The objective of guests at such a party is, of course, to have fun. The type of fun may vary for different classes of party goers.

This woman who is called "Ma" was giving the party. . . . It seems she considers herself the mother to all those kids in the area, and everybody calls her "Ma." She gives these parties. Charges 25 cents.

There was a lot of drinking—inside, outside, in the cars, in the alleys, everywhere. There were Rattlers and a bunch of boys from the [housing] projects. They had two rooms, neither of them very large. There was some friction going on when I got there—boys bumping each other, and stuff like this.

There were a lot of girls there. Must have been about 50 to 75 people in these two rooms, plus another 20 or 25 outside. There were some older fellows there, too—mainly to try and grab one of these younger girls.

The girls were doing a lot of drinking—young girls, 12- and 13-year-olds. This one girl, shortly after I got there, had passed out. I took her home. Nobody there, but two of the other girls stayed with her.

The age group in this party amazed me—must have been from about 11 to the 30's. There were girls there as young as 11, but no boys younger than about 15. The girls are there as a sex attraction, and with the older boys and men around, you know the younger boys aren't going to do any good.

We had one real fight. One of David's sisters was talking to one of these boys from the projects—a good-sized boy, bigger than me. I guess she promised to go out to the car with him—this is my understanding. Anyhow they went outside. To get outside you had to go out this door and down this hall, and then out on the porch and down the stairs. She went as far as the porch. As she got out there, I guess she changed her mind. By this time the guy wasn't standing for any "changing the mind" business, and he started to pull on her—to try and get her in the car. She yelled for David, and he came running out. All he could see was his sister and a guy he didn't know was pulling on her. David plowed right into the guy. I guess he hit him about 15 times and knocked him down and across the street, and by the time I got there the guy was lying in the gutter. David was just about to level a foot at him. I yelled at David to stop and he did. I took him off to the side and told Gary to get the guy out of there.[10]

The worker walked down the street with David, trying to cool him down. What happened next very nearly precipitated a major gang conflict:

Duke, Red, and Mac were standing eight or ten feet away, sort of watching these project boys. This one boy goes up the street on the other side and comes up *behind* David and me. We don't see him. All of a sudden Duke runs right past me. I was wondering what's going on and he plows into this guy—crashed the side of his mouth and the guy fell flat. Duke was about to really work the guy over when I stopped him.

Duke said, "Well look, man, the guy was sneaking up behind you and I wasn't gonna have him hit you from behind! I did it to protect you."

I got the guy up and he said, "I wasn't going to hit you—I just wanted to see what was going on," and this bit.

By now Duke says, "Well, the heck with it. Let's run all these project guys out."

They banded together and were ready to move, but I talked them out of it. I said, "Look, don't you think you've done enough? The police aren't here yet, but if you start anything else they'll be here. Somebody is bound to call them. The party is still going on so why don't we all just go back inside. No sense in breaking up a good thing—you paid your quarter."

I finally got them all back inside, but Duke says, "We've been laying off fighting for the last year or so. Looks like we'll have to start again."

"What for? You haven't been in trouble for the last year or so." They had to admit this was right, that if they started fighting again they're going to be in trouble, and they agreed with me.

The aftermath of this fight illustrates further the manner in which such institutions contribute to gang conflict. Two weeks earlier this same worker had reported an altercation between another of his boys and a boy from the projects. Again, there had been pushing and shoving in the crowded rooms, ominous glances, and muttered threats. The fight had begun innocently enough, with two boys playfully boxing with one another. One boy hit a little too hard, and soon they were hard at it. The worker intervened, but not until tempers were high and a window had been broken.[11]

[10] Interview, 2/16/61 (Dillard).
[11] Interview, 1/31/61 (Dillard).

By way of contrast, white gang boys are more openly at odds with the adult community, particularly concerning rowdyism, drinking (which is well nigh universal) and drug use (which is rare), and sexual delinquency. These boys were more often at odds with proprietors of local hangouts and with other local adults than were the Negro gang boys. Thefts may be tacitly condoned by adult "fences" and other purchasers of stolen goods, so long as local residents are not victimized. In communities undergoing racial transition—during the period of study this included nearly all lower class white communities in Chicago—the rowdyism complained of may be turned to advantage by adults and encouraged. An apposite case is an incident which occurred shortly after midnight on a weekend in late summer, 1959. The scene is a typical late evening gathering of boys and girls at "their" park in a southside neighborhood which was unsuccessfully resisting invasion by Negro residents. A detached worker's "incident report" provides the data:[12]

At approximately 12:30 at night, this worker was loitering with a group of teen-age white kids at the corner of [the park], which is immediately across the street from . . . Catholic Church. The group was a mixed one of boys and girls ranging in age from 16 to 20. There were approximately 15–20 teen-agers, and, for the most part, they were sitting or reclining in the park, talking, drinking beer, or wrestling playfully with the girls. The worker had parked his car adjacent to where the group was gathered and was leaning on the fender of his auto talking to two youths about the remainder of the softball season. The group consisted of members of the Amboys, Bengals, Sharks, and a few Mafia. They were not unusually loud or boisterous this particular hot and humid evening because a policeman on a three-wheeler had been by a half-hour earlier and had warned them of the lateness of the hour.

While the worker was talking to two of the Amboys, he noticed a solitary teen-age figure ambling along on the . . . sidewalk . . . , heading toward X Avenue. The worker paid no particular heed, thinking it was just another teen-ager walking over to join the park group. However, as the figure neared the group, he made no effort to swerve over and join the group but continued by them with no sign of recognition. This was an oddity, so the worker watched the youth as he passed the gathered teen-agers and neared the curb where the worker was sitting on his car fender. At this point, the worker suddenly realized that the teen-ager was a Negro and in danger, if detected. The worker did not dare do or say anything for fear of alerting the teen-agers sitting in the park, and for a few minutes thought the Negro youth could pass by without detection. However, Butch, a Bengal who had been drinking beer, spotted the youth and immediately asked some of the other teen-agers, "Am I drunk or is that a Nigger on the corner?" The attention of the entire group was then focused on the Negro youth, who by this time had stepped off the curb and was walking in the center of the street toward the opposite curb. The youth was oblivious to everything and was just strolling along as if without a care in the world. Behind him, however, consternation and anger arose spontaneously like a mushroom cloud after an atom explosion. Muttered threats of "Let's kill the bastard," "Get the mother-fucker," "Come on, let's get going" were heard by the worker. Even the girls in the crowd readily and verbally agreed. . . .

Within seconds, approximately twelve youths arose and began running in the direction of the Negro youth. The worker, realizing that he was unable to stem the tide of the enraged teen-agers, yelled out to the Negro youth something to the effect of "Hey man, look alive." The Negro boy heard the worker as he paused in mid-stride, but did not turn around. Again the worker found it necessary to shout a warning as the white teen-agers were rapidly overtaking him. At the worker's second outcry, the Negro youth turned around and saw the white teen-agers closing in on him. Without hesitation, the Negro youth took off at full speed with the white mob at his heels yelling shouts of "Kill the bastard—don't let him get away."

The worker remained standing by his car and was joined by three Amboys who did not participate in the chase. The president of the Amboys sadly shook his head, stating that his guys reacted like a bunch of kids whenever they saw a colored guy, and openly expressed his wish that the Negro boy would get away. Another Amboy in an alibi tone of voice, excused his non-participation in the chase by explaining that he couldn't run fast enough to catch anybody. Harry merely stated that the Negro didn't bother him, so why should he be tossed in jail for the assault on a stranger.

As we stood by the car, we could hear the actual progress of the chase from the next block. There were shouts and outcries as the pursued ran down X and his whereabouts was echoed by the bedlam created by his pursuers. Finally, there was silence and we waited for approximately fifteen minutes before the guys began to straggle back from the chase. As they returned to the worker's car and to the girls sitting nearby, each recited his share of the chase. Barney laughlingly related that Guy had hurdled a parked car in an effort to tackle the Negro, who had swerved out into the street. He said that he himself had entered a coal yard, looking around in an effort to find where the Negro boy had hidden, when an adult from a second floor back porch warned that he had better get out of there as the coal yard was protected by a large and vicious Great Dane.

The Negro youth [apparently] had decided that he couldn't outrun his tormentors and had begun to go in and out of back yards until he was able to find a hiding place, at which point he disappeared. His pursuers then began to make a systematic search of the alleys, garages, back yards, corridors, etc. *The boys were spurred on to greater efforts by the adults of the area who offered advice and encouragement.* One youth laughingly related that a woman, from her bedroom window, kept pointing out probable hiding places in her back yard so that the youth below would not overlook any sanctuary. This advice included looking behind tall shrubbery by the fence, on top of a tool crib by the alley and underneath the back porch. Other youths related similar experiences as the adults along X Avenue entered gleefully in the "hide-and-seek." Glen related that as the youths turned onto X, he began to shout to the people ahead in the block that "a Nigger was coming" so that someone ahead might catch or at least head off the Negro. The other pursuers also took up the hue and cry, which accounted for the loud noises heard by the worker.

Examples of such adult support were not uncommon and provided a rationale for some of the boys' continued participation in racial violence. But conflict gangs comparable to some of our Negro gangs were not to be found in Chicago during the years of study. White gangs fought occasionally, but there was no sustaining conflict orientation among them, no pride in their conflict "rep" such as was common with several Negro gangs.[13]

With respect to the racial contrast we are studying, the point seems clear. The nature of delinquency-supporting relations between adults and adolescents differs in lower class Negro and white communities. Negro communities provide a flow of common experiences in which young people and their elders share, and out of which delinquent behavior emerges almost imperceptibly, albeit at times dramatically. In this sense our Negro communities "look" a good deal like Miller's description of lower class culture.[14] The white community is more concerned, and with notable exceptions more effectively controls the excesses of their young people, supporting them in specific types of delinquency which are equally continuous with the ordinary pattern of adult-adolescent relations, but more purposive and specifically motivated than is the case in the Negro communities we have studied. Beyond such instances in which delinquency is "approved," the white

[13] The nature of differing delinquency orientations is further discussed in Chapter 9.

[14] Walter B. Miller, "Implications of Urban Lower-Class Culture for Social Work," *Social Service Review* (September, 1959), pp 219–36.

community is deeply disturbed and acts, not always successfully, to curb youthful misbehavior. Here the dimensions of control suggested by Cloward and Ohlin seem more appropriate than the "focal concerns" and other aspects of Miller's analysis.[15] But social control is relative, and the institutions of lower class white communities—the churches, families, political and illegitimate, even settlement houses and other welfare establishments—are more capable of concerted effective action than is the case for Negroes. The extent to which this is true varies, and the reasons doubtless are many. Certainly they are complex. Among them, however, are the greater economic stability of white communities and the existence of indigenous institutions with established leadership. The failure of Negro communities, generally, and lower class Negroes especially, to generate strong and effective leadership is a well documented and much lamented fact, and it bears upon the problems we are discussing.

Whatever the causes, community-level differences clearly influence patterns of juvenile behavior, and in some measure account for differences in our gangs. A more detailed examination of these influences is beyond the scope of this chapter.

[15] Richard A. Cloward and Lloyd E. Ohlin, *Delinquency and Opportunity* (Glencoe Ill.: The Free Press, 1960).

CHAPTER 6

The Analysis of Self-descriptions by Members of Delinquent Gangs

The primary data for this chapter, the self-descriptions of respondents from a delinquent gang of Negro boys, were obtained in a Chicago Park District field house. The boys lived in an adjacent public housing project and hung on the corner near the field house and in the playground. The data were collected by a Youth Studies Program staff member who had spent a number of days as an observer of the gang. He was assisted by the gang's detached worker. Following administration of the questionnaire to the gang boys, these men joined efforts and located twenty-three non-gang boys of similar ages, who also lived in the same project, to serve as control subjects. Administration required about an hour and a half; the paired-comparison instrument in which we are primarily interested, about twenty minutes.

The instructions read: "We want to know how you and your friends describe yourselves. Place an X in the box beside the one of each of the following pairs of words which best describes you and your friends." For example, see Figure 6.1

    1. ☐ SMART   as compared to   COOL ☐

    91. ☐ LOYAL   as compared to   RELIGIOUS ☐

FIG. 6.1

The set of fourteen adjectives chosen for the instrument included items believed to be especially salient to lower class (troublesome, tough, mean, smart, cool, sharp) and middle class (clean, obedient, religious, helpful, polite) "focal concerns" and items which were assumed to be universal among adolescents and relatively neutral with

This chapter was previously published with Ellen Kolegar as co-author, in *The Sociological Quarterly*, III (October, 1962), 331–56.

respect to social class (strong, athletic, loyal).[1] It was originally believed that these terms would provide helpful information concerning the relation between self-description and behavior of street-corner groups with different delinquency orientations (e.g., "parent-delinquent subculture," conflict, criminal, and retreatist) and of non-gang and middle class control groups.

In this study, as in most studies, the theoretical concerns which guided the creation of the instrument and the selection of the sample did not extend to a specification of the steps involved in analysis. Following data collection, data analysis is viewed as a process which requires many decisions, some of which must necessarily be made on inadequate grounds. It is believed that the number of such decisions involved, even in a modest study, is quite large and that the emphasis upon brevity in scientific publication generally discourages thorough discussion of these matters.

While it is possible that in sharply focused studies the provision of greater detail of analysis would not be necessary, this is almost certainly not true in a study which, like the present, is intended to provide broad documentation of the adaptations of adolescent boys in the inner city.

In this particular chapter, the objective is to determine what, if any, relation exists between behavior—both observer reports and self-reports by the boys—and the boys' descriptions of themselves in a peer-group context. One would not guess in advance that there would be much latitude for surprise as one follows out the quite typical sequence of decisions concerning validity, technique of analysis, and the routine statistical operations. In practice it is found that with closer scrutiny the universe of what is taken for granted contracts; one becomes more aware of unexplored paths and of steps, quickly taken, which set the limits of discovery and, therefore, deserve later review.

If it is surprises in the data which characteristically stimulate the construction of new hypotheses, and if, in some areas of research, new hypotheses are actively sought, then there is in all probability some way of proceeding in the analysis of data which results in more new

[1] For a discussion of the concept of "focal concerns" and their specification within lower class culture, see Walter B. Miller, "Lower Class Culture as a Generating Milieu of Gang Delinquency," *Journal of Social Issues*, XIV (1958), 5–19; more specifically related to teen-age gangs is Walter B. Miller, Hildred Geertz, and Henry S. G. Cutter, "Aggression in a Boy's Street Corner Group," *Psychiatry*, XXIV (1961), 283–98.

hypotheses than others. This question is not treated in general in this chapter. However, the self-descriptions analysis is used to illustrate the retroductive premise that what is being looked for becomes more specific and takes new directions as analysis proceeds. More generally, it is suggested that the questioning of the micro-details of the analysis of one segment of a set of parallel data is a good way to proceed when discovery is an important objective.

The Consistency of Paired Comparisons

When questionnaire data are collected from poorly educated boys in a field situation, there is always the gnawing question of the confidence one can safely place in them. To cope with this concern, it was particularly advantageous to be working with the paired-comparisons instrument. The very burden of simulating for the $n(n-1)/2$, or 91, paired comparisons would seem to encourage straightforward self-reports. And, in the event that the psychologically more demanding course of simulation were undertaken, it would probably result in many inconsistencies in the non-polar terms which might be detected as circular triads.

To illustrate, let us consider the number of times one term is preferred over other terms for two randomly selected gang boys (see Fig. 6.2). The full matrix of choices for Boy 18 reveals that five circular triads exist. These are:

$$\text{tough} > \text{athletic} > \text{cool} > \text{tough}$$
$$\text{smart} > \text{tough} > \text{mean} > \text{smart}$$
$$\text{sharp} > \text{mean} > \text{clean} > \text{sharp}$$
$$\text{mean} > \text{smart} > \text{sharp} > \text{mean}$$
$$\text{athletic} > \text{smart} > \text{tough} > \text{athletic}.$$

His most preferred construct (troublesome) is preferred over all others and his least preferred construct (loyal) is less preferred than all other alternatives. In this sense, these two terms are separated by a maximum distance. For Boy 16, there are thirty-one circular triads present. The separation between his most and least preferred (athletic and religious) is equal to 18's, but there is more overlapping in the intermediate range.

This first glance at the responses from two boys both raises a question and answers a question. The question raised relates to the circular triads. There is no established convention concerning how many one should tolerate. It is not clear whether they arise from non-

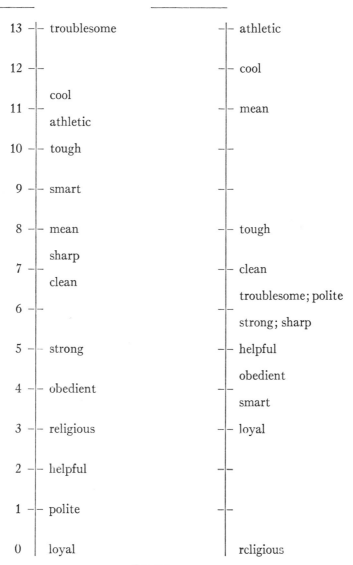

Number of
times word
chosen over
others   BOY 18   BOY 16

	BOY 18	BOY 16
13	troublesome	athletic
12		cool
11	cool / athletic	mean
10	tough	
9	smart	
8	mean	tough
7	sharp / clean	clean
6		troublesome; polite / strong; sharp
5	strong	helpful
4	obedient	obedient / smart
3	religious	loyal
2	helpful	
1	polite	
0	loyal	religious

Fig. 6.2

discriminable differences (note for 18 it is adjacent terms which are confused), deliberate deception, or careless errors. While it did not seem wise to use resources to stop and investigate this question, it was possible to tabulate the distribution of circular triads for the total population of 537 boys tested.

Number	Frequency
0–4	44
5–9	64
10–14	79
15–19	74
20–24	62
25–29	28
30–34	30
35	6
36–39	19
40–44	22
45–59	41
60–74	32
75–89	26
90–104	10
	537

After inspecting this distribution and the protocols of some boys who were well known to us, we arbitrarily decided that any respondent who had more than thirty-five circular triads would be assumed to have not understood and worked consistently on the ranking or to have erred in his effort to be deceptive. For these respondents we assume that no consistent self-conception report has been obtained. While our respondent, Boy 16 above, who has a total of thirty-one circular triads, is retained, nearly 30 per cent of the sample is lost by this criterion.

An investigator experiences the arbitrary decision on the number of circular triads as a sort of esthetic compromise, rather than a substantively important decision. If such instances of mild discomfort are not too frequent, one tends to forget them in time. It is, however, possible that some later finding may have the character such that it could be biased by the absence of the rejected 30 per cent. If this is the case, this decision will have to be reopened. The clear understanding that early decisions can be reopened in the light of later findings may generally be an important factor which frees an investigator to move ahead through the preliminary inspection of his findings.

Social Desirability

The question answered by the responses relates the willingness of respondents to describe themselves in terms which have negative connotations. The most self-descriptive term according to Boy 18 is *troublesome,* and for Boy 16, the third-place term is *mean.* Both also describe themselves as *cool* and *athletic.* For 18 the four lowest terms are *loyal, polite, helpful,* and *religious.* The strength of *cool,* implying uninvolvement and awareness of self-interests, is consistent with the low rank of *loyal,* which implies involvement in the interests of others.

Since the appearance in 1957 of Edwards' book concerned with the "social-desirability" variable, investigators have felt some compunction to follow his dictum and equate paired terms for their social desirability.[2] It is quite apparent that the paired-comparison instrument we have used does not equate terms for social desirability. Thus, even though Edwards' suggestion was in the literature at the time the instrument was constructed, the suggestion was ignored. This creates tension, for one feels that he will be forced either to contest the soundness of the suggestion or to suffer the consequences of having ignored it. In fact, the finding that boys do describe themselves with negative terms places the whole controversy in a new light.

One can argue that if social desirability had been controlled by matching, then this response disposition would not have been discovered. It does not weaken this position to say that what is socially desirable for middle class persons is not the same as what is socially desirable for gang boys, for Edwards' dictum carries the premise of a cross-stratum[3] and, to some extent, a cross-cultural generality. On the other hand, it also does not follow that we know what a person who describes himself as *troublesome* believes to be "socially" desirable. What we have discovered is simply what Dicken reports is being discovered by others who study mentally ill and deviant persons; namely, social desirability may better be studied than corrected for.[4]

[2] Allen L. Edwards, *The Social Desirability Variable in Personality Assessment and Research* (New York: Dryden Press, 1957).

[3] It may be noted that we have established that Osgood's semantic-differential factors are very similar for this group and for middle class subjects; see Chapter 3.

[4] Charles F. Dicken, "Psychological Assessment Techniques," to be published in *Progress in Neurology and Psychiatry,* XVIII (New York: Grune and Stratton, 1964), 604–21.

Similarity of Rankings

Returning again to the two randomly selected gang members' scores, the rho for the correlation of the rank orders of terms for boys 18 and 16 is 0.66. An alternative measure of similarity could be obtained by mapping the responses of the boys on the same matrix, using 1's to indicate identical entries (see Fig. 6.3). When this is done it may be seen that 71 per cent of the entries are identical. There are no investigations of the relative merits of these two indices of similarity known to the writers. In the absence of authoritative guidance, we selected the latter measure because it seemed more directly related to the individual pairing operation and because it had

	a	b	c	d	e	f	g	h	i	j	k	l	m	n
troublesome—a	...	0	0	0	1	0	0	0	0	1	1	1	1	1
cool—b		...	1	1	1	1	1	1	1	1	1	1	1	1
athletic—c			...	0	1	1	1	1	1	1	1	1	1	1
tough—d				...	1	0	1	1	0	1	1	1	1	1
smart—e					...	1	0	0	1	0	1	0	0	1
mean—f						...	0	1	1	1	1	1	1	1
sharp—g							...	1	1	1	1	1	0	0
clean—h								...	1	1	1	0	0	1
strong—i									...	1	1	1	1	0
obedient—j										...	1	0	1	1
religious—k											...	0	0	0
helpful—l												...	0	1
polite—m													...	1
loyal—n														...

FIG. 6.3

the slight advantage of avoiding negative signs. It is not clear that any later development in the analysis of the data would arise which would cause the reversal of this decision. However, since more time is required to compute this similarity measure than rho, the decision to use it might be reopened on the pragmatic grounds of the time available if other groups were to be similarly analyzed.

The Study of One Gang

At the time of the design of the field instrument it was known that the self-descriptions of lower class gang and non-gang boys would be compared with one another and with middle class boys. For such comparisons there are qualitative hypotheses which may be drawn from current delinquency theories and tested in the traditional hypothetico-deductive manner.[5] The present chapter came to be written as we faced the prospect of testing hypotheses over additional groups available to us and recognized that an improved set of hypotheses could be formulated if we could make more specific use of relationships within the gangs. We needed more specific experience with the self-descriptions of one gang so that we could in time employ this knowledge as an empirical guide to a model which would relate differential-delinquent behavior, rank in the group, and self-descriptions.[6]

Newcomb's work shows that persons with similar interests elaborate their acquaintance through time.[7] This is similar to the way in which homogamy of background is a positive factor in mate-selection.[8] At the same time, the self-descriptions may be viewed as indicators of personality needs, and as Winch's work has shown, needs may be best gratified by complementarity in dyads. With questions of this type in mind, the similarity measure given in Table 6.1 was obtained for all pairs of the 25 Garden Gang boys (reduced from 36 when 11 were eliminated for excessive circular triads).

The previously obtained value of 71 per cent for boys 18 and 16 is shown in the corresponding column and row in Table 6.1. It may be noted that each of them is more similar to boys 2, 8, and 23 than they are to one another. In addition, it may be noted that they are both quite different from boys 4 and 37, for example. To determine more generally how similar gang and non-gang boys are to one another, a parallel matrix was prepared for 15 non-gang boys (8 other non-gang boys were rejected, 5 for excessive circular triads and 3 for incomplete returns). Finally, a matrix was prepared for the comparison of gang and non-gang boys. We did not take pains to write down our predictions, but there is no doubt that it was our clear expecta-

[5] Intergang variations, and variations between gang, non-gang, and middle class subjects on this instrument are reported in Patricia Hodge, "Self-Descriptions of Gang and Nongang Teen-Aged Boys," unpublished Master's thesis, Department of Sociology, University of Chicago, 1964.

[6] Among more recent attempts to include the elements of behavior, self-concepts, and role relations in delinquency typologies, see John W. Kinch, "Self-Conceptions of Types of Delinquents," *Sociological Inquiry*, XXXII (Spring, 1962), 228–34; and Don C. Gibbons, "Prospects and Problems of Delinquent Typology," *Sociological Inquiry*, XXXIII (Spring, 1962), 235–44.

[7] Theodore M. Newcomb, *The Acquaintance Process* (New York: Holt, Rinehart, and Winston, 1961).

[8] See Robert F. Winch, *Mate-Selection: A Study of Complementary Needs* (New York: Harper and Brothers, 1958).

tion that the operation of group processes would in some way increase the similarity of self-descriptions for the boys who were members of the gang in contrast to those who were not. We therefore were sharply surprised to find the following:[9]

	Average Similarity
Gang Boys with Gang Boys	57.1
Gang Boys with Non-Gang Boys	57.0
Non-Gang Boys with Non-Gang Boys	60.9

TABLE 6.1

THE AGREEMENT MATRIX FOR MEMBERS OF THE GARDEN GANG*

	2	4	6	7	8	10	11	13	14	16	17	18	23	24	26	27	28	32	33	36	37	38	40	41	42
2		32	56	66	85	44	64	79	58	76	75	82	81	86	79	50	49	73	46	72	30	48	40	25	38
4			56	62	38	75	66	35	54	36	40	36	38	37	41	57	75	40	48	43	75	69	67	71	78
6				68	59	69	60	55	49	58	55	49	58	55	54	53	62	52	48	64	68	66	64	60	58
7					70	65	80	65	59	66	54	62	72	65	66	54	76	68	49	71	53	69	65	56	61
8						52	64	81	58	71	70	81	87	79	85	49	55	76	40	77	40	53	42	36	42
10							62	50	58	44	54	38	47	48	47	50	77	52	56	55	81	68	72	72	74
11								60	42	60	52	60	66	60	70	58	71	61	38	66	47	67	58	55	68
13									59	66	71	68	79	75	79	52	49	71	45	76	36	52	45	33	44
14										53	64	49	58	57	56	55	59	58	48	55	55	55	64	48	58
16											70	71	76	75	67	54	49	67	44	64	37	48	44	41	47
17												68	74	78	70	56	44	59	45	67	43	54	46	42	50
18													75	70	76	52	48	69	37	69	31	48	33	34	36
23														81	82	53	54	72	40	75	37	53	43	36	47
24															70	56	45	64	54	74	32	54	47	27	48
26																50	55	74	30	72	38	53	46	36	48
27																	47	46	38	43	44	58	41	49	56
28																		62	45	50	69	60	69	74	63
32																			42	56	42	44	52	44	40
33																				47	49	50	63	46	46
36																					42	66	50	42	48
37																						62	67	80	67
38																							63	59	70
40																								66	66
41																									64
42																									

* Average agreement 57.1%.

The original expectation was of the character that, if it had been confirmed, it might have been reported but without particular elaboration. When it was unconfirmed we were confronted with the previously unanticipated need to formulate an alternative hypothesis in order to continue the analysis. We reasoned that if group process does

[9] In testing the significance of the differences between 57.1 and 60.9, an intriguing question is encountered. If we use the entire n_1 $(n_1 - 1)/2 + n_2$ $(n_2 - 1)/2 - 2$ (where $n_1 = 25$ and $n_2 = 15$) degrees of freedom, we will be erroneously assuming independence between each of the comparisons. On the other hand, if $n_1 + n_2 - 2$ is used, the df are certainly underestimated. Since $t(.05)_{38}$ df = 2.06, $t = 2.56$, and $P(t_{obs}) < .05$, we are not in doubt about rejecting the null hypothesis. It is also clear, though, that the degrees of freedom should be higher, and the criterion value closer to the level of 1.96 for an infinitely large number of degrees of freedom.

not operate to increase homogamy among these boys, then the self-descriptions must either be unaffected by group membership and based upon common experience in the parent culture or, more likely, there may be within the gang more clearly defined subgroups of boys with different self-descriptions.

The first interpretation suggested that the similarity measure was unrelated to the gang process we were studying; the second suggested that boys with contrasting self-descriptions might be identified within the gangs. The first interpretation suggested that we may have been wasting our time, the second that we might be on to something interesting. Faced with these two possibilities, it was apparent that we needed to examine the possibility of important subgroup differentiation before deciding on an interpretation. To do this, we needed a method of characterizing within-gang similarity or differentiation.

Attitude Clique Differentiation

To speak of similarity of attitudes without any implication of the amount of interaction between members of the set, we propose the term "attitude clique." For gang boys the evidence from which inferences are to be made about the existence of attitude cliques is given in Table 6.1. The problem is the reorganization of these data (and the comparable data for the non-gang boys) so that unequivocal decisions can be made concerning the nature of the cliques. Brief consideration will be given to three alternative methods which have previously been described in the literature.

The Katz Sociomatrix Interchange. If one takes the values in Table 6.1 and writes them on small movable blocks (in our case, sugar cubes), it is possible to interchange the rows and then the columns of the matrix so that the identity of the original values is maintained and the relative distance of the original row and column intersections from the main diagonal changed. When one systematically carries this interchange out with the objective of placing the large values as close as possible to the main diagonal, one then defines along the rows and columns an order of persons such that the greater the consensus, the closer the position.[10]

In practice, even with no more than twenty-five persons, this interchange process proves to be very laborious. More than this, when one has made all of the interchanges which appear plausible, he is still

---

[10] Leo Katz, "On the Matrix Analysis of Sociometric Data," *Sociometry*, X (1947), 233–41.

not sure that he has achieved the best placement. As a rough check, one can compute the weighted sum of the squared distance of a given cell from the main diagonal and strive to make this sum a minimum. The original percentages placed as they are in Table 6.1 give a value of 16.9×10^8 and at the point at which we stopped in the matrix manipulation (see Table 6.2) the value is 12.8×10^8.

TABLE 6.2

PARTITION INTO ATTITUDE CLIQUES OF THE GARDEN
GANG BOYS BY KATZ SOCIOMATRIX METHOD

	2	24	23	8	18	26	13	32	16	17	36	7	6	11	14	28	27	33	37	10	40	4	38	42	41
2		86	87	85	82	79	79	73	76	75	72	66	64	56	58	49	50	46	30	44	40	32	48	38	25
24			81	79	70	70	75	64	75	78	74	65	60	55	57	45	56	54	32	48	47	37	54	48	27
23				87	75	82	79	72	76	74	75	72	66	58	58	54	53	40	37	47	43	38	53	47	36
8					81	85	81	76	71	70	77	70	64	54	58	55	49	40	40	52	42	38	53	42	36
18						76	68	69	71	68	69	62	60	49	48	48	52	37	31	38	33	36	48	36	34
26							79	74	67	70	72	66	70	54	56	55	50	30	38	47	46	41	53	48	36
13								71	66	71	76	65	35	60	59	49	52	45	36	50	45	35	52	44	33
32		73.9							67	59	56	68	52	61	58	62	46	42	42	52	52	40	44	40	44
16		(I×I)								70	64	66	58	60	53	49	54	44	37	44	44	36	48	47	41
17											67	54	55	52	64	44	56	45	43	54	46	40	54	40	42
36												71	64	66	55	50	43	47	42	55	50	43	66	48	42
7													68	80	59	76	54	49	53	65	65	62	69	61	56
6														60	49	62	53	48	68	69	64	56	66	58	60
11															42	71	58	38	47	62	58	66	67	68	55
14		54.7										55.2				59	55	48	55	58	64	54	55	58	48
28		(I×II)										(II×II)					47	45	69	77	69	75	60	63	74
27																		38	44	50	41	57	58	56	49
33																			49	56	63	48	50	46	46
37																				81	67	75	62	67	80
10																					72	75	68	74	72
40																						67	63	66	66
4		42.8										58.9							69.8				69	78	71
38		(I×III)										(II×III)							(III×III)					70	59
42																									64
41																									

NOTE: Inset values are average agreement figures for corresponding sectors of the matrix.

It may be seen that boys 16 and 18, who were previously discussed, are placed in the same quadrant, but they are not adjacent. The average similarity in the I × I segment is 73.9 and it is comparably high in III × III at 69.8. Elsewhere it is clearly lower.

Unfortunately, it is not possible to say that there is not some other ordering which would slightly improve the grouping. The empirical interchanging on the desk top had proceeded for about a week when it was concluded that this solution was about as good as could be obtained. The location of the dividing lines is completely arbitrary. Thus, one concludes with a desire to confirm the conclusions reached by this ingenious process by some other technique—preferably one which is less laborious and, if possible, more certain.

The Wright-Wallace Pairing Technique.[11] This technique is programmed for UNIVAC and is built on the principle of the successive grouping of persons with the greatest similarity. For example, the first step in the program, represented by the vertical mark between 10 and 15 in Table 6.3, makes two pairings: 8 and 23 with a similar-

[11] See Benjamin Wright, David Wallace, and Frances Moore, "Step-Wise Grouping" (mimeographed), the University of Chicago, December 1961. See also Jack Sawyer and Terrance A. Nosanchuk, "Analysis of Sociometric Structure: A Method of Successive Grouping," *Proceedings of the Social Statistics Section, American Statistical Association,* 1960.

TABLE 6.3

PARTITION BY STEPWISE GROUPING COMPARED
WITH KATZ SOCIOMATRIX SOLUTION

PERSON NUMBER	KATZ GROUP	VARIANCE REDUCTION DUE TO COMBINATION
8	I	
23	I	
26	I	
13	I	
36	I	
2	I	
24	I	
17	I	
16	I	
14	II	
18	I	
32	I	
27	II	
10	III	
37	III	
41	III	
6	II	
40	III	
4	III	
42	III	
38	III	
7	II	
11	II	
28	II	
33	II	

(Scale: 0 5 10 15 20 25 30 35 40 45 50 55 60 65 70)

ity value of 87 per cent and 2 and 24 with a similarity value of 86 per cent. The scale at the top represents the reduction in variance due to combination.

The second step in the program combines 8 and 23, now considered as a unit, with 26—the similarity for this set is 85 per cent. Simultaneous with this secondary pairing there are two primary pairings of 10 and 37 at 81 per cent and 7 and 11 at 80 per cent. The last primary pairing is between 6 and 40 on about the sixth step. Their similarity is 64 per cent. By scanning down the column for 40 in Table 6.1, it may be seen that 40 has a similarity value with 10 of 72 per cent but, as we have indicated above, 10 is not available because it has been grouped with 37 on the basis of their 81 per cent similarity. Eventually, 40 and 10 are united, but it is an intrinsic limitation of the program that it does not scan all possible sets of three or

80	23	26	
13	36	02	These were all in Class I by the Katz method.
24	17	16	

10	37	41	
6	40	4	These, excluding 6 only, were in Class III by the Katz method.
	42	38	

FIG. 6.4

more before it pairs, hence it may proceed by steps which should be retraced in order to achieve the optimal solution.

To illustrate the convergence between this method and the Katz method, it may be noted that at the eighth step, there are two groups which closely correspond to Katz's I and III partition (Fig. 6.4). The Katz method Class II cases, which are admittedly heterogeneous, are at this point in the stepwise program split into three units (Fig. 6.5). In support of this method, it is to be indicated that the operations are very rapid on a computer, the print-out is easy to read and understand, and the results are substantially in agreement with the previous method. At the same time, at just the point at which one wants unequivocal guidance, this method leaves much to the judgment of the investigator.

Direct Factor Analysis of the Similarity Scores. By use of direct factor methods it is possible to factor the similarity matrix in Table 6.1 into an arbitrary number of factors, then rotate the orthogonal factors until the included factors explain a roughly proportional amount of the variance. The fact that the similarity scores derived from the paired comparison operation have very similar means and variances enables us to proceed with a substantive interpretation of the first factor, as if covariances or correlations had been involved. If non-standardized scores had been used, the direct factor approach would result in a first factor essentially descriptive of the mean level of effects.[12]

$$
\begin{array}{cc}
14 & 18 \\
32 & 27
\end{array} \Bigg\} \quad
\begin{array}{l}
\text{Cases which eventually} \\
\text{go into Class I.}
\end{array}
$$

$$
\left.
\begin{array}{cc}
7 & 11 \\
 & 28 \\
 & 33
\end{array}
\right\} \quad
\begin{array}{l}
\text{Cases which eventually} \\
\text{go into Class III.}
\end{array}
$$

FIG. 6.5

On the basis of a preliminary inspection of four factors and a varimax rotation, it was concluded that two factors accounting for 71 per cent of the variance would adequately describe the factoring of Table 6.1. The rotated loadings are given in Table 6.4. Three groups may then be defined as follows:

Group I   Individuals with weights higher than .72 on I and lower than .38 on II.

Group II   Individuals with weights between .34 and .72 on I and between .38 and .72 on II.

Group III   Individuals with weights lower than .38 on I and higher than .72 on II.

This partitioning is both economical in time required, given a computer, and the most unequivocal. It is in close agreement with the Katz solution given in Table 6.2. Only two cases, 28 and 38, which are there adjacent, are in this solution interchanged. This same result might have been reached with further iterations by the Katz method.

---

[12] Henry R. Kaiser, "The Varimax Solution for Analytic Rotation in Factor Analysis," *Psychometrika*, XXIII (1958), 187–200; and Duncan MacRae, Jr., "Direct Factor Analysis of Sociometric Data," *Sociometry*, XXIII (December, 1960), 360–71.

The near equivalence of the two solutions can be shown by comparing the average similarity scores:

Attitude Cliques	Katz	Direct Factor
I×I.............	73.9	73.9
I×II............	54.7	55.2
I×III...........	42.8	42.7
II×II...........	55.2	55.4
II×III..........	58.9	58.1
III×III.........	69.8	72.5

The only appreciable change is the increase in similarity, from 69.8 to 72.5, for Group III × Group III.

TABLE 6.4

THE VARIMAX ROTATION TO TWO FACTORS FROM
DIRECT FACTOR ANALYSIS OF THE
AGREEMENT MATRIX

Attitude Cliques	Person No.	I	II	h^2
I..............	02	.92	.18	.88
I..............	18	.84	.19	.74
I..............	08	.89	.26	.86
I..............	24	.85	.26	.79
I..............	23	.88	.27	.85
I..............	13	.84	.27	.78
I..............	26	.84	.28	.78
I..............	16	.78	.29	.69
I..............	17	.76	.33	.69
I..............	36	.75	.37	.70
I..............	32	.73	.35	.66
II.............	07	.62	.60	.74
II.............	11	.57	.58	.66
II.............	14	.51	.54	.55
II.............	27	.47	.50	.47
II.............	06	.46	.65	.63
II.............	33	.34	.55	.42
II.............	38	.40	.71	.66
III............	28	.36	.78	.74
III............	40	.27	.79	.70
III............	42	.27	.80	.71
III............	10	.29	.85	.81
III............	41	.13	.85	.74
III............	37	.14	.87	.78
III............	04	.16	.88	.80
Percentage variance explained	—	.38	.33	.71

For the 15 non-gang boys, a parallel factor solution was completed. It resulted in a distribution of boys which compares with that for gang boys in the following way:

	Gang	Non-Gang
I	11	2
II	7	4
III	7	9

The fact that non-gang boys had 9/15 of their total in one partition accounts for their higher average similarity score. It may also be noted that there is a near significant difference in the allocation to the different partitionings: the gang boys are more frequently in I and the non-gang boys in III.[13]

TABLE 6.5

ATTITUDE CLIQUE DIFFERENTIATION IN
SELF-DESCRIPTIVE TERMS

DESCRIPTIVE TERM	MEAN NUMBER OF INSTANCES WORD CHOSEN OVER ANOTHER FOR EACH ATTITUDE CLIQUE		
	I	II	III
Cool	11.6	8.6	3.6
Tough	9.8	6.1	3.3
Troublesome	9.6	2.8	0.9
Mean	6.6	4.1	1.1
Athletic	11.9	9.6	11.0
Strong	7.3	8.7	7.1
Sharp	5.4	7.3	4.6
Obedient	4.7	3.3	7.1
Religious	0.5	4.3	7.4
Polite	2.4	5.8	8.0
Smart	4.9	7.6	8.6
Loyal	3.6	6.6	8.7
Helpful	5.0	8.3	9.1
Clean	7.4	7.8	10.4

The Polar Self-descriptions

The analysis thus far suggests that, if self-descriptions do make a difference in behavior, then the difference should be greatest and most observable between attitude Cliques I and III. The terms which were differentially preferred by these cliques are shown in Table 6.5.

[13] $\chi^2(.05)_{2df} = 5.99$, $\chi^2 = 5.15$, $P = .08$.

Clique I (in comparison with Clique III) favors *troublesome, cool, tough,* and *mean.* For convenience in later discussion we shall refer to Clique I as the "cool aggressives." Clique III favors *religious, polite, loyal, helpful, smart, clean,* and *obedient.* This pattern contains most of the elements of the Scout Pledge: "On my honor I will do my best: to do my duty to God and to my country, and to obey the Scout Law; to help other people at all times; to keep myself physically strong, mentally awake, and morally straight." Hence, we describe Clique III as the "scouts."[14]

From the manifest content emphasized, cool aggression suggests overt delinquent acts. In this connection it will be recalled that more than 60 per cent of the non-gang boys, who are in general less delinquent than the gang boys, were scouts, in contrast with only 28 per cent of the gang boys. The original interest in the behavioral correlates of self-descriptions can now be phrased: What are the behavioral differences between cool aggressives and scouts?

To clear away non-discriminating differences it may be reported that there is no difference in the average age (around 17) or average intelligence (around 84) between the cliques.[15]

With regard to sociometric choices, it may be reported that between boys with positively reciprocated friendship choices, the average similarity score is significantly higher than that for boys with an unreciprocated choice, or no choice at all (see tabulation near top of p. 133).[16]

Knowledge that likes choose one another leaves open the question whether this is more true for scouts than for cool aggressives. In most groups one would guess that persons who, in fact, were troublesome

[14] The work on a typology of inmate subcultures initiated by Schrag has resulted in the identification of various inmate roles, including "square Johns," somewhat like our "scouts" and "right guys" somewhat like the "cool aggressives." This work also utilizes self-description of a deviant population and is concerned with ways in which such self-conception may be related to behavior. See Donald L. Garrity, "The Prison as a Rehabilitation Agency," in *The Prison: Studies of Institutional Organization and Change,* edited by Donald R. Cressey (New York: Holt, Rinehart and Winston, 1961).

[15] Testing of individual personality characteristics, values, motivation, and intelligence was included in an assessment program independent of the sociometric and self-description data of primary concern to this chapter. See Desmond S. Cartwright and Kenneth I. Howard, "Psychological Assessment of Street Corner Youth," unpublished manuscript, Youth Studies Program, University of Chicago, 1961 (mimeographed). Intelligence data were obtained for eight "cool aggressives," five "scouts," and five of the mixed group.

[16] For $++$ vs. $0+$, $t(.025)_{64df} = 2.0$, $t = 2.3$, $P(t_{obs}) < .025$. There is no significant difference between $0+$ and 00.

and cool might be underchosen, but in the world of delinquent gangs they might actually be overchosen. Although the differences are not great, the latter interpretation is suggested by findings reported in Table 6.6. The cool aggressives are not only overchosen by boys with similar attitudes, they are overchosen by scouts as well.

Pattern	Number of Pairs Involved	Average Similarity
++...........	22	67.2
0+...........	44	58.8
00...........	165	57.1

In view of the above finding, one might guess that cool aggression within the gang might carry with it positive connotations for self-image. In fact, when compared with the other two attitude cliques, they prove to give themselves a slightly higher evaluative score on the semantic-differential responses to the concept "myself as I usually am" (6.2 in contrast with 5.5 for mixed and 6.0 for scouts). Their average evaluation score for GANG, 5.5, was lower than the 5.9 for the scouts but higher than the 5.1 for the mixed clique. Therefore, there are no grounds for believing that the cool aggressives are consciously more self-rejecting, but neither are they conspicuously higher.

When asked to compare their group with other boys in the neighborhood, cool aggressives saw their own group as being more *cool, troublesome,* and *mean.* When scouts made the comparison, they saw

TABLE 6.6

RELATIVE INTERCHANGE OF "FRIEND" CHOICES BETWEEN ATTITUDE CLIQUES

	Cool Aggressives I	Mixed II	Scouts III
I	110*	82	105
II	127	52	97
III	141	32	111

* An index value of 100 would represent the expected number of votes corrected for the number of boys in a group (exclusive of the respondent in main diagonal cells).

their own group as being more *helpful, loyal,* and *polite.* There are three observations to be drawn from this. First, since the "other boys" are a constant referent, there must be some systematic bias such that gang boys see non-gang boys as having contrasting rather than similar characteristics.

Second, if this contrasting conception does obtain, it is possible that cool aggressives might well have been expected to see their gang as being less good than scouts simply because of the characteristics they imputed to it. The fact that the gang emerged only slightly less highly evaluated for cool aggressives than for scouts means they must not have thought that being *cool, troublesome,* and *mean* was unequivocally bad (in the sense that it emerges from applications of the semantic differential). This adds up to a small bit of evidence that cool aggressives think of being *mean* and *troublesome* as being somewhat "good."

Finally, for scouts and cool aggressives to simultaneously hold contrasting conceptions of the common "other" must imply that there is little opportunity for discussions in which they reach consensus on what kinds of persons they or other boys are.

When these boys were asked, in the same battery which included the paired-comparison instrument, what kinds of activities "you and your friends" participate in each day, cool aggressives reported that they gambled, made money illegally, necked, signified,[17] played truant, and fought more than did scouts, whereas scouts reported a higher frequency of singing, playing cards for fun, and individual sports.[18] The cool aggressives reported both that they work slightly more than scouts, and that they regarded work as more important than did scouts. The cool aggressives reported slightly more heterosexual activity and a greater importance for quarter parties, necking, and intercourse. The self-reported activities are undoubtedly touched by the bias toward internal self-consistency which characterizes individual self-descriptions. The fact that cool aggressives reported both more illegitimate *instrumental* and illegitimate *expressive* behavior than scouts is consistent but not definitive, particularly since they

[17] Signifying, or playing the dozens, is a form of systematic exchange of insults, ordinarily carried out in the presence of an audience. It serves as a social-control mechanism and a device for display of verbal virtuosity. See Ralph F. Berdie, "Playing the Dozens," *The Journal of Abnormal and Social Psychology,* XLII (January, 1947), 120–21.

[18] All these differences are significant at the .05 level except individual sports which misses the .05 level by .05 of a point.

also reported more involvement in the legitimate instrumental activity of work and regarded it as more important than did the scouts.

Self-description and Observed Behavior

Behavior factor scores (from Chapter 4) by attitude cliques for the Garden Gang boys are given in Table 6.7. The Conflict factor which relates to individual and group fighting, as well as carrying a concealed weapon and assault, is very low for all three cliques. The slight excess of the scouts over the cool aggressives is not significant.

The Stable Corner-Activities factor which loads on individual sports, team sports, signifying, dancing, and gambling shows that all three cliques have scores around the mean of the sixteen groups and are not differentiated from one another.

TABLE 6.7

AVERAGE FACTOR SCORES BY ATTITUDE CLIQUES FOR
BEHAVIOR REPORTED BY DETACHED WORKERS

Factor Designation	Cool Aggressives I	Mixed II	Scouts III
I. Conflict.............	−11.3	−6.6	−7.7
II. Stable corner-activities.	0.2	1.4	1.4
III. Stable sex-maturity....	6.1	5.9	2.9
IV. Retreatism...........	− 6.0	−4.6	−5.1
V. Auto theft–authority protest...............	− 8.0	−4.7	−8.0

The Stable Sex-Maturity factor which loads on sexual intercourse, statutory rape, petting, signifying, hanging on the corner, buying and selling alcohol and work experience shows the cool aggressives to be higher than the scouts, but this difference is not significant due, in part, to the relatively high variability of the boys on this score.

The Retreatism factor which loads on the use, buying, and selling of marihuana and "hard narcotics," homosexuality, common-law marriage, attempted suicide, and pimping is quite low for all cliques of this gang and not differentiating.

Finally, Factor V, which loads on auto theft, driving without a license, public nuisance, truancy, theft, the use, buying, and selling of alcohol, and running away from home is quite low for both cool aggressives and scouts, and is slightly but not significantly higher in the mixed group.

Discussion

The analysis, as it has worked out, has converged on the test of whether or not the observed behaviors of the contrasted attitude cliques were similar, or differentiated in a manner parallel to the attitude differences. The comparison of the eleven cool aggressives with the seven scouts provides no basis for rejecting the hypothesis of sampling variation from a pool of common behavior. There is a sizable risk of a Type II error because of the small number of boys which were available within the gang. There is, in addition, the possibility that this gang—which is among the least delinquent of the set of actively delinquent gangs included in the study—has a different relationship between self-description and behavior than exists for more delinquent gangs. In terms of the objectives of the analysis of this segment of the data, certain questions of method have been solved, and in terms of these solutions certain further questions of interpretation may be raised.

The principal gain from the methodological exploration has been to adapt multivariate methods to the characterization of the similarity of self-descriptions. The problem of interpretation is the explanation of the meaning of the contrasting self-descriptions. It is to be noted that cool aggressives, in their responses to questions about their own activities, report that they engage in significantly more illegitimate activity than do scouts. This difference in magnitude may be valid but, turning on differential frequency rather than prevalence, it may be of a character which is not accurately perceived by the detached worker assigned to this gang. The worker with the Garden Gang is known to have one of the stronger middle class orientations toward the objective of work with gang boys of all of the somewhat more than a dozen workers in the program.[19] This orientation could have influenced both his perception of the boys and their willingness to confide illegitimate activities. From an independent study, we know the extent to which in his interviews this detached worker reports delinquent involvement for his gang in excess of information available from police records. In this case, the excess is *smaller* for

[19] Social class orientation of workers has been observed by the Youth Studies Program since the inception of the research. Formal testing of these orientations was undertaken by Desmond S. Cartwright and James F. Short, Jr., in consultations with R. W. Boone, then Director of the Program for Detached Workers of the YMCA.

the Garden Gang than for any other gang under observation.[20] This is, of course, only evidence that delinquency may be underestimated, not that it is differentially underestimated between the two cliques. It is, however, possible that scouts would be more cautious about permitting illegitimate behavior to become known to the detached worker than would cool aggressives.

On the other hand, if one assumes that the many sources of information available to the detached worker results in valid delinquency assessment, then one can entertain some doubt about the self-reported activity which shows consistency with the self-description on the grounds that it is cut from the same cloth and may arise from a tendency toward internal self-consistency. However, if the boys were simply trying to be self-consistent, it would be hard to account for the fact that cool aggressives, who report that they make money illegally more often (and have more sexual activity), also hold work to be highly important.

This joining of emphasis upon illegal money and delinquent sexual activity—"bads" for middle class society—with work, interests us. We note for development in the next chapter that a heavy emphasis upon sports, which is viewed as carrying middle class boys through a moratorium on work-related activities while they are being educated, may actually arrest the gang boy's movement into lower-status jobs and family commitments. In the same way, getting illegal money and having illegitimate premarital liaisons with girls which requires money may indirectly lead to getting "hooked" at an earlier time into a lower class adjustment.

Unlike Kaufmann's image of keeping one's analytic system at low tension by either accepting or rejecting each scientific statement,[21] one experiences quite the opposite feeling in the face of the need to validate fallible measures concomitantly. In this case, for example, since the evidence is not clear enough with regard to either the observer or self-reports to grasp firmly or let go, one continuously turns over in his thinking what he knows about the whole process. This is true for the self-descriptions also.

20 See John M. Wise, "A Comparison of Sources of Data as Indexes of Delinquent Behavior," unpublished Master's thesis, Department of Sociology, University of Chicago, 1962.

21 Felix Kaufmann, *Methodology of the Social Sciences* (New York: Oxford University Press, 1944), pp. 229–44.

The fact that both cool aggressives and scouts received many sociometric votes probably reflects the fact that these boys do not behave with indiscriminate cool aggression or with over-zealous morality toward members of their gang. The fact that the cool aggressives were somewhat overchosen by the gang is interpreted as reflecting a positive value accorded toughness in the face of threat within lower class culture generally rather than "tough" behavior with in-group members.

It seems that the scout and cool aggressive constellations of self-description are not deep-seated personality characteristics but more of the character of political conservatism in contrast with radicalism, or of optimism in contrast with pessimism. In the larger society, one can always select aspects about which one can be conservative, or optimistic, or other items about which radicalism or pessimism is appropriate, but such characterizations do not strongly influence overt behavior. Lodged as they are between the lower class culture of the gang world and the demands of middle class institutions, the pluralism of the alternative orientations may be easily come by, even adaptive for the group,[22] yet not highly predictive for any individual. This contrasts with the conscious role-specialization, for example, of individuals who are prized for their athletic skill when competition with other groups is involved. The scouts and cool aggressives identifications seem not to be badges by which the boys are known to one another; they seem to be less conscious adjustments to the group environment.[23] Thus, even though the attitude cliques may not be closely associated with differential delinquent behavior as a collective phenomena, they can be thought of as arising out of the cultural cross-pressures in the relevant social environment.

Thus, the search for new hypotheses (to guide the analysis of the remaining data has led us to a position which contrasts with work in the field of delinquency (i.e., by Reckless and his associ-

[22] See John M. Roberts' discussion of parallel mechanisms among the Zuni in Florence R. Kluckhohn and Fred L. Strodtbeck, *Variations in Value Orientations* (Evanston, Ill.: Row, Peterson, 1961), pp. 285–316.

[23] It is possible, also, that they are unique to the Garden Gang, and that other gangs will not be characterized by "attitude cliques" of this type, or by any other divisions on the basis of self-description. Hodge has found that, of all gangs studied, the Garden Gang evidenced the least consensus concerning self-descriptions. Kendall's coefficient of concordance for Garden Gang members' self-descriptions was .27, while for other gangs this measure varied from .30 to .57. Kendall's coefficient of concordance varies from 1.0, indicating perfect agreement to 0, indicating complete lack of agreement. See Hodge, *op. cit.*

ates)[24] which emphasizes the predictive value of self-descriptions. We would predict that the differential self-descriptions elicited from gang boys will *not* be associated with marked delinquency differences. We come to this conclusion not because of our doubt about method errors (of the type complained about by Wylie)[25] but because of a more externalized conception of the locus of causation. We view both the delinquent and non-delinquent behavior of gang boys as arising in the interplay of group expectations and situational requirements in such a manner as to overdetermine delinquency to the degree that, when the contribution of self-description to the prediction of behavior is added, no improvement results. This conclusion, derived from preliminary analyses of self-reports, is modified considerably, however, in the following chapter.

[24] See Walter C. Reckless, Simon Dinitz, and Ellen Murray, "Self Concept as an Insulator Against Delinquency," *American Sociological Review*, XXI (December, 1956), 744–46; and Walter C. Reckless, Simon Dinitz, and Barbara Kay, "The Self Component in Potential Delinquency and Potential Non Delinquency," *American Sociological Review*, XXII (October, 1957), 566–70.

[25] See Ruth C. Wylie, *The Self Concept: A Critical Survey of Pertinent Research Literature* (Lincoln: University of Nebraska Press, 1961).

CHAPTER 7

Self-description and Delinquent Behavior

In the preceding chapter it was found that in one set of Negro gang boys differences in self-conceptions did not discriminate between degrees of delinquency involvement. Moreover, there was a suggestion that it was the boys who described themselves as "scouts" who were most involved in conflict delinquency. In this chapter we wish to check the hunch that within delinquent gangs, boys who describe themselves in terms of more conventional values are more delinquent. To open this question we will again factor paired-comparison self-descriptions to see if the earlier "scout" v. "cool aggressive" typology exists for the full set of boys with which our study is concerned. By virtue of the availability of a broader sample, the distribution of self-descriptions can be checked for conformity to plausible concomitants of social position: race, class, and gang status. Intertwined with substantive considerations is a methodological question relating to whether boys responded to the instruments primarily with reference to themselves, their friends, or both. We will seek to justify our confidence that they are reporting about themselves. The correspondence between self-reported behavior and self-descriptions will be checked and related to the delinquency factor scores developed in Chapter 4. To achieve these objectives, it will be necessary to introduce a number of new measures. We have evolved these from tests administered to the more than five hundred boys who completed the paired-comparison task (see Chapter 6). All of the instruments discussed in this chapter were completed by the boys in non-school settings in their home neighborhoods, and under the supervision of Youth Studies Program personnel.

Background

As a first step, it is desirable to look for a moment at prior attempts to use self-reports in the understanding of delinquency. We referred briefly in the last chapter to the studies, between 1956 and 1962, of Reckless, Dinitz, and others at Ohio State University who have found self-concept to be related to "delinquency proneness" among public school children, and to actual delinquency in longitudinal studies.[1] Their self-concept measures are derived from questions involving good and bad projections of oneself among peers, family members, and teachers—e.g., whether one expects to get into trouble and whether one perceives others as having these expectations. Delinquency proneness has been measured by scales from the California Psychological Inventory. Actual delinquency has been inferred from self-reports and court records and followed up over a period of years. Precisely how self-concept is related to delinquency is not made clear in these reports, for their interpretation does not go beyond the suggestion that self-concept differences result from differential socialization and that, in turn, differences in delinquency result from the relative "insulating" qualities of self-concept.

Referring to these studies, Wylie has pointed out that "their results do not warrant these conclusions because (a) there were a number of important objective differences between the groups (e.g., number of broken homes, parents' reported attitudes toward the boys); and (b) in any event we cannot know to what extent the boys' reports (self-concepts) reflect rather than cause the differences in behavior which lay behind their teachers' nominations of them."[2] Wylie's implied criteria are quite stringent—so stringent, in fact, that they appear to cause Wylie to overlook the interesting demonstration that teachers were able to identify boys who get in trouble and that, whatever their origins, these boys held negative self-assessments. The

[1] Walter C. Reckless, Simon Dinitz, and Ellen Murray, "Self Concept as an Insulator Against Delinquency," *American Sociological Review,* XXI (December, 1956), 744–46; Walter C. Reckless, Simon Dinitz, and Barbara Kay, "The Self Component in Potential Delinquency and Potential Non-Delinquency," *American Sociological Review,* XXII (October, 1957), 566–70; Simon Dinitz, Barbara Ann Kay, and Walter C. Reckless, "Group Gradients in Delinquency Potential and Achievement Scores of Sixth Graders," *American Journal of Orthopsychiatry,* XXVIII (July, 1958), 588–605; Jon E. Simpson, Simon Dinitz, Barbara Kay, and Walter C. Reckless, "Delinquency Potential of Pre-Adolescents in High Delinquency Areas," *British Journal of Delinquency,* X (January, 1960), 211–15; Frank R. Scarpitti, Ellen Murray, Simon Dinitz, and Walter C. Reckless, "The 'Good' Boy in a High Delinquency Area: Four Years Later," *American Sociological Review,* XXV (August, 1960), 555–58; and Simon Dinitz, Frank R. Scarpitti, and Walter C. Reckless, "Delinquency Vulnerability: A Cross Group and Longitudinal Analysis," *American Sociological Review,* XXVII (August, 1962), 515–17.

[2] Ruth Wylie, *The Self Concept: A Critical Survey of Pertinent Research Literature* (Lincoln: University of Nebraska Press, 1961), p. 219.

sixth-grade classrooms of Columbus, Ohio, provide a reference frame such that if a boy believes others think he will get into trouble, his chance of doing so is increased. If our findings differ from these, the explanation may be given by differences in reference group benchmarks and by group processes which tend to be unique to members of delinquent gangs.

At the same level of use of self-reports without reference group specification, a great deal of work has been done with the Minnesota Multiphasic Personality Inventory—an instrument which combines self-reports of experiences, attitudes, and feelings.[3] The MMPI consists of 550 statements which are then reduced to ten clinical and four validity scales. When scored, these provide "personality profiles" of respondents. Hathaway and Monachesi, principal investigators of delinquency with the MMPI, have described these profiles as revealing "the self-perception of the subject in relation to others in his social world as well as some of the various roles he plays. In other words, an individual's MMPI profile constitutes a personal and social self-evaluation."[4]

It has been demonstrated that both the clinical and validity scales of the MMPI are related to "delinquency proneness" in adolescent boys.[5] Nearly two thousand ninth-grade boys attending Minneapolis public schools during the 1947–48 year were tested with the MMPI and checked after two years against public and private agency records for evidence of delinquent behavior. Boys with elevations on scales 4, 8, and 9 (Psychopathic deviate, Schizophrenia, and Hypomania, respectively) were found to have higher delinquency rates than the over-all rate established by the study for Minneapolis boys, while boys high on scale 0 (Social introversion), 2 (Depression), and 5 (Masculinity-femininity) had exceptionally low delinquency rates.

One of the most interesting aspects of this analysis was the finding that among these three sets of scales the inhibitory appeared to be the most powerful, for when one of the inhibitory scales (0, 2, 5) was paired

[3] Starke R. Hathaway and Elio D. Monachesi, eds., *Analyzing and Predicting Juvenile Delinquency with the MMPI* (Minneapolis: University of Minnesota Press, 1953).

[4] From the "Foreword" to John C. Ball, *Social Deviancy and Adolescent Personality: An Analytic Study with the MMPI* (Lexington: University of Kentucky Press, 1962).

[5] The following analysis is taken from Starke R. Hathaway, Elio D. Monachesi, and Laurence A. Young, "Delinquency Rates and Personality," *Journal of Criminal Law, Criminology, and Police Science*, L (February, 1960), 433–40.

with one of the variable scales (1, 3, 6, 7), or even with one of the excitatory scales to comprise the two most deviant scales in the same profile, the delinquency rate for the combination tended to be below the rate for all Minneapolis boys [p. 434].

A second follow-up on the original sample four years after testing and replication of the entire study on a statewide sample of 11,329 ninth graders in 1953–54 (this time with a three-year follow-up check on delinquency records) confirmed these findings and provided a further basis for exploration of the usefulness of the MMPI for delinquency-prediction purposes. The over-all findings are summarized as follows:

. . . delinquency rates of 40.9 and 34.6 are the totals for all boys of each sample. In both cases, the boys who obtained codes with deviant excitatory scales . . . have a delinquency rate 20 per cent larger than the general rate. Contrastingly, the boys with inhibitory codes . . . have delinquency rates that are only 6 to 8 tenths of the general rate. Those boys with no deviant score on their profiles also show a lower rate. Finally, in both cases, boys who had invalid profiles . . . have an elevation of rate.

All these trends are even more marked among the girls. . . . Here the personality test data so closely relate to the delinquency rate that the rate among girls with excitatory code profiles . . . is up to twice the general rate, and the rates for the most normal profiles . . . are zero for the 41 Minneapolis girls and only 2.4 per cent among the 84 girls in the statewide sample.

The authors are quite candid in their assessment of these findings: "We do not find these figures to be startling or highly explanatory of the personality factors in delinquency. . . . We have recovered some from our earlier disappointment that we seem to discover such relatively weak predictors and analyzers of the personalities of delinquents. At any rate, these factors . . . are much less powerful and apply to fewer cases among the total samples than would be expected if one reads the literature on the subject. . . . Surely we cannot say that these data put us far ahead either in prediction or understanding" (p. 439). Hathaway and Monachesi hold some hope that the findings "convey valid information which may provide a modest base upon which a scientific knowledge of the interrelationships of personality and delinquent behavior can be founded," however, and indicate that they hope "to find new relationships and new analytical approaches that will sharply increase and extend the validity of the findings" (p. 439).

The Present Case

We share the conviction of Hathaway and Monachesi that the "response to the (test) item is neither simple statement of obvious facts nor simply lying nor random answering." We agree, also, with their stated belief that "our difficulty lies in the objectivity, broad sampling, and longitudinal method of study" (p. 439). The problem of predicting a phenomenon so heterogeneous as delinquency in Minnesota is indeed great. Their study, like virtually all studies in this tradition, has attempted to predict a gross measure of delinquent behavior—"the" delinquency rate as measured by police contact, court appearance, or some combination of official and unofficial agency bookkeeping. While dependence upon such measures has been much lamented in recent theoretical and in some empirical work, little has been done about it. It is in this particular detail that our study narrows the gap between report and criterion. Our multivariate reduction of detached-workers' reports of gang boys' behavior provides measures which are both more finely scaled and more substantively differentiated than those ordinarily employed.

The question of the fineness of the grain and detailed validity of measurement becomes a concern, for it will be recalled (in Chapter 6) that a brief allusion was made to self-reports of behavior being related to self-description reports in the "expected" direction, while observer reports of behavior were not. This finding and the knotty problems of recall, definition, and possible distortion, for whatever reasons, of self-reports lead us in this chapter to figuratively "take a clean sheet of paper" and go again through our operations to explain them fully. We know that self-concepts and action interact continuously, and we therefore will loosen our premises and avoid a rigid definition of which variable is the predictor and which the criterion.

In the attempt to achieve greater precision we must always deal with a kind of Heisenberg phenomenon—the more delinquent boys in life may be the more delinquent boys in filling out our instruments. In Chapter 3 we have described the care we took to motivate the boys at the laboratory. The present instruments were administered in the field, and similar motivational gambits were employed (e.g., refreshments and the good offices of detached workers). Again, great care was taken to insure that boys who had reading problems were helped with the instruments, though the testing atmosphere was less formally structured than was the case in the laboratory. We have tried in each instance to eliminate obviously faked and inconsistent responses. These procedures raise the question of the representativeness of boys who successfully completed the assigned tasks. One check on this is to look at boys whose paired-comparison protocols were retained on the basis of the circular-triad criterion (e.g., tough > cool, cool > religious, religious > tough). The 240 gang boys for whom relevant detached-worker reports were available were distributed as follows, by category of gang membership:

Response Consistency	Core Members	Fringe Boys	N
Retained = <35 circular triads.....	84.5%	15.5%	142
Rejected = >35 circular triads......	83.6%	16.4%	73
Too poorly completed to code......	80.0%	20.0%	25

Hathaway, Monachesi, and Young report that boys who have some public record of delinquency have a tendency to underrate their frequency of "trouble with the law" (only 80 per cent of a group of known delinquents admitted this fact on the MMPI), while one-third of the boys with no known delinquency, and 61 per cent of boys who acquired police records only *after* MMPI testing answered "false" to the statement, "I have never been in trouble with the law." Data in this same article indicate that "invalids" (youngsters with excessive "don't know" responses, or those who are adjudged to be "faking good" or "faking bad" in test performance) have the highest delinquency rates of all among the Minneapolis boys (58.1 per cent, compared to 49.3 per cent of those with elevations on excitatory scale codes). For the state-wide sample the delinquency rate of boys with high excitatory scale codes is about the same as the "invalids" (41.9 per cent compared to 39.1 per cent). Thus, in their research, evidence of dissimulation on tests is predictive of delinquency.

We can essentially replicate this aspect of the MMPI study by looking at mean behavior factor scores of boys in the three categories of adequacy in filling out the paired-comparison instrument:

Response Consistency	Conflict	Stable Corner-Boy Activity	Stable Sex-Maturity	Retreatist	Authority Protest	N
Retained....	−.08	.44	.20	−.08	−.11	137
Rejected....	−.24	.23	.06	−.09	−.03	65
Not coded...	.24	.16	.05	−.05	.24	25

When one checks the significance of the observed differences, the twenty-five boys with non-coded responses are more conflict oriented than the rejected boys, but not more than the retained boys. Between the "retained" and the "not coded" boys, the latter are to a lesser degree "stable corner boys" and are higher on "authority protest"— these have P levels of .10 and .20, respectively. Since the only significant difference observed occurred between "rejected's" and "not coded's," and since these were on opposite sides of the "retained," we conclude on the hopeful note that within a population of gang boys, poor instrument completion is *not* predictive of differences in observed criterion behaviors. If one had mixed together delinquent and non-delinquent populations, the results obtained by simply looking at instances of poor instrument completion might well have been consistent with the MMPI findings. For present purposes, the anticipated poorer reporting by more delinquent respondents does not appear to be present.

The Paired-Comparison Terms as Attitude Measures

Shortly after the boys completed the paired-comparison task in the field, a further attitude instrument, asking for in-group, out-group comparisons on a seven-point scale, was administered to them. While it was our intention only to use this as a basis for measuring how boys compared themselves with others independently of the first instrument, the presence in the in-group, out-group comparisons of the fourteen adjectives used in the paired comparisons came to be perceived as a further asset. This measure yields information on the way in which the race and status of the boy are involved in the process of self-describing. The boys were instructed as follows:

INSTRUCTIONS: We want to know how you and your friends compare yourselves with boys in this same neighborhood who do not belong to any group such as yours. Suppose the circle in the middle of each of the following items represents boys in this neighborhood who do not belong to your group or to any group like yours. Please place an X beside each word where you believe you and your friends are in comparison with such boys.[6]

	MORE			SAME		LESS	
COOL	___	___	___	0	___	___	___
BRAVE	___	___	___	0	___	___	___

[6] Non-gang boys were instructed specifically to compare themselves with gang boys in their neighborhoods.

In the analysis of these materials arbitrary weights were used such that "MORE" was 7, 0 was 4, and "LESS" was 1, with the places in between being given the appropriate intermediate numbers. The adjectives used were presented in this order:

cool	cowardly	square	weak	unlucky	dirty
brave	tough	sad	smart	cheerful	unfriendly
lazy	dumb	polite	truthful	obedient	strong
sharp	soft	free-spending	troublesome	womanly	religious
loyal	mean	clean	manly	good	squealer
rude	thrifty	disobedient	bad	exciting	lucky
helpful	kind	studious	friendly	athletic	boring

For the fourteen adjectives which were the same as the ones used in the paired-comparison self-description task, there were ten opposites (one pair within the set, troublesome-helpful, and eight others):

Original 14	Opposite Term
mean	kind
troublesome	helpful
tough	soft
cool	square
strong	weak
sharp	(no opposite)
athletic	(no opposite)
clean	dirty
smart	dumb
obedient	disobedient
religious	(no opposite)
helpful	(see troublesome above)
polite	rude
loyal	(no opposite)

In addition to the opposites involving the original paired-comparison terms, nine other pairs can be made up from the list of forty-two. These are:

studious	lazy
friendly	unfriendly
good	bad
thrifty	free-spending
lucky	unlucky
cheerful	sad
exciting	boring
brave	cowardly
manly	womanly

To complete the listing, mention is made of the concept, "truthful" which is unmatched, as are the four listed along with the original fourteen above. The eighteen paired terms provide a simple reliability check when the opposites are valid opposites and the attitude processes the same for socially desirable and socially undesirable terms. If the ranking of one term is not roughly the complement of the ranking of the opposite term, there is probably a confounding of elements of unreliability with indication that the prescriptive and proscriptive mechanisms do not perfectly mesh. To illustrate this ap-

Race	Gang	Lower Class	Middle Class
Negro........	(203)	(133)	(33)
polite......	4.7	5.5	6.5
rude.......	3.8	2.2	1.4
	.9	3.3	5.1
White........	(70)	(68)	(54)
polite......	4.7	5.8	6.2
rude.......	3.4	2.2	1.5
	1.3	3.6	4.7

proach we take the two terms which produced the sharpest differentiation by status; *polite* and *rude:* Viewed in this way the "status gradient" among Negroes is steeper than that of whites:

$$\text{Negro} \quad (5.1 - 0.9)/2 = 2.2$$
$$\text{White} \quad (4.7 - 1.3)/2 = 1.7$$

We are particularly pleased with the economy of these measures, for they compress into two values the responses of more than five hundred boys on a trait which is a key prerequisite for mobility of lower class persons through educational processes or service occupations. It is just those boys, who on the basis of other information would be assumed to profit most from greater politeness, who see themselves as being maximally disadvantaged. It could not have been known in advance that those who were rude would see themselves as being rude. Pairs for which status gradients are steeper for Negroes than whites are grouped together in Table 7.1.

TABLE 7.1

ADJECTIVE PAIRS FOR WHICH OWN-GROUP V. OTHER-GROUP COMPARISONS
INCREASE WITH CLASS AND GANG STATUS—STATUS GRADIENTS FOR
NEGROES GREATER THAN FOR WHITES

PAIRS OF OPPOSITE ADJECTIVES	GANG		LOWER CLASS NON-GANG		MIDDLE CLASS	
	Negro (203)	White (70)	Negro (133)	White (68)	Negro (33)	White (54)
Friendly	4.8	5.2	5.8	5.7	6.3	5.9
Unfriendly	3.4	3.0	2.2	2.5	1.8	2.4
	1.4	2.2	3.6	3.2	4.5	3.5
Clean	5.1	5.0	5.8	5.8	6.6	6.2
Dirty	3.0	2.8	2.0	2.4	1.3	2.0
	2.1	2.2	3.8	3.4	5.3	4.2
Polite	4.7	4.7	5.5	5.8	6.5	6.2
Rude	3.8	3.4	2.2	2.2	1.4	1.5
	.9	1.3	3.3	3.6	5.1	4.7
Smart	4.9	5.0	5.6	5.8	6.2	6.2
Dumb	2.9	2.4	1.9	2.2	1.2	1.6
	2.0	2.6	3.7	3.6	5.0	4.6
Kind	4.6	5.0	5.8	5.8	6.4	6.0
Mean	4.0	3.6	2.8	2.8	2.2	1.8
	.6	1.4	3.0	3.0	4.2	4.2
Helpful	4.7	4.9	5.4	5.6	6.4	6.0
Troublesome	3.7	3.8	2.3	2.6	1.9	2.0
	1.0	1.1	3.1	3.0	4.5	4.0
Good	4.8	4.8	5.6	5.4	6.0	5.8
Bad	4.0	3.6	2.4	2.6	2.0	2.0
	.8	1.2	3.2	2.8	4.0	3.8

Computed in the same way as was done for polite and rude, the
status gradients for these are as follows:

Adjective Pairs	Negro Status Gradient	White Status Gradient	Difference
friendly–unfriendly.........	1.6	.6	1.0
clean–dirty...............	1.6	1.0	.6
polite–rude...............	2.2	1.7	.5
smart–dumb..............	1.5	1.0	.5
kind–mean...............	1.8	1.4	.4
helpful–troublesome........	1.8	1.5	.3
good–bad.................	1.6	1.3	.3

There are three pairs in which there is a marked status gradient, but in which the previously noted racial difference does not appear (see Table 7.2).

TABLE 7.2

ADJECTIVE PAIRS FOR WHICH OWN-GROUP V. OTHER-GROUP COMPARISONS INCREASE WITH CLASS AND GANG STATUS—STATUS GRADIENTS EQUAL OR SLIGHTLY GREATER FOR WHITES

PAIRS OF OPPOSITE ADJECTIVES	GANG		LOWER CLASS NON-GANG		MIDDLE CLASS	
	Negro (203)	White (70)	Negro (133)	White (68)	Negro (33)	White (54)
Studious.......	3.9	4.1	4.8	5.1	6.2	6.4
Lazy...........	3.4	3.4	2.8	2.4	2.5	2.0
	.5	.7	2.0	2.7	3.7	4.4
Obedient.......	4.6	4.4	5.5	5.4	6.2	6.0
Disobedient....	3.4	3.4	2.6	2.8	2.2	2.0
	1.2	1.0	2.9	2.6	4.0	4.0
Thrifty........	4.7	4.2	4.8	4.6	5.8	5.2
Free-spending...	4.8	4.8	4.4	4.0	4.0	3.8
	− .1	− .6	.4	.6	1.8	1.4

The status gradients from Table 7.2 are as follows:

Adjective Pairs	Negro Status Gradient	White Status Gradient	Difference
studious–lazy..............	1.6	1.8	.2
obedient–disobedient.......	1.4	1.5	.1
thrifty–free-spending.......	1.0	1.0	0.0

It is difficult to explain these differences in terms either of reference group theory or theories treating of social comparison processes. The terms, particularly of Table 7.1, seem so primordial that if Negro gang boys are in fact so fundamentally disadvantaged—both in comparison with lower class non-gang Negroes and white gang boys—as the scores indicate, major modification of the social situation would be required to remove this negative self-image. On the other hand, why should the middle class Negro boy see himself so much better (i.e., *good, clean, smart*, and *friendly*) than middle class white boys in comparison with neighborhood others? We know that Negro middle class persons are less residentially segregated than are whites, and these findings may reflect the fact. Also, Drake and Cayton make much of the existence, side-by-side, of "respectables" and "shadies" throughout the class structure in *Black Metropolis*.[7] Perhaps the middle class Negro boys are at the top of a system looking back, while the white middle class boys still see steps ahead to white upper class. There is no clear explanation to be read from the data available, but the empirical findings bring to mind also Frazier's assertions concerning the narcissistic preoccupations and escapist concerns of Negro "society," and Wilson's diagnosis of the ambivalent position of middle class Negroes with respect to their lower class colleagues and racial advancement.[8]

It is interesting to note that the two adjective pairs which correspond to Miller's focal concerns of lower class culture are comparatively non-discriminating by status groups. (See *lucky-unlucky* and *exciting-boring* in Table 7.3.) The *cheerful-sad* differences show status differentiation only for white boys. For Negroes, *cheerful* shows a clear gradient, *sad* does not. The ambivalence of middle class Negro boys once again is apparent. Inkeles' study of surveys in industrial societies, and more recent work by Bradburn,[9] show consistent status

[7] St. Clair Drake and Horace R. Cayton, *Black Metropolis: A Study of Negro Life in a Northern City* (New York: Harcourt, Brace and Co., 1945).

[8] E. Franklin Frazier, *Black Bourgeoisie* (Glencoe: The Free Press, 1957); and James Q. Wilson, *Negro Politics: The Search for Leadership* (Glencoe: The Free Press, 1959).

[9] Alex Inkeles, "Industrial Man: The Relation of Status to Experience, Perception, and Value," *American Journal of Sociology*, LXVI (July, 1960), 1–31; and Norman S. Bradburn, "In Pursuit of Happiness," National Opinion Research Center, University of Chicago, May, 1963, Report #92. "Very Happy" responses decline from 29 per cent for college graduates to 19 per cent for less than eighth

TABLE 7.3

ADJECTIVE PAIRS FOR WHICH OWN-GROUP V. OTHER-GROUP COMPARISONS DISCRIMINATE WEAKLY AND SHOW NO SIGNIFICANT TREND

PAIRS OF OPPOSITE ADJECTIVES	GANG		LOWER CLASS NON-GANG		MIDDLE CLASS	
	Negro (203)	White (70)	Negro (133)	White (68)	Negro (33)	White (54)
	Trend Positive with Status					
Lucky.........	4.5	4.8	5.0	4.4	4.6	5.0
Unlucky.......	3.6	3.8	3.4	3.6	2.8	3.1
	.9	1.0	1.6	.8	1.8	1.9
Cheerful.......	5.1	4.8	5.6	5.4	5.8	5.6
Sad...........	2.7	2.9	2.4	3.0	3.0	2.5
	2.4	1.9	3.2	2.4	2.8	3.1
Exciting........	5.0	4.7	4.8	4.8	5.3	4.8
Boring.........	3.2	2.8	2.7	2.6	2.6	2.8
	1.8	1.9	2.1	2.2	2.7	2.0
Cool..........	5.0	5.4	5.0	4.6	5.4	5.5
Square........	2.8	2.6	2.7	2.9	2.6	3.2
	2.2	2.8	2.3	1.7	2.8	2.3
	Trend Negative with Status					
Strong.........	5.1	5.1	4.8	4.6	4.9	4.4
Weak..........	3.0	3.0	3.0	3.3	3.0	3.3
	2.1	2.1	1.8	1.3	1.9	1.1
Brave..........	5.0	4.6	4.7	4.4	4.4	4.3
Cowardly......	2.8	2.9	2.6	3.0	3.1	3.4
	2.2	1.7	2.1	1.4	1.3	.9
Tough.........	4.8	4.7	4.0	3.6	3.8	3.0
Soft..........	3.5	3.4	3.6	3.2	3.4	3.8
	1.3	1.3	.4	.4	.4	− .8

gradients for "happiness." These studies, however, are for older respondents, and attention has not been directed to racial differentials. The troubled role of the Negro middle class person in our society is a complex matter. In addition to the Frazier and Wilson suggestions, these boys may feel that although they are *good, clean,* and *smart,* there is a good deal missing in society's response. A recent study in Chicago by Duncan and Hodge finds considerably less occupational mobility among non-whites than "expected" on the basis of correlations between mobility and education among other segments of the population.[10] Among Negro boys in this study the finding is relevant particularly for NMC since they have the most successful school adjustments and the best prospects for further educational achievement.[11]

Particular attention should be directed to the negative gradients associated with strength, bravery, and toughness. The higher the status, the less the attribute distinguishes one's own group from outgroups in the neighborhood milieu. There is a suggestion here of greater dependence upon physical strength in interpersonal relations, even among close friends, as one descends the social ladder. We shall return to this theme in later chapters.

For the eighteen adjective pairs investigated, only one showed the characteristic of a positive trend for Negroes and a negative for white. Such an adjective pair is of particular interest because such opposing slopes would indicate differing centrality of the implied value theme in Negro and white subcultures. The terms are *manly* and *womanly* (see tabulation near top of p. 154). For Negroes, the higher one's status, the *greater* one's masculinity; for whites, the higher one's status, the less one's masculinity by this criterion.

It would have taken great sophistication to anticipate this result in advance. Once it is before us, the general line of the Whiting-Miller

---

grade, and the older one is, the less happy (30 per cent at under 30; 18 per cent over 70).

[10] O. D. Duncan and Robert W. Hodge, "Education and Occupational Mobility: A Regression Analysis," *American Journal of Sociology,* LXVIII (May, 1963), 629–44.

[11] Jonathan Freedman and Ramon Rivera, "Education, Social Class, and Patterns of Delinquency," paper read at the annual meetings of the American Sociological Association, 1962.

argument concerning identity problems in female-dominated, lower class, Negro homes, and Frazier's description of the importance placed on sexual prowess by Negro middle class males come to mind.[12] We know that about one-half of our Negro gang boys report a father figure in the home. This figure is two-thirds for white gang boys.[13] This small difference in availability of fathers surely would

Race	Gang	Lower	Middle
Negro:			
manly............	4.6	4.8	5.3
womanly.........	3.4	3.2	2.4
	1.2	1.6	2.9
White:			
manly............	5.0	4.7	5.0
womanly.........	2.4	2.6	3.8
	2.6	2.1	1.2

not account for the differences in masculinity conceptions. One might guess that what is involved is a cultural difference in the degree to which being manly is a focal concern in the respective cultures. It is not possible to say just what being manly implies, but there are two bits of evidence which suggest that it means more than being overpowering as a sex figure with females. It will be recalled from Chapter 3 that Negro and white evaluations (on the Osgood evaluation scales) of the construct GIRL ("makes out with every girl he wants") differed considerably:

Race	Gang	Lower	Middle
Negro..............	5.3	5.1	5.0
White..............	4.3	4.2	3.5
	1.0	0.9	1.5

[12] See Roger V. Burton and John W. M. Whiting, "The Absent Father and Cross-Sex Identity," *Merrill-Palmer Quarterly*, VII (1961), 85–95; Walter B. Miller, "Implications of Lower Class Culture for Social Work," *Social Service Review*, Vol. XXXIII (September, 1959); and Frazier, *op. cit.*

[13] Data from our study populations are discussed in Ray A. Tennyson, "Family Structure and Delinquent Behavior" in *Juvenile Gangs in Context: Theory, Research and Action,* Malcolm W. Klein and Barbara G. Myerhoff, eds. (Conference Report, Youth Studies Center, University of Southern California, 1964).

Also in terms of *smartness*—a single rating based upon one of Miller's focal concerns:

Race	Gang	Lower	Middle
Negro.............	6.1	5.6	5.8
White.............	5.2	4.5	3.8
	0.9	1.1	2.0

In both cases there is just a slight negative status gradient for Negro boys' evaluations while for white boys it is steeper. Negroes are higher than whites, and the disparity is greatest between the Negro and white middle class respondents.

In terms of *potency* (also by Osgood scales),

Race	Gang	Lower	Middle
Negro.............	4.5	4.5	4.7
White.............	4.4	4.4	4.2
	0.1	0.1	0.5

there is no significant difference between Negroes and whites, or by classes, on the perceived potency of someone who "makes out."

One must reason with care in a region with so many imponderables, but certainly the evidence above, bearing narrowly on heterosexual behavior, would not cause one to believe that Negro middle class males were very different from Negro lower class and gang males in their assessment of their role in heterosexual behavior. For this reason we guess that more than heterosexual behavior is involved.

The non-acceptance, or non-reporting, of womanly traits by middle class Negroes represents a change from both lower class gang and non-gang evaluations, but a change—if one is to infer from the contrast with the trend of white middle class response—of a character which is not likely to facilitate occupational and educational mobility.[14]

To account for all of the forty-two adjectives, we include in Table 7.4 the remaining six for which no opposites were available, arranged

[14] Cf., once more, Dollard's discussion of the perceived relation between control of sexuality and mobility. John Dollard, *Caste and Class in a Southern Town* (New Haven: Yale University Press, 1937).

by the clarity of the status gradient. *Religious, truthful,* and *athletic* show positive trends with status for boys of both races. Gradients for the first two adjectives—among the most "middle class" in our entire battery—are substantial. *Sharp* and *loyal* are slightly positive with status for Negro boys, but not for whites, due to the falling off of middle class boys. *Squealer* is positive with status for white but not for Negro boys, due to higher ratings given by gang youngsters.

Recapitulating in terms of the original fourteen adjectives used for the paired comparison, we find that positive terms such as *polite, obedient,* and *helpful,* and negative terms such as *mean* and *troublesome,* when joined with their opposites work clearly as indices of race,

TABLE 7.4

UNPAIRED ADJECTIVES, PRESENTED WITH OWN-GROUP V. OTHER-GROUP
COMPARISONS FOR NEGROES AND WHITES

UNPAIRED ADJECTIVES	GANG		LOWER CLASS NON-GANG		MIDDLE CLASS	
	Negro (203)	White (70)	Negro (133)	White (68)	Negro (33)	White (54)
Religious.......	4.0	4.0	5.0	5.2	5.8	6.3
Truthful.......	4.3	4.8	5.3	5.4	6.0	6.0
Athletic.......	5.0	5.2	5.7	5.2	5.8	5.6
Sharp.........	4.8	4.4	5.3	5.4	5.4	5.0
Loyal.........	4.8	5.0	5.2	5.4	5.4	5.0
Squealer.......	3.1	2.2	2.6	2.6	3.0	3.6

class, and gang status; the term *clean* discriminates more for Negroes than whites (see Table 7.1). The lower the class, the greater the emphasis upon *strong* and *tough* (see Table 7.3). *Loyal* shows little variation and is positively related to status only for Negro boys. *Cool* varies little and unsystematically in relation to status. One thus concludes that the direction of the differences obtained are both discriminatory and congruent with expectation in 12 of the 14 instances, the two exceptions being the terms *cool* and *loyal,* which do not discriminate by the race, class, gang-status criterion.

You and/or Your Friends

Although this result assures us, it still leaves a question as to whether boys reflected a cultural stereotype when describing "_____ and your friends"—leaving himself, the "you" out—or whether the "you" is fused collectively with "and your friends" and whether indeed boys might be describing their friends rather than themselves. We have satisfied ourselves on this question by returning once more to the eleven "cool aggressives" and the seven "scouts" of the Garden Gang described in Chapter 6.

It will be recalled that these boys and the non-gang boys with whom they were asked to compare themselves lived in the same housing project. It was possible that both "cool aggressives" and "scouts" might have described the non-gang members in the same way. If this had proved to be the case, the argument that self-descriptions referred primarily to friends would have been enhanced. This was precluded by the fact that "cool aggressives" and "scouts" in fact described the non-gang members in non-similar ways. For both groups the "others" were described as lacking attributes with highly ranked self-descriptions. Hence one can conclude that both "cool aggressives" and "scouts" were ethnocentrically describing others by a stereotyped, negative projection. The evidence supporting this interpretation is given in Charts 1 and 2. "Cool aggressives" see their own group as being more *cool, troublesome,* and *mean,* and less *helpful, polite,* and *religious;* "scouts" see themselves as more *clean, helpful, loyal, smart, polite, obedient,* and *cool,* and as less *tough, mean,* and *troublesome.*

It was demonstrated in Chapter 6 that the "scouts" and "cool aggressives" were *not* friendship cliques; hence it could not be the case that the friends they incorporate into their collective identity were in fact all "cool aggressives" or "scouts" respectively. Nor could it be the case that 'scouts" and "cool aggressives" among the Garden Gang boys were comparing themselves with completely different sets of "others"—both were referring to non-gang boys in the same housing project. We conclude, therefore, that boys responded to the self-description question of "you and your friends" (and to own-group, other-group comparisons) in terms of feelings about themselves. In the own-group, other-group comparison, apparently they buttress these responses by assuming that fellow gang members share, and non-gang members lack, these same characteristics. In so doing, gang boys behave very much like other groups which "typically perceive the group's opinion to be closer to their own opinions than it actually

CHART 1.—Decreasing Importance of Term as Self-description
by "Cool Aggressives," Garden Gang

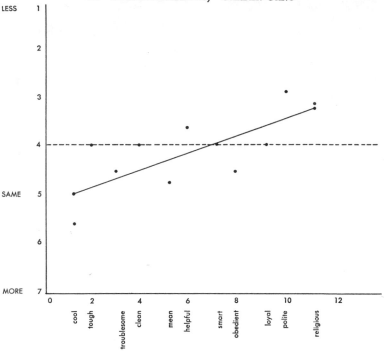

CHART 2.—Decreasing Importance of Term as Self-description
by "Scouts," Garden Gang

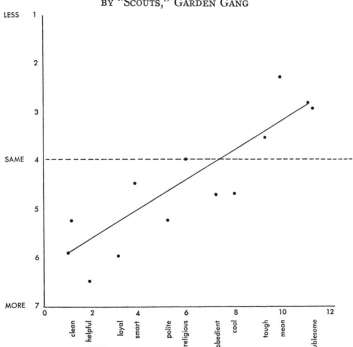

is."[15] We interpret this finding as putting to rest the possibility that boys chose to describe "their friends" rather than themselves. And with this, we return to the central task.

Self-description Factors

The essential description of the paired-comparisons task has been discussed earlier. With the 387 non-circular cases available to us it is not practicable to proceed by inspecting the similar responses of pairs of boys. For this reason we have approached the problem by determining for each respondent how many times each adjective was chosen over another adjective (from 0 to 13, for the 14 adjectives), then producing a matrix of the correlations. In this process seven additional cases were eliminated because of incomplete identification, so that the resultant 14 $\times$ 14 matrix was made up of correlations over 380 respondents.

The factor analysis was done by the principal components method, and the rotation carried out by the Kaiser varimax routines cited in previous chapters. Four factors were sufficient to permit each adjective to be displayed with a loading greater than 0.5 on at least one factor. The analysis of the previous chapter was based upon 25 boys, and while these 25 were included again in this sample of 380, this small fraction would not have caused the re-emergence of the Scouts v. Cool Aggressive factor if in fact it were not a predominant factor for the entire population. It may be seen in Table 7.5 that the ordering of the adjectives is very similar to the ordering in Table 6.5 of the preceding chapter.

The Scouts v. Cool Aggressives factor is bipolar and appears to involve as its principal dimension a characterization of the nature of association with others. All of the positive loading adjectives, for example, carry with them the implication of *responsible* relations with

[15] Bernard Berelson and Gary A. Steiner, *Human Behavior: An Inventory of Scientific Findings* (New York: Harcourt, Brace and World, Inc., 1964), p. 336. The authors go on to cite Kelley and Thibaut to the effect that "Whether this is due to association with a biased sample of like-minded individuals in the group or to an attempt to allay anxiety about non-conformity by minimizing deviation from the group standard remains a problem for further research," from Harold H. Kelley and John W. Thibaut, "Experimental Studies of Group Problem Solving and Process," in Gardner Lindzey (ed.), *Handbook of Social Psychology* (Vol. 2, New York: Addison-Wesley, 1954), p. 768. Berelson and Steiner add: "By virtue of the informality in the operations of most small groups, issues may be kept from being put to clear test." Our data suggest that knowledge of group norms counter to individual attitudes is a more powerful deterrent to open discussion of issues than is the informality of the groups. See Chapters 2 and 10.

associates, and recognition of *obligations* implied by such relations. This is perhaps the essence of *loyalty*. *Politeness* is predicated upon the recognition of conventions based upon mutual respect. *Helpfulness* carries with it the implication of personal obligations and non-exploitativeness in personal relations. The *religious* person may be many other things as well, but it seems likely that he also regards relations with others as involving obligations to his fellow man. And

TABLE 7.5

FACTOR ANALYSIS OF PAIRED-COMPARISON SELF-DESCRIPTIONS

Adjectives	Scout v. Cool Aggressive Factor	Sharp-Smart Factor	Strong Factor	Clean v. Athletic Factor	h²
Mean.............	−78*	−17	18	04	.67
Troublesome........	−74*	−33	−04	−18	.69
Tough............	−68*	−08	52	−08	.74
Cool.............	−65*	30	19	−14	.46
Strong............	−20	01	84*	10	.76
Sharp............	−19	76*	06	−13	.63
Athletic...........	−16	−04	−16	−83*	.74
Clean............	00	04	−47	56*	.54
Smart............	14	65*	−09	26	.52
Obedient..........	50*	−34	−34	30	.57
Religious..........	56*	−06	−27	12	.40
Helpful...........	56*	−25	−12	12	.40
Polite............	66*	−08	−39	10	.60
Loyal............	72*	−10	22	−12	.59
Per cent variance explained..........	.28	.10	.12	.09	.59

* Adjective used in factor score.

obedience is almost by definition the recognition of personal obligations, not indiscriminately, but obligations to persons of legitimate authority.

By contrast, each of the four negative loading items on Factor I (*mean, tough, troublesome,* and *cool*) carry strong overtones of disruption or disregard of obligations to one's associates or to convention, perhaps of detachment from associations which require reciprocity.

The second factor, Sharp-Smart, is connotatively richer than the most general meaning of the two adjectives involved. Each of the adjectives has a spectrum of legitimate to illegitimate meanings. For example, *sharp* can connote alert, well-dressed, or able to cheat without being discovered. *Smart* can connote intelligence or possession of inside information, and invulnerability to being tricked or conned by others. Boys who are high on Sharp-Smart are neither *obedient* (—0.34) nor *troublesome* (—0.33), so one would guess that they wish to avoid both positive and negative involvement with others. The positive loading of *cool* (.30) adds to this interpretation of detachment in relations with others.

The third factor is nearly specific to *strong*, although it has overtones also of *toughness*. In addition, it is negatively defined by its opposition to *cleanliness, politeness,* and *obedience*. It seems clear, therefore, that this factor does *not* define strength of character, but rather refers to physical strength which may or may not also involve athletic skill and may or may not involve *troublesomeness* and *meanness*, as indicated by the relatively low loadings of these adjectives.

The fourth factor is bipolar between *athletic*, accounting for nearly all of the variance, and *clean*. Eleven of the fourteen adjectives have the same sign on this factor as on the first factor, but the loadings are low. One might have preferred a three-factor solution, but this would have obscured the interesting opposition of *athletic* and *clean* in this factor. This opposition is of interest primarily because of a hypothesized difference between middle and lower class, with respect to the relation between athletics and "character-building." A close connection between these activities often is posited as a rationale for "delinquency prevention" activities of agencies working with children across the entire social-class spectrum. It is our hypothesis, however, that such a connection is warranted chiefly for middle class boys, or for lower class boys where an adult-sponsored institutional context is a recognized part of the activity. Where this is not the case, and it seems particularly not to be the case among gang boys, athletic activity appears to be quite neutral with respect to "character-building" of the type involving attitudinal or behavioral characteristics of obedience, religiosity, helpfulness, or politeness. Cohen has noted that middle class athletics in contrast with lower class are likely to involve such middle class virtues as discipline, subordination of self to a team, practicing for relatively remote goals rather than immediate gratification, and planful organization of time.[16] Gang athletics, in particular, tend to be less well organized, to emphasize individual

[16] Albert K. Cohen, *Delinquent Boys: The Culture of the Gang* (Glencoe, Ill.: The Free Press, 1955.)

performance, and to serve immediate rather than long-run goals. "Rules of the game" are likely to be subordinated to victory or to face-saving in defeat.

Self-descriptions and Other Measures

The determination of the four factors arising from self-descriptions completes the tool-making for the central objective of the chapter— the determination of the relationship between self-described factor

TABLE 7.6

MEAN SELF-DESCRIPTIONS FACTOR SCORES FOR RACE,
SOCIAL CLASS, AND GANG STATUS

Background	Scout v. Cool Aggressive Factor[a]	Sharp-Smart Factor[b]	Strong Factor[c]	Clean v. Athletic Factor[d]	Number of Boys
			Negro		
Gang...............	15.7	14.0	6.6	1.1	127
Lower class, non-gang	21.2	13.2	5.3	2.1	81
Middle class.........	25.6	14.8	5.2	3.4††	26
			White		
Gang...............	9.4	14.2	7.5	0.5	40
Lower class, non-gang	20.7	14.6	5.7	1.8	57
Middle class.........	25.5	16.6	5.5	1.4	49
			All boys		
	18.9	14.3	6.0	1.6	380

[a] NG < NLC (or NMC)**; NG > WG**; WG < WLC (or WMC)**.
[b] No significant differences.
[c] NG > NLC (or NMC)**; WG > WLC (or WMC)**.
[d] NMC > NG (and WG)**.
†† $p < .01$.

scores and delinquency. We turn to this task first by examining variations of the self-descriptions over the major population categories; next, we examine relations to known delinquency; finally, we examine the relations between self-description and self-reports of delinquent activity. From the preliminary analysis of the adjectives in the own-group, other-group comparisons we expect clear differences by social status. More importantly, if the hunch of the previous chapter is to be confirmed, we require an absence of a strong relationship between "cool aggressive" self-descriptions and known delinquency. The relation between self-description and self-reported delinquency is a matter of interest for which we have no precise prediction save that we would guess that the individual's disposition to be consistent would cause this correlation to be higher than that between self-description and detached-worker reports of delinquency.

Mean self-description factor scores are presented in Table 7.6 in terms of the, by now, familiar distinctions of race, social class, and gang status. The scores are formed by summing the number of times an adjective is preferred and taking note of the algebraic sign determined by the factor analysis. For the first factor one proceeds as follows:

Adjectives	Theoretically Possible Low Score	Theoretically Possible High Score
(−) Mean.	13 ⎫	0 ⎫
(−) Troublesome.	12 ⎪ −46	1 ⎪ −6
(−) Tough.	11 ⎪	2 ⎪
(−) Cool.	10 ⎭	3 ⎭
Obedient.	4 ⎫	9 ⎫
Religious.	3 ⎪	10 ⎪
Helpful.	2 ⎬ 10	11 ⎬ 55
Polite.	1 ⎪	12 ⎪
Loyal.	0 ⎭	13 ⎭
	−36	49

Under the assumption of purely random response, the expected mean would be 6.5 rather than zero. Since the actual mean is 18.9, it is apparent that there is a composite preference for "scout" terms. The value for Negro gang boys, 15.7, is significantly lower (more toward the "cool aggressive" extreme) than is the score for Negro lower class non-gang boys. The next gap, between the last named and the Negro middle class, is not significant. This pattern is repeated for whites, and the two gaps, significant at the .01 level, are indicated by the pair of asterisks in footnote "a," Table 7.6. White gang boys' self-descriptions are more "cool aggressive," or less "scoutish," than are the other groups, at the .01 level. Scores for both gang groups are above the "expected" mean of 6.5, however, indicating that gang boys' self-descriptions are a good deal more "scoutish" than might be inferred from their behavior. Hodge reports further that product-moment correlations between scales constructed for members of each race-by-class-by-gang-membership category range between .79 and .97, thus indicating a high level of agreement among all boys.[17] These findings are consistent with "values" data discussed in Chapters 2 and 3. We conclude that these results, obtained from the *combination* of adjectives produced by the factor analysis, warrant further analysis.

For the Sharp-Smart factor the expected score under random assumptions would be 2 times 6.5, or 13. Between race and status groups there are no significant differences in these scores.

The Strong factor is measured by only one adjective, hence the expected value is 6.5. Within race, gang boys describe themselves as stronger than other boys studied. Having seen and been in contact with the gang and non-gang boys, we cannot believe that this is realistically related to physical strength. Perhaps those high on this factor "protest too much," or the result may simply be a reflection of the degree to which strength is a focal concern. We feel this adjective is also related to the personal meaning of collective membership and that the strength involved is not the strength of the individual boy, but of numbers.

The Clean v. Athletic factor score has an expected value under random expectations of 6.5 less 6.5, or zero. To avoid negative scores in Table 7.6 we have added a constant of 3 to all scores. There is only one significant effect. Middle class Negro boys rank themselves as *cleaner* than do Negro gang or white gang boys. It may be noted in passing that at each status level, Negroes report themselves as *cleaner* than do whites.

Stability of Paired-Comparison Self-descriptions

One of the great problems of working with sets of corner boys over time is that the boys available for a first test often drift away by the time a second test is desired (see Chapter 1). In later chapters we have confronted problems of inconsistent or incomplete response to various instruments. The degree to which we have suffered from such difficulties becomes apparent when we wish in the present chapter to relate three different measures:

[17] See Patricia Hodge, "Self-descriptions of Gang and Non-Gang Teen-aged Boys," unpublished Master's thesis, Department of Sociology, University of Chicago, 1964.

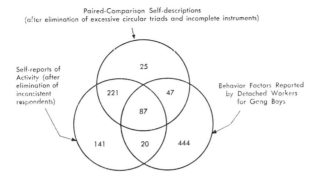

In the section just completed, it was noted that the factoring of the self-descriptions was based upon 380 responses. Since the Venn diagram indicates that the crucial comparison will involve only 87 cases, one wonders if in narrowing to 87 from 380 the factor structure has remained relatively unchanged. That it has can be illustrated from this matrix of self-concept factor scores:

Factors	Sharp-Smart	Strong	Clean v. Athletic
Scout v. cool aggressive........	−03 (−05)	−32 (−29)	31 (41)
Sharp-smart......	....	−01 (−05)	18 (29)
Strong..........	....	....	−08 (−15)

This shows that values for the subset of 87 (in parentheses) are very similar to those based upon the larger set of 380.[18] With this result in hand, we turn next to an accounting for the Self-reported Activity measure.

Activity Self-reports

The strategy behind this instrument was simple. One of the authors had previously worked with self-reported delinquency scales for high

---

[18] The matrix of behavior factor correlations for the 87 compared with the full set of 598 gang boys (see Chapter 4) is similarly reassuring.

school and training school populations.[19] In this case, we wished to do something similar after making appropriate changes for the range of activities expected. It was highly desirable to include a set of activities sufficiently within the range of allowable behavior (like playing cards and listening to rock-and-roll) so that some inferences about styles of activity participated in could be made before defensive reactions were encountered. In addition it was hoped that by stressing the frequency of activities per week, we would have an operational measure which might logically vary quite widely from the more abstract paired-comparison self-description. The boys were given a list of activities and asked: "How often do you and your friends do these things?" There were five response alternatives:

☐ almost every day
☐ 1 to 3 times a week
☐ 1 or 2 times a month
☐ 1 to 2 times a year
☐ never

As a check for consistency in response to this instrument, the list of activities was presented a second time and each boy was instructed to indicate how important each activity was to him. Boys who had indicated they never engaged in an activity or did so only one or two times a year but then checked this activity as being very important to them were eliminated. By this means and by eliminating obviously patterned responses, such as checking the same degree of involvement or importance for all items, the original 537 completed instruments were reduced to 469.

The twenty-three activities which were checked by the boys were presented in the order indicated by the numbers at the extreme left of Table 7.7. However, they have been ordered in the table so that their dominant weights on the six principal factors cascade from left to right. Correlations of these activities were factored by the principal components method supplemented by a varimax rotation. The resultant activity factors may be described as follows:

Corner-Boy Delinquent (I)—With highest loadings of gambling, signifying, hanging, drinking, riding in cars, fighting, and making money illegally; also involves truancy, lower class party behavior (quarter parties)

[19] See, for example, James F. Short, Jr., and F. Ivan Nye, "Reported Behavior as a Criterion of Deviant Behavior," *Social Problems,* IV (Winter, 1957–58), 207–13; and F. Ivan Nye and James F. Short, Jr., "Scaling Delinquent Behavior," *American Sociological Review,* XXII (June, 1957), 326–31.

TABLE 7.7

FACTORS IN THE SELF-REPORTS OF ACTIVITIES*

Item No.	Activity	Corner-Boy Delinquency I(X_1)	Lower Class Social and Sexual II(X_2)	Non-retreatist Conventional III(X_6)	Early Adolescent Heterosexual IV(X_3)	Mature Vocational V(X_5)	Organized Individual Sports Activities VI(X_4)	Communalities
8	Gambling (playing cards or pool for money, shooting dice, penny pitching)	−72	02	−19	−02	04	−23	60
6	Signifying or playing the dozens	−71	−04	20	02	−14	04	56
4	Hanging (being with the boys on the street)	−67	11	−12	−22	−05	−02	53
18	Drinking beer, wine, whiskey	−58	14	−41	−16	−09	21	60
14	Riding in cars	−56	−02	−18	−02	27	09	43
15	Fighting (humbug or rumble)	−52	30	−13	−16	−19	−13	46
11	Making money (bread) illegally	−42	35	−23	07	−06	−17	39
21	Playing cards for fun (no money involved)	03	72	18	15	05	−04	58
7	Dancing	−01	68	−03	−39	−11	−06	62
20	Sexual intercourse	−27	56	−43	−31	−04	−06	68
10	House or quarter parties in the area	−39	47	−05	−18	07	−23	47
12	Going to school	19	08	72	18	−23	07	66
1	Team sports (such as softball, basketball, football)	−04	03	62	−17	08	−26	50
13	Smoking marihuana (pot)	−18	10	−54	−00	−33	−26	52
2	Singing	10	05	−09	−66	−22	−20	55
3	Trying to impress (rapping to) the girls	−38	12	18	−53	14	07	49
17	Smooching, necking, petting	−32	34	−24	−45	15	06	50
22	Listening to rock-'n-roll music	−31	01	10	−34	−30	07	31

* Horizontal lines separate items utilized for scoring each factor. Thus, items 8, 6, 4, 18, 14, 15, and 11 were combined for Factor I; items 21, 7, 20, and 10 for Factor II; items 12, 1, and 13 for Factor III, etc.

TABLE 7.7—*Continued*

Item No.	Activity	Corner-Boy Delinquency I(X₁)	Lower Class Social and Sexual II(X₂)	Non-retreatist Conventional III(X₆)	Early Adolescent Heterosexual IV(X₃)	Mature Vocational V(X₅)	Organized Individual Sports Activities VI(X₄)	Communalities
5	Working or job..	−08	09	08	07	65	04	45
16	Skipping school (truancy).....	−43	26	06	01	−55	04	56
9	Individual sports (such as pool, boxing, swimming)........	−11	04	−02	−26	06	−78	70
19	Club meetings...	08	25	11	27	−18	−56	50

and a good deal of heterosexual play. It is most incompatible, as evidenced by opposite sign loadings, with school attendance and club meetings.

Lower Class Social and Sexual (II)—As evidenced by its four highest loading behaviors, playing cards (not for money), dancing, sexual intercourse, and quarter parties, this factor is less delinquent than Factor I, and more formally "organized," in the sense that it is more likely to involve club meetings and less likely to involve hanging, although it is not incompatible with fighting and stealing.

Non-retreatist Conventional (III)—This configuration is high on school attendance and team athletics of the more traditional middle class pattern of school activities. It is incompatible with drinking, use of marihuana, and delinquency generally. Note, here, that sexual intercourse and smooching split away from trying to impress girls, the former being bipolar with school and team sports, while the latter has a small but positive association with these behaviors.

Early Adolescent Heterosexual (IV)—Characterized by highest loadings of singing, trying to impress the girls, smooching, dancing and listening to rock 'n roll. This pattern is not club or school oriented. It has a strong sexual orientation, but is not otherwise delinquent.

Mature Vocational (V)—This factor separates work behavior from nearly all the traditional adolescent pursuits both delinquent and non-delinquent.

Organized Individual Sports Activities (VI)—Here, for the first time in the entire analysis, individual sports and club meetings load highly together. Delinquent activities have no close association with this pattern, though several load in the same direction. Drinking is bipolar with it, but the loading is low.

Factor scoring was accomplished by adding together boys' scores on individual behaviors included in each factor, weighting frequency responses from "every day" $= 1$ to "never" $= 5$. For initial confirmation of the meaning of these scores we turn to Table 7.8, where

TABLE 7.8

MEAN SELF-REPORTED ACTIVITY FACTOR SCORES
BY RACE, CLASS, AND GANG STATUS

Race, Class and Gang Status	Corner-Boy Delinquency (Low Score More Delinquent) $I(X_1)$	Lower Class Social and Sexual (Low Score More Delinquent) $II(X_2)$	Early Adolescent Heterosexual (Low Score More Delinquent) $IV(X_3)$	Organized Individual Sports (Low Score More Active) $VI(X_4)$	Mature Vocational (Low Score More Work, Less Skipping School) $V(X_5)$	Non-retreatist Conventional (Low Score More School Involved) $III(X_6)$
			Negro			
Gang (N=153).....	17.3	8.6	6.8	4.5	−0.2	0.7
Lower class non-gang (N=111).....	22.7	10.5	7.6	5.7	−0.1	−0.4
Middle class (N=29)......	23.8	11.8	8.2	5.1	−1.3	−1.2
			White			
Gang (N=55)......	15.8	12.2	7.4	5.6	−0.1	0.7
Lower class non-gang (N=71)......	21.0	13.7	9.9	5.2	−0.0	−0.3
Middle class (N=50)......	27.9	15.1	10.2	4.6	−1.7	−2.1

the self-reported activity scores are displayed by race and status. To facilitate comparison we have rearranged the factor columns in terms of their decreasing apparent relation to delinquency. Both the slopes of values within strata of the social groups and the observed mean levels deserve attention.

TABLE 7.9

SELF-REPORTED ACTIVITY FACTOR SCORES WHICH ARE LOWER FOR ROW SAMPLE THAN FOR COLUMN SAMPLE

	NG	NLC	NMC	WG	WLC	WMC
NG		I*** II*** IV** VI***	I*** II*** IV** VI**	II*** IV VI***	I*** II*** IV*** VI**	I*** II*** IV***
NLC	III***		II**	II*** III**	II*** IV***	I*** II*** IV***
NMC	III*** V*	III V* VI		III*** V	II*** III IV** V*	I*** II*** IV**
WG	I*	I***	I***		I*** II*** IV***	I*** II*** IV***
WLC	III**	I*	I** III VI	III*		I*** II***
WMC	III*** V***	III*** V*** VI***	III VI*	III*** V*** VI***	III*** V*** VI*	

*** p < .001; ** p < .01; * p < .05; p < .10.

For Factors I, II, and IV, "lower than" means "more delinquent." A lower score on Factors III and V has a positive connotation, i.e., "more school involved" and "more work," and a lower score on Factor VI simply means more active in sports.

Consider first Corner-Boy Delinquency, Factor I. White gang scores are very different from white middle class scores (27.9, less 15.8 equals 12.1) in contrast with the lesser range for Negroes (6.5 points). Thus, while gang boys are more delinquent for both Negro and white respondents, Negro gang responses are not so differentiated from (Negro) middle class responses as are white gang boys (from white middle class).

If one looks at the five scales from the standpoint of their delinquency implications, gang boys are always most delinquent and white middle class the least delinquent. To facilitate discussion, Table 7.8 data are presented in terms of significant differences between our samples in Table 7.9.

Several variations are of interest. Consider *Corner-Boy Delinquency (I)*:

> gambling
> signifying
> hanging
> drinking
> riding in cars
> fighting
> making money illegally

Gang boys are more involved than every other group, as are White gang boys more than their Negro counterparts.

On *Lower Class Social and Sexual (II)*:

> playing cards for fun
> dancing
> sexual intercourse
> house or quarter parties

within race, G > LC > MC; and except for NMC v. WG, all three categories of Negroes are more involved than any category of whites. This racial difference in matters sexual is similar to that reported in Chapter 3.

The same racial differential occurs for *Early Adolescent Heterosexual (IV)*:

> singing
> rapping to the girls
> smooching, necking, petting
> listening to rock and roll

Within race, gang boys are most active, but lower class boys do not differ from their middle class counterparts. WLC and WMC boys clearly are less active.

Paradoxically, *Organized Sports*, (*VI*), which is made up of only:

> individual sports
> club meetings

is highest for NG and WMC populations, on all other factors our extreme groups. The apparent paradox may be due to differences in detached worker activity among gang boys and to greater Hi-Y Club attachment of WMC as compared to NMC boys. Detached workers with NG boys tended, during our period of study, to hold club meetings more regularly than did workers with white gangs. And WMC boys were involved to a much greater degree in YMCA and school sponsored activities and they were more involved in sports than were the NMC boys.

For the *Mature Vocational* (*V*) cluster made up of:

> working
> (absence of) truancy

middle class boys of both races report they skip school less and/or work more, but gang and non-gang boys are not differentiated within race.

Finally, and not unexpectedly, for *Non-retreatist Conventional* (*III*) behavior:

> going to school
> team sports
> (not) smoking pot

gang boys of both races are least involved in the conventional and most in the retreatist activity.

Self-description and Activities

There are now available ten separate factor scores based on self-reports: four from the paired comparisons; six from the self-reported activity. The relationship between these measures for gang boys only is shown in Table 7.10. Four significant relationships emerge:

a) The Scouts report that they are involved in fewer Corner Boy Delinquent activities (r = 0.44**).

b) Respondents high on Sharp-Smart report less activity of a Lower Class Social and Sexual nature (r = 0.22*), and they are more involved in Mature Vocational experience (the r = —.20 is just short of significance).

c) Boys who stress Strong in their self-description are more heavily involved in going to school and in team sports (r = —.27*).

d) Scouts report *more* Mature Vocational experience and less truancy (r = —0.24), but they are more involved in Lower Class Social and Sexual behavior (r = —0.19).

e) The Cleans (in contrast with the Athletics) report less Corner-Boy Delinquent involvement (r = —0.19) and more Mature Vocational experience (r = —0.19)—these values fall just short of significance.

TABLE 7.10

CORRELATIONS BETWEEN SELF-DESCRIPTION AND
SELF-REPORTED ACTIVITY FACTOR SCORES

	SELF-DESCRIPTION FACTORS			
ACTIVITY FACTORS[a]	Scout v. Cool Aggressive X_7	Sharp-Smart X_8	Strong X_9	Clean v. Athletic X_{10}
X_1 Corner-boy delinquent.......	44**	05	—07	19
X_2 Lower class social and sexual..	—19	22*	08	—15
X_3 Early adolescent heterosexual.	10	16	04	—05
X_4 Organized individual sports...	05	08	—01	14
X_5 Mature vocational..........	—24*	—20	—01	—19
X_6 Non-retreatist conventional...	—10	06	—27*	13

[a] Low score means more delinquent on Activity Factors X_1, X_2, and X_4; on X_3 it means more school involved; on X_5 more work involved; and on X_6 less active in organized individual sports.
* p < .05.   ** p < .01.

The four significant and the four near-significant findings fit together sufficiently well to suggest essential consistency. Or, putting it more conservatively, whatever the distortions in self-reported data, the distortions either are present in the same way in, or are absent from, the sets of responses here considered. The remaining sixteen correlations which are not significant, and the low level of all but one of the significant correlations, suggests that, as a result of our prior factoring, we have produced a set of relatively uncorrelated measures.

The next step is to search by multiple correlation and regression techniques for combinations of self-reported characteristics which correlate highly with observed delinquency. Our approach is not limited to a search for plausible relationships. Consistent with the spirit of the inquiry throughout the book we wish to expose ourselves to the possible discovery of unanticipated findings. This intention should not be confused with planless empiricism.

Regression Analysis

Were it possible to digest at a glance the information in 50 correlation coefficients, Table 7.11 would tell the story of the relationship between the five behavior dimensions and the ten self-reported scores quite adequately. Roughly viewed, if one wished to consider the behavior outcomes as a product of the boys' attitudes and self-descriptions, one could view the column headings as dependent variables to be predicted by row entries. This conventional model is not appro-

TABLE 7.11

CORRELATIONS BETWEEN BEHAVIOR DIMENSIONS,
ACTIVITY REPORTS, AND SELF-DESCRIPTION

SELF-REPORTS	BEHAVIOR DIMENSIONS				
	Conflict Y_1	Stable Corner-Boy Activity Y_2	Stable Sex-Maturity Y_3	Retreatist Y_4	Authority Protest Y_5
	Activity				
X_1 Corner-boy delinquent..	-03	-31^{**}	16	-16	-09
X_2 Lower class social and sexual...............	-14	-09	-32^{**}	04	18
X_3 Early adolescent heterosexual...............	-09	-02	-21^*	00	-03
X_4 Organized individual sports...............	17	10	09	10	19
X_5 Mature vocational.....	-10	00	-07	10	01
X_6 Non-retreatist conventional...............	42^{**}	09	23^*	39^{**}	17
	Self-descriptions				
X_7 Scout v. cool aggressive.	32^{**}	-07	01	-02	17
X_8 Sharp-smart..........	05	-15	-13	08	23^*
X_9 Strong...............	-11	01	05	-13	07
X_{10} Clean v. athletic......	51^{**}	-09	17	18	23^*

* p .05.
** p .01.

priate, for it is known that the behavior represented by row entries does not precede outcomes in the columns. The crucial concern is not to define the direction of effect, but to identify those effects which operate concomitantly. In this sense, we regard the behavior outcome as the dependent variable in order to use the compression of the regression approach.

Conflict

An overview of what will be learned from the regression analysis can be obtained by inspecting the significant correlations in Table 7.11. For example, with regard to the Conflict factor:

> individual fighting
> group fighting
> concealed weapons
> assault

the computation routine first extracts the Clean v. Athletic score—$r = 0.51^{**}$. The second score extracted is Non-retreatist Conventional (a high score indicates less school and team sports involvement, $r = 0.42^{**}$) and the third is Scout v. Cool Aggressive ($r = 0.32^{**}$). Taken together, these three produce a multiple correlation of $R = 0.65^{**}$:

Multiple R	Factor Utilized	First-Order Correlation
0.51	Clean v. Athletic	0.51
0.63	Non-retreatist Conventional	0.42
0.65	Scout v. Cool Aggressive	0.32

The two paired-comparison self-descriptions clearly oppose common sense expectation. Boys who give 'Clean" and "Scout" responses are *more* active in Conflict. The third component, lack of contact with organized sports and possible use of marihuana is—and this time, plausibly—related to Conflict activity. That is, boys who report going to school, participating in team sports, and less pot smoking are less involved in conflict. Thus, despite the general correspondence between negative self-evaluation and delinquency by status level suggested in Tables 7.8 and 7.9, this relationship within the gang is reversed. The hunch from Chapter 6 is confirmed.

We were fearful that our results might be an artifact arising from the presence of eighteen of the eighty-seven boys who were Rattlers, a seriously delinquent gang in a marginal commercial area. From observation of their style of relating to officialdom, this gang appeared to be strongly disposed to give socially acceptable self-descriptions. With this gang eliminated, however, the results of the regression analysis were unchanged. This clears the way for further consideration of the process by which the finding arises.

Perhaps the verbal aggressiveness of the "Cool Aggressive" self-description is compensatory for lesser skill and involvement in Conflict; and, by the same reasoning, these boys apparently emphasize being *athletic* as more descriptive than being *clean*. The importance of *clean*, i.e. "Clean v. Athletic," whatever its meaning, is the pragmatic fact that it correlates so highly with Conflict. It suggests a desire for the "clean appearance," perhaps also the avoidance of the dirt associated with lower class occupations. One might speculate that preference for "clean" in the "clean v. athletic" distinction may

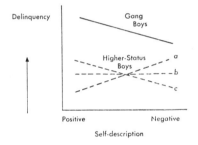

be an adaptation to blocked mobility aspirations for *obedient* (r = 0.30 in Table 7.5), perhaps effeminate, personally fearful boys who find gang association to be *smart* (r = .26 in Table 7.5) in compensation for a variety of personal shortcomings.

It should be emphasized that it was within the scope of our data to demonstrate that positive self-descriptions were associated with greater delinquency only for gang boys. No adequate criterion measure—like the detached-worker reports—was available for non-gang or middle class boys. We are quite sure that the delinquency rates are lower for non-gang boys.[20] The hypothetical lines a, b, and c in the figure above indicate simply that we do not know the slope of the

[20] A record search of all boys studied finds the following mean numbers of offenses known to the police per boy in each group: NG = 3.14, WG = 2.73, NLC = .47, WLC = .31, NMC = .06, WMC = .02. See John M. Wise, "A Comparison of Sources of Data as Indexes of Delinquent Behavior," unpublished Master's thesis, University of Chicago, 1962.

relationship. It is our guess, however, that for non-gang populations the slope would not parallel the gang-boy slope. We would expect to find negative self-descriptions associated with increasing delinquency among non-gang boys (slope a)—in line with the Reckless and MMPI results cited earlier.

For the gang boys, greater involvement in this first behavior dimension, conflict—the one of greater public concern—occurs for boys whose *clean*-oriented, scout-like self-conceptions and rejection of athletics make them especially vulnerable to the group process. It may be suggested that the scoutish element, involving as it does greater responsibility in interpersonal relations, enables these boys to facilitate cohesive relations in these loosely structured gangs. This in turn places them in positions and situations which expose them to the operation of group processes which involve heightened exposure to delinquency episodes. The fact that this factor includes individual as well as group fighting is not inconsistent with this interpretation, as some readers might assume. Within the gang very much the same processes operate wth respect to both types of fighting.

Stable Corner Boy

Returning to Table 7.11, it may be seen that Stable Corner-Boy activities:

> individual sports
> team sports
> social activities
> gambling

are most significantly correlated with the boys' own reports of their Corner-Boy Delinquency (r = —0.31**) where a low score indicates more delinquent involvement in gambling, signifying, hanging, drinking, riding in cars, fighting, making money illegally, and thus accounts in a plausible way for the correlation being negative. In this case, as in each of the regression analyses, the computation begins by taking out first the larger correlation, then correlating the predicted Y value with the remaining self-report scores. When the next score is significantly correlated, it is then taken out and the inspection repeated. This ordinarily results in a termination of the regression computation after two or three self-report scores have been utilized. However, in the present case, the application of these criteria stops after one clearly important predictor variable has been included. Using the previous convention, the multiple R is the same as the r reported above.

When the entire nine remaining scores are added, the R rises only to R = 0.38. Since only the Corner-Boy Delinquency score makes a significant contribution to the reduction of the variance, the a priori wisdom in selecting the Corner-Boy designation both for the Behavior and Activity factors is empirically confirmed, even though the percentage of the variance accounted for remains very low.

Stable Sex-Maturity

The third column in Table 7.11 relates to sexual intercourse, petting, signifying, and work experience as perceived by the detached worker. While there are three significant correlations with self-reported activity factors in the column, only two of these work out in the multiple regression:

Multiple R	Factor Utilized	First-Order Correlation
0.32........	Lower Class Social and Sexual	−0.32
0.41........	Non-retreatist Conventional	0.23

The interpretation is quite straightforward: the more card playing for fun, dancing, sexual intercourse, and house or quarter parties the respondent says he participates in, and the less involved he reports himself to be in individual sports and club meetings, the more the detached worker perceives him to be active in Stable Sex-Maturity. In this case there is a positive and significant relationship between "saying" and, if not doing, at least being perceived to "do" the activity in question.

Retreatist

The fourth column in Table 7.11 shows only one high correlation, the r = 0.39** with X_6, Non-retreatist Conventional Behavior, again a plausible relationship. The items so related are:

Y_4		X_6
narcotics		(absence of participation
pot		in school and in
homosexuality		team sports)
common-law marriage	and	(participation in
attempted suicide		smoking pot)
pimping		

The R = r as given above. The next score considered is X_{10}, the "Clean" v. "Athletic" distinction, but since the correlation is non-significant it is rejected and the extraction stops. The explanation contributed by one score, the self-reported disposition to smoke pot and to engage infrequently in school and team sports activities accounts for relatively little of the observed variance.

Authority Protest

Finally, the fifth column in Table 7.11 is best predicted by X_{10}, "Clean" v. "Athletic" and X_8, the "Sharp-Smart" emphasis which in combination produce an R = 0.32.

Multiple R	Factor Utilized	First-Order Correlation
0.23.......	Clean v. Athletic	0.23
0.32.......	Sharp-Smart	0.23

In this case the next two scores, X_4 and X_2, are interesting. If they were included (R = 0.410) an appreciable gain would result from the fact that Authority Protest is associated with less participation in organized sports and club meetings and in less Lower Class Social and Sexual Activity. Taken together, this suggests that reactions to constraint of Authority Protest boys operate against the positive involvement which club meetings and organized sports entail. The criterion behaviors (auto theft, driving without license, and running away) suggest working class, non-slum adaptations involving both the auto culture of youth and attempted family controls of a type with which Negro boys, in contrast with white, are less familiar.

Discussion

To reverse the order of the chapter in recapitulation, we note that two findings have emerged from the chapter which are "surprising" by "common sense" criteria. Boys who described themselves as *clean* rather than *athletic* and as "scouts" rather than "cool aggressives" were more, rather than less, involved in conflict behavior. On the basis of this finding we have argued that in the loosely structured and highly aggressive gang situation scoutish characteristics promote group cohesion and so throw scoutish boys into roles and situations which are especially vulnerable to group-process determinants of gang delinquency. Boys who eschew athletic activity, preferring to stay *clean*, lack the status-giving opportunities which accrue to skill in sports and so must achieve status in other ways. Among the gangs we have studied, aggressive and other delinquent skills are likely to be among the few alternatives available for status gain.

These interpretations are not mutually exclusive; indeed they may reinforce one another. That is, while the "scouts" possess virtues which make possible group cohesion, these virtues are not intrinsically rewarding on the street. Polite, helpful, religious, obedient—these attributes do not especially commend themselves in the rough and tumble, body punching, signifying, drinking, and "making out" which are the hallmarks of street life. They may even suggest effeminacy. Even loyalty may expose one to danger, but loyalty to the group by at least some of its members is a necessary condition for group existence. The other attributes, in combination with loyalty, make possible a measure of group cohesion by counteracting the divisive tendencies suggested by the cool-aggressive adjectives and manifest in much of the behavior of the boys. Loyalty is the one attribute possessed by the scouts upon which they may expect to establish a "rep." One way to demonstrate loyalty is by engaging in conflict, heeding the call to arms or perhaps stirring up a little conflict, thereby creating the occasion for status-rewarding display of a masculine self. Thus, *both* "scouts" and "cleans" may be responding to status demands of the group, but for somewhat different reasons related to nuances of self-attributes.

With these exceptions, gang boys' behavior matched their self-reported activities and self-descriptions in a manner plausible by lay expectations. It may be pertinent to note, however, that the exceptions are of sufficient magnitude that they may help to explain the positive but low predictions obtained with the mmpi, cited at the beginning of the chapter. That is, if the Chicago experience is repeated in other cities, negative self-descriptions of aggressive gang boys would not be highly correlated with delinquency and would, therefore, attenuate correlations between self-descriptions and delinquent behavior among more general populations.

For behavior other than conflict delinquency, our data are of little pragmatic value and they may not help theoretically. Even though statistically significant multiple correlations were obtained, only a small portion of the variance was explained:

Behavior Dimension	Self-reports	R (Where We Stopped)	Maximum Attainable if All Predictors Used
Y_1 Conflict	X_{10} Clean v. athletic X_6 Non-retreatist conventional X_7 Scout v. cool aggressive	.654	.701
Y_2 Stable corner boy	X_1 Corner-boy delinquent	.305	.382
Y_3 Stable sex-maturity	X_2 Lower class social and sexual X_6 Non-retreatist conventional	.413	.530
Y_4 Retreatist	X_6 Non-retreatist conventional	.392	.492
Y_5 Authority protest	X_{10} Clean v. athletic X_8 Sharp-smart	.323	.488

If one reasons that the percentage of the variance explained can be derived from R^2, the self-reports account for nearly half of the variation in conflict behaviors, but much less than this of the other behavior patterns. Since we are here capitalizing on some adventitious correlations, we could not expect to do as well as 40 per cent if our self-reports were used to predict delinquent behavior among more general populations. It is apparent, therefore, that we have identified better guidelines for theoretical development than for the "practical" implications of predictive efficiency.

Our search has demonstrated very clearly that lower class boys are more disadvantaged than middle class boys, if one grants the operational efficacy of negative self-reports as a measure of disadvantage. By extension of the argument, gang boys are more disadvantaged than non-gang boys within the lower class and Negroes more than whites. While documentation of this status gradient is not a startling discovery, it is something of a technical contribution to be able to demonstrate that the gradient was elicited with such regularity and precision from boys who have the social and educational characteristics of those in our sample.

It is precisely the regularity of the status gradient in general which gives special importance to departures which are noted in particular instances. The first of these involves the consistency with which middle class Negroes as compared to WMC boys feel they are cleaner, better (higher on *good*), and friendlier than others. We have noted earlier Frazier's allusion to the cultivation of "personality" among middle class Negro males as a means of achieving influence among whites and distinction in the Negro world; this, against a background of insecurity and frustration as a result of the "mark of oppression" of being Negro. The ambivalence of the NMC boys about themselves is seen in the *combination* of positive and negative self-references. We suggest that this is due in part to "relative *gratification*" compared to other Negroes, but *deprivation* relative to the white world which serves as an ultimate status criterion.[21]

One other racial difference in status gradients was especially striking—among Negro boys the gradient for *manly* was direct with social level (there was no gradient among whites); the gradient for *womanly* was inverse for Negroes, but direct for whites. This difference, plus examination of evaluation, "smartness" and potency ratings of an image of high heterosexual activity suggested that the implied Negro middle class boys' protestations concerning their manhood were likely to impede social mobility.

Most primitively, the technique of attitude assessment permitted respondents to select adjectives as self-descriptive and then independently to judge the degree to which others possessed these attributes. The discovery that Scouts among the Garden Gang judged non-gang boys to be less "scoutish" while Cool Aggressives judged the same boys to be less "cool aggressive" led us to the conclusion that the boys were projecting a self-image both in describing themselves and their friends and in comparing their gang with non-gang boys. This seemed especially likely since neither Scouts nor Cool Aggressives were homogeneous friendship cliques—that is, each "attitude clique" (Scouts and Cool Aggressives) chose close friends from the other—and both gang and non-gang boys lived in the same housing project; hence, it was likely that they were to a high degree utilizing the same boys as a comparison group.

Table 7.12 demonstrates that this same tendency is present for the larger set of boys—that is, respondents say they have more of characteristics which they have identified as self-descriptive, and conversely, they assign to out-group boys attributes which they feel

---

[21] See James A. Davis' discussion of the "American Soldier" findings concerning relative deprivation and relative gratification, in "A Formal Interpretation of the Theory of Relative Deprivation," *Sociometry*, XX (December, 1959), 280–96.

are not descriptive of themselves. The only perturbation in the entire table is the slight drop in level of the term *mean* between boys who have chosen this term 4–9 times and those choosing it 10–13 times over other adjectives. The small number of boys (18) who choose *mean* as self-descriptive 10–13 times makes this exception of little importance in view of the overwhelming consistency of the table.

Table 7.12 lumps together the full set of boys after elimination of excessive triads (but before boys who had failed to check only one

TABLE 7.12

MEAN ON IN-GROUP/OUT-GROUP COMPARISON FOR
FOURTEEN TERMS BY NUMBER OF TIMES TERM
PREFERRED OVER OTHERS ON PAIRED COMPARI-
SONS (ALL BOYS)

TERM	NUMBER OF TIMES WORD PREFERRED OVER OTHERS ON PAIRED COMPARISONS		
	0–3	4–9	10–13
Athletic......	4.4 (17)	5.1 (127)	5.8 (212)
Clean........	4.2 (6)	5.5 (200)	5.8 (149)
Loyal........	4.5 (38)	5.0 (177)	5.5 (141)
Cool.........	4.5 (54)	4.9 (181)	5.5 (123)
Helpful.......	4.1 (29)	5.4 (202)	5.6 (122)
Polite........	4.4 (55)	5.3 (182)	6.0 (118)
Religious.....	3.8 (130)	5.5 (126)	5.6 (101)
Smart........	4.8* (26)	5.0 (242)	5.8 (88)
Obedient.....	4.6 (88)	5.3 (191)	5.5 (80)
Sharp........	4.4 (25)	4.6 (276)	5.3 (55)
Strong........	4.2 (64)	4.8 (242)	5.2 (48)
Tough........	3.6 (209)	4.4 (108)	5.0 (37)
Troublesome..	2.6 (263)	3.2 (76)	4.1 (23)
Mean........	2.6 (276)	4.6 (64)	4.4 (18)

* Ns in parentheses. The higher the value of the means, the *more* a boy thinks his group has this quality in comparison with out-group boys.

or two paired comparisons were scored in order to bring the full set to 380). In Table 7.13, mean in-group, out-group comparisons on the five scout and four cool aggressive adjectives are presented for Scouts and Cool Aggressives in each population group. Again, Scouts see

TABLE 7.13

MEAN OWN-GROUP/OTHER-GROUP COMPARISONS FOR SALIENT PAIRED-
COMPARISON ADJECTIVES, "COOL AGGRESSIVES" AND
"SCOUTS," IN SIX POPULATION GROUPS

PAIRED-COMPARISON ADJECTIVES	NEGRO						WHITE					
	Gang		Lower Class Non-Gang		Middle Class		Gang		Lower Class Non-Gang		Middle Class	
	C.A.*	Sc.*	C.A.	Sc.	C.A.	Sc.	C.A.	Sc.	C.A.	Sc.	C.A.	Sc.
N =	24	101	12	69	0	26	10	30	9	48	3	46
Mean	4.1	3.4	4.1	2.5	....	2.2	5.6	3.3	3.9	2.4	1.3	1.8
Troublesome	4.2	3.4	2.1	2.1	....	2.0	4.0	3.3	3.3	2.1	2.0	2.0
Tough	4.5	4.2	5.0	3.6	....	3.6	5.6	4.4	4.7	3.4	3.0	3.1
Cool	4.5	4.6	5.4	4.6	....	5.4	5.9	5.4	5.1	4.3	6.0	5.5
Obedient	3.3	4.2	4.9	5.6	....	6.1	4.4	4.5	4.4	5.3	6.0	5.9
Religious	2.4	3.9	4.6	5.2	....	5.9	3.4	4.2	4.7	5.3	7.0	6.4
Helpful	3.2	4.6	5.2	5.5	....	6.4	4.6	4.6	5.6	5.6	6.0	5.9
Polite	2.5	4.6	5.5	5.8	....	6.5	4.3	4.8	4.8	5.6	6.3	6.2
Loyal	3.5	4.7	4.5	5.4	....	5.3	3.9	5.5	5.3	5.2	5.7	4.9

* Cool Aggressives are boys whose Factor I scores are negative; Scouts are positive.

themselves as more "scoutish" than out-group boys while Cool Aggressives see themselves as more "cool aggressive." The one major exception occurs among middle class white boys where it is clear that the three "cool aggressives" really aren't, after all!

Having thus concluded the analysis of self-reports, we turn in Chapter 8 to an examination of the nature of group processes which are involved in delinquency episodes.

The Response of Gang Leaders to Status Threats: An Observation on Group Process and Delinquent Behavior

With this chapter we make more explicit our concern with group process and gang delinquency and with empirical identification of the nature of this relationship. The chapter describes a particular type of delinquent episode which arises when a gang leader acts to reduce threats to his status by instigating out-group aggression. Our view is that leaders resort to this action because of the limited resources they have for internal control of their group—particularly when their status is attacked.

Unlike other syndrome explanations, such as that of Bloch and Flynn[1] who related delinquency to particular types of parent-child relations, or the various theories that are concerned with the emergence of delinquent subcultures,[2] this paper attempts to provide a clearer understanding of the precipitation of episodes within "delinquent gangs." The focus is on the ongoing relations of group members rather than on the boys' family backgrounds or the position of lower class adolescents within the social structure. The argument is not that family background and social class position are unimportant, but rather that these factors cannot explain the emergence of particular instances of aggressive delinquency from the ongoing, largely non-delinquent, behavior of gang boys.

Liberal use of illustrative instances will correct the impression

This chapter is a revision of a paper read at the annual meeting of the American Sociological Association, 1961, and was previously published under this same title in the *American Journal of Sociology*, LXVIII (March, 1963), 571–79.

[1] Herbert A. Bloch and Frank T. Flynn, *Delinquency: The Juvenile Offender in America Today* (New York: Random House, 1956), pp. 151–75.

[2] See Albert K. Cohen, *Delinquent Boys: The Culture of the Gang* (Glencoe: The Free Press, 1955); Albert K. Cohen and James F. Short, Jr., "Research in Delinquent Subcultures," *Journal of Social Issues*, XXIV (1958), 20–37; and Richard A. Cloward and Lloyd E. Ohlin, *Delinquency and Opportunity: A Theory of Delinquent Gangs* (Glencoe: The Free Press, 1960).

that would exist if William Foote Whyte's superb description of Doc and the Nortons in *Street Corner Society*[3] were permitted to carry the full burden of our need for knowledge about subinstitutionalized elementary social behavior of corner groups.[4] Whyte's corner boys were not delinquents, they were older, and they were much more stable as a group than are adolescent delinquent gangs. Considering the narrative materials of delinquency literature, it comes as a surprise to find how little illumination of group process they provide. For any but the most broadly formulated hypotheses concerning the nature of group life among the boys studied, we find these materials inadequate. By contrast, the strength of *Street Corner Society* lies exactly in the fact that the descriptions are given in such a way that the group process is explicit.

One notable instance of experimental research specifically related to delinquency is the investigation of Lippitt, Polansky, Redl, and Rosen in which deliberately frustrated camp boys followed in delinquent activity an impulsive boy who was ordinarily given low rank in the group.[5] These authors did not intend to suggest, however, that the mechanism revealed by this ingenious experiment is the typical process for delinquent groups in their natural setting. Similarly, Polsky and Kohn's description of the process by which "delinquency in its collective form" emerges "out of the interaction of a group of youngsters" within a juvenile correctional institution[6] is not meant to serve as the model for collective delinquency outside of a "total institutional" context.[7]

[3] *Street Corner Society* (Chicago: University of Chicago Press, 1943; 2d ed., 1955).

[4] See George Homans, *The Human Group* (New York: Harcourt, Brace & Co., 1950) ; and George Homans, *Social Behavior: Its Elementary Forms* (New York: Harcourt, Brace & Co., 1961).

[5] Ronald Lippitt, Norman Polansky, Fritz Redl, and Sidney Rosen, "The Dynamics of Power: A Field Study of Social Influence in Groups of Children," in *Readings in Social Psychology,* ed. Eleanor Maccoby, Theodore M. Newcomb, and Eugene S. Hartley (New York: Henry Holt & Co., 1958).

[6] See Howard Polsky, "Changing Delinquent Subcultures: A Social Psychological Approach," reprinted from *Social Work* (October, 1959), pp. 1–15; and Howard Polsky and Martin Kohn, "Participant Observation in a Delinquent Subculture," *American Journal of Orthopsychiatry,* XXIX (October, 1959), 737–51.

[7] Erving Goffman, "On the Characteristics of Total Institutions: The Inmate World," and "Staff-Inmate Relations," in *The Prison: Studies in Institutional Organization and Change,* ed. Donald R. Cressey (New York: Holt, Rinehart & Winston, 1961), Chaps. 1 and 2, pp. 15–106.

The closest parallel to our concern with group factors in delinquency outside the context of a camp or treatment institution is Jansyn's study of the social system of a gang with whom he worked as a "detached worker."[8] He found that, for this group of boys, delinquent behavior, on both an individual and a group basis, served to increase the solidarity of the group, and that group leadership and membership varied according to specific group goals being implemented. Further, the boys' perceptions of who was and who was not a member of the group, how large the group was, the importance and even the existence of a conception of "turf" or "territory" were responsive to the situation in which the group found itself.

The shifting character of the group structure that Jansyn describes for the white gang he worked with is present in the white gangs contacted in the present project and in the Negro gangs as well. Central to our present argument is the proposition that flux in membership and amorphous group boundaries reduces the latitude the leader has in dealing with status threats. But, as the case material illustrates, the disposition of the threatened leader to use out-group aggression to deal with the threat involves further premises about group norms and the required fluctuation in role behavior by the leader. Eight cases, followed by brief interpretative sections, will be presented.

Detached Worker Case Reports

Interviews with detached workers were reviewed by the research staff and representative selections made for this chapter.[9] In proceeding with the selection, we reasoned somewhat as one would in the review of cases in law. The principle is illustrated as it emerges in different form over the range of specific fact situations that might be encountered with street corner groups.

Case 1.—Duke is the leader of the King Rattlers, a conflict-oriented group of approximately fifty Negro boys, aged fifteen to nineteen, who live on the periphery of a commercial area in the inner city. Duke is a good fighter, having risen to his leadership status in the group by being quick and effective with his fists while, at the same time, playing it very cool. Duke does not get caught. The detached

[8] Leon Jansyn, "Solidarity and Delinquency in a Street Corner Group: A Study of the Relationship between Changes in Specified Aspects of Group Structure and Variations in the Frequency of Delinquent Activity," unpublished Master's thesis, University of Chicago, 1960.

[9] See Chapter 1 for discussion of detached workers as sources of data, and Chapters 2, 5, and 9 for material relative to detached workers' roles.

worker reaffirmed Duke's status by working through him and was quickly successful in suppressing intergang fighting. Duke's leadership style capitalizes on his coolness and on his ability to both negotiate in intergang councils and to control his boys.

Despite his coolness, Duke did become implicated in a shooting incident that involved other members of the Rattlers and was sent to jail. The boys eventually "beat the rap," but they were held in detention for two and one-half months. While Duke and the others were absent from "the scene," new officers were "elected" by the worker and the group. It was understood that when Duke returned he would be president again. Upon Duke's return, despite the celebrations attending it, no formal recognition was made of his leadership. It was shortly after this that the detached worker with the Rattlers made the following observations in a weekly interview:

A: . . . Duke is acting very unusual. It's not the same Duke.
Q: What's happened?
A: I don't know. I feel maybe it's because he's been in jail and he's trying to release a lot of energy. Maybe after a while, he'll settle down. As of yet he hasn't setted down. He is one of the real instigators in fightin'. They say, "You know, Duke is acting like us now." The boys even notice the difference in him. It isn't just me.
Q: Do they appreciate this or don't they like this?
A: They appreciate it because now they have no more problems. All of them like to fight. If Duke chips in, that's better yet. But they notice the change in him. I keep tellin' Duke, "Be careful, boy, you'll be right back in jail."

The worker then described Duke's behavior at a basketball game which had been scheduled with the Jr. Lords.

A: Duke was calling them "mother-fucker," and "The Lords ain't shit." Duke walked up to them—Duke doin' all the talkin'—instigator. Bill next to him and Harry listening. Everybody was listening but Duke, and I was having a problem trying to get Duke down there so he could get himself dressed and leave. Duke walked up and said, "You ain't shit. The Jr. Lords ain't shit. Are you a Jr.? The boys said, "No." And he said, "A fuckin' old Lord, I'm King Rattler." Duke walked all through all of them, "You ain't shit," trying to get a fight. "Come on, Duke," I said, trying to push him down the stairs. But each time he'd get away and go over there, "You Lords ain't shit . . . we're Rattlers. We're Eastside Rattlers."
Q: Was he drunk?

A: No, he's sober but he's changed. Big change. Bill was watchin' him and goin' along. I told Harry to grab him and told Henry to get Duke and take him. I had to grab him—he wouldn't listen. The rest of the Rattlers wanted to fight too. So I had to take Duke downstairs, and while they were getting their clothes on we had a problem with hats. They wanted the new hats of the other team which they could see on the rack. Duke owns a brown hat, but he had worn a gray one over there. By mistake, I gave him a brown hat which belonged to the Lords. When I saw what had happened, I tried to get it back but no one knew where it was.

The prognosis one would make from the hat and fighting incidents would be one of a growing gap between the detached worker and Duke. Such a gap did not, in fact, materialize. Just a week later, the worker took Duke to a large department store where he secured a job as messengerboy. Duke's behavior was exemplary. His "strange behavior" did not recur, and he resumed a steadying, essentially non-aggressive and non-delinquent influence on the group.

It is to be noted in the detached worker's report quoted above that the boys approved of Duke's aggressiveness, were willing to fight, and, against the expressed desires of the detached worker, were willing to help Duke conceal the stolen hat. After this brief period of catering to the most broadly held norms of aggressive behavior, Duke resumed the "cool" image that had distinguished him from the group he led. The Duke incident occurred despite the conscious intention of the detached worker to support Duke's leadership.

It is our interpretation that the tough, highly aggressive, behavior was adopted by Duke to clarify the uncertain leadership situation that had arisen as a result of his detention. In the next case, the status threat arises from a detached worker's failure to understand the previously existing leadership structure.

Case 2.—A worker who had been successful in reaching and in reducing the delinquency of a leadership clique known as the "Big Five," suddenly found that a group of his boys were following another boy in predatory and assaultive delinquency. It developed that this new leader had been in jail during the several months that the worker had been with the group. The worker was only dimly aware of the boy's existence and not at all aware of his former leadership position. Upon release from jail, this boy gathered "lower-echelon" boys about himself and led them in a variety of aggressive delinquencies. This situation was well under way before it was understood by the worker but, when he did turn his attention to the errant group, he brought the aggressive behavior of the subgroup under relative control by "capturing" their leader.

Case 3.—A contrasting case involves the return from Army duty of a leader of the Midget Lords, a segment of a large conflict-oriented gang complex known as the "Nation of Lords." It resulted in what we call "The Great Train Robbery."

Johnnie was by far the strongest leader of the Lords. When a new worker was assigned to the group, Johnnie was in the service. The worker was told about Johnnie, however, and upon the latter's return to the group late in the summer of 1960, he was introduced to the worker. The worker was not able to "capture" Johnnie immediately and, in fact, found that he was somewhat uncomfortable with Johnnie and the clique of boys who were most directly involved with him. The worker continued, therefore, to spend the majority of his time with the less delinquent boys who were not Johnnie's immediate followers.

One evening Johnnie and his clique asked the worker to take them "out South" to a party. Figuring that this would at least remove a troublesome element from the area, the worker agreed to the request. Rather than staying with the boys, however, the worker returned to the area where he contacted other members of the Midgets.

On their own return trip, Johnnie and his boys made a spur-of-the-moment decision to hold up the car on the elevated train on which they were traveling. They beat one man and took cash from passengers.

If this dramatic demonstration of toughness and daring had been successful, it would have reaffirmed Johnnie's leadership role in his clique, solidified the subgroup, and, in all probability, have drawn the worker into closer work with Johnnie's clique. The interpretation of this incident in terms of status implications is by no means unequivocal but, since the robbery cannot be understood as the actions of boys rationally oriented toward crime as a way of life, the need for an alternative interpretation is clear.

Case 4.—The protagonist, Lawrence, was an influential member of a group for which there was no single and most powerful leader. To maintain his position of influence, Lawrence was required to play a central role in many of the varied activities of the group. The incident in question turned around a "quarter party" which Lawrence was "putting down" primarily out of his embarrassment over having no money. Several of the other Chiefs were employed at this time, but Lawrence was not. He deprecated the party and urged the Chiefs to join him in "turning it out," that is, in breaking it up.[10] When the other Chiefs refused to go along with the suggestion despite his urging, Lawrence did not pursue the issue further. Instead, he borrowed money from the worker because, we believe, his position in the group made asking for money from another group member untenable.

During the course of the evening, Big Daddy, another member of the Chiefs, started after a member of the Cobras with a hammer. The detached worker grabbed Lawrence and, in recognition of his status and ability to control the other boys, said, "Look, I don't want no crap. What about you?" Lawrence replied, "Don't worry, ain't gonna be no crap," and proceeded to help the worker bring about order.

If we view Lawrence's threat to turn the party out as a way of "saving face" when his financial dilemma further complicated the status ambiguity attendant upon the entry of a new worker into the group, then the resolution of status ambiguity by the loan and the request from the worker for help may be regarded as having prevented the delinquency.

The next two cases are parallel. They both involve a detached worker's problem in dealing with a highly aggressive boy who had an established role of instigating delinquent episodes.

Case 5.—In the first case, the boy, Commando, was known for his daring and for being in the middle of whatever was happening. When the Lords came together as a fighting group, under pressure from a rival gang who were "wolf-packing" in the area, Commando became one of the boys who was most difficult to control. He instigated trouble in a way that captured attention, and he set a style of violence by sometimes carrying a shotgun.

The worker decided to "put down" Commando in front of the rest of the group by telling him that he really was not tough or brave. He concluded by saying, "You ain't nothin'." Commando reacted by being even more reckless in his actions, particularly when members of the rival group were on the scene. He continued to demonstrate to the group that he was not chicken and that he *was* somebody until the worker ceased his public ridicule.

[10] Whyte reports Doc's similar plight, though Doc did not suggest a delinquent way out of his dilemma (see Whyte, *op. cit.*).

When the worker shifted to a nurturant relation and impressed Commando privately with his responsibility, as a leader, for curbing conflict, the boy became less aggressive and aided the worker. The worker still feels, however, that in a conflict situation, without a worker present, Commando would find it difficult not to "sell wolf tickets" (i.e., challenge) to rival gang members and instigate conflict. Commando appears not to be motivated to convert status won by aggression to a more stabilized rank in the group.

Case 6.—A comparable case involved Bill, a tough and influential member of the Pizza Grill Boys. These boys lived in an area where organized crime was firmly entrenched. The boys stole automobiles, auto parts, and many other articles, hot-rodded their cars, and drank excessively. They were not a fighting gang. The worker with these boys had been an intercollegiate boxing champion and had engaged in a brief professional career as a boxer. He taught Bill and others in the group a great deal about boxing. Bill proceeded to employ these skills in beating up boys in the area. The worker strongly and publicly reprimanded Bill for doing this, indicating that this behavior was stupid and cowardly rather than brave, tough, and skilled. Bill's subsequent action was to drink excessively and then proceed to get into fights that demonstrated how tough he was.

After winning a fight, Bill did not have the skills to convert the advantage to generalized rank. Cases 5 and 6 both involve inflexibility in role shift after aggression, thus suggesting that flexibility is required if a boy is to cope successfully with leadership demands of groups such as these.

The next case is interesting from two perspectives. First, it indicates that the outcome of competitive sports activities, even when supervised, may release a need for status equilibration that results in overt aggression. Second, it provides a commentary on what the participants understand concerning their own motivation.

Case 7.—Gary, one of the three top "influentials" among the King Rattlers, was captain of one of the two pool teams from this gang. The other Rattler team won their division play while Gary's team placed second in their division. In the championship playoffs, Gary's team was eliminated in the first round of play, while the other group, which had advanced to the semifinals, wound up in fourth place. Feelings ran high at the playoffs; and individual and team winners received a great deal of praise.

Gary and his team watched first the finals, then the presentation of the individual trophies to the other team from their gang. The trophies, which were proudly displayed upon the return to the Rattler area, re-emphasized Gary's failure in this formal leadership role. The timing was particularly bad because Gary had emerged as one of two major influentials among the Rattlers since the employment and marriage of Duke, the former leader, who was at this time spending less time with the group. But Gary himself had recently obtained a job and had not spent much time on the streets. Gary had been paid on the day of the tournament and, at the tournament, he had the substantial sum of between $50 and $80 in his pocket. For this reason, the gang, which placed a high value on strong-arming, was not clear whether Gary would continue to lead them in this activity.

Although we should like to have more detailed information, we know only that after the tournament sessions were over Gary and two members of his team strong-armed a man. The team members held the man and Gary hit him; the take was $18. Gary's subsequent comment to the worker was, "Shit, I wasted my time." This was as far as he could go to explain why he had strong-armed with money in his pocket. He told the worker simply, ". . . saw him walking down the street and just got him—for no reason, just got him."

The salient elements in Gary's case are these: (a) he was adept at strong-arming, (b) strong-arming was status-conferring in the group, and (c) Gary played a crucial role in the incident in question. While these facts are not sufficient to establish the relationship, they are all consistent with the interpretation that Gary's action was specifically related to his need for status reaffirmation following the perceived loss in connection with the pool tournament.

Case 8.—On a note of caution, we shall close with an observation concerning a drug-using group of white boys who resisted taking up an invitation to aggressive behavior under highly provocative circumstances. The group was oriented primarily around the use of drugs in pill form, though the boys smoked marihuana heavily, drank excessively, and, when they could afford it (and it was available), used heroin. According to the worker, these boys "looked upon fighting as being 'square.'"

The incident to be reported concerns the summer, 1961, "wade-ins" by Negroes and whites at "white" beaches on Chicago's South Side in protest against the segregation of beach facilities. When the possibility of the "wade-ins" became known to a large white gang from the same area as the drug-users, they immediately took up a battle cry and proceeded to plan the co-ordination of groups in opposition to the "wade-ins." Excitement ran high and they admonished the drug-using group to lend support to the cause. The worker reported that the drug-using group "expressed considerable racial hostility" and "talked about getting into the coming battle," but when the "wade-ins" occurred they chose to separate themselves from the milling hostile crowd that gathered on the beach. Instead, they proceeded to get "high" on pills. While six of them did go to the beach, they chose to sit beneath a tree—at the far end of the beach, away from the "wade-in"—and play cards. In the words of the worker, "they could hardly have been less concerned with who was going to occupy the beach."

These boys, in contrast to previous cases cited, had been urged to fight, with clear insinuations that anyone who did not was "chicken," yet they chose to turn away. Their reaction to this threat was withdrawal from the larger group and participation in activity expressive of the norms which distinguished them from the conflict-oriented boys, namely, drug use. This instance does not involve any separate threat to the leader of this group, for all members seemed to agree easily on the course of action. However, this response, in this situation, suggests that, in groups in which the leader's prestige is bound up in competence at enjoying esoteric "kicks," it may well be doubted that status threat would result in aggressive behavior.

From the practical standpoint of understanding of gang functioning, this reservation may not be important, for it is the observation of our group and other workers that individual boys who adopt strong retreatist adaptations (such as drug use) do not continue as prominent members of large gangs. They drift off into small cliques, and in many cases appear to behave as an isolated individual who moves (without developing strong interpersonal ties) into loci of heightened collective emphasis on retreatist norms. From the theoretical standpoint, this instance suggests a possible dependence between group norms and modes of status reaffirmation and, at the same time, reminds us that there was a high evaluation of aggression in the functioning of the groups from which the other examples were collected. By an extension of this thinking, if one doubts that aggression would confer higher status in retreatist groups, it is also plausible to doubt that aggression would confer higher status in middle class adolescent groups—though for different reasons.

Targets and Functions of Aggression

Miller and his associates suggest that verbal aggression "was an essential element of behavioral mechanisms which operated to delineate standards of personal worth, to facilitate effective collective functioning, to maintain relations of reciprocity and equality, to define attitudes toward those outside the group and their values, to indicate the *limits* of acceptable behavior and to provide effective sanctions against deviation from group-supported standards."[11] For our groups, also, the level of intragroup aggression in such forms as "body-punching" and "signifying" is high but intragroup dominance-seeking aggressive behavior by gang members, including acknowledged leaders, is not supported by group norms and is rarely resorted to by gang leaders.

Leaders we have observed are cautious not to exercise their leadership arbitrarily, and often overtly disavow that they lead the gangs. The percentage of total activities that are formally organized is low, and leaders are, in general, very careful to obtain clearance from other high status group members before staking their prestige on a given course of action. We do not, in many cases, know how the original hierarchy of status was established, but clearly it is not maintained by aggressive dominance-seeking by leaders.[12] Except when other boys in the gang directly challenge their status, leaders of even the toughest fighting gangs do not engage in dominating, aggressive interpersonal relationships within the gang. Among conflict gangs the leaders are known to have the capacity to function aggressively against other members when necessary to maintain their dominance, but the overwhelming preponderance of their actions is co-ordinating and nurturant.

Discussion

In cases 5 and 6, the principals, Commando and Bill, made their bids for attention through aggressive behavior but, when the tension was past, they were not able to shift roles. Neither maintained a

---

[11] Walter B. Miller, Hildred S. Geertz, and Henry S. G. Cutter, "Aggression in a Boys' Street-Corner Group," *Psychiatry,* XXIV (November, 1961), 283–98.

[12] Mandel recently discussed the severe sociometric costs of interpersonally aggressive dominance-seeking among the boarding-school boys he studied. See Rudolf Mandel, *Die Aggressivität bei Schulern: Beobachtung und Analyse des Aggressiven Verhaltens einer Knapengruppe im Pubertätsalter* (Bern and Stuttgart: Verlag Hans Huber, 1959) ; also Miller *et al., ibid.*

following. The observation that a good suitor may not make a good husband, or a good campaigner a good president, is applicable in other contexts. It is our thought that similar shifts in system requirements occur with great frequency on the corner. The leaders who persist over long periods, like Duke (Case 1), do have aggressive skills as well as the ability to use them selectively.

The quickened tempo of the testing of relationships on corners, in contrast with, for example, work groups, arises in part because leaders do not control important amounts of property, because there are few privileges or immunities they can bestow, and because there are no external institutional pressures that constrain members to accept the discipline of the gang. Gang membership is very fluid,[13] particularly among fringe members. The leader cannot crassly dominate a person who is dissatisfied with the allocation of rewards within the group because of the effectiveness of the threat of splintering away. The result is that the successful gang leader is surprisingly conciliatory in his corner relations.

The recourse to aggressive behavior toward an out-group object is viewed as being a part of the sensitivity to role requirements. Out-group aggression does not undercut the gratification that membership confers and does not expose the relationship to the threat of splintering. The foray provides excitement, a heightened need for leadership, and a non-disruptive way for the leader to exercise his aggressive skills.

We do not mean to imply that all attempts at status re-equilibration through out-group aggression are successful. Sometimes they are not, and when they are not, the consequences can be grave. Kobrin and Finestone describe a case in which a boy withdrew from the gang and began to smoke marihuana,[14] and another case, known to us by correspondence, resulted in suicide. Most failures are unquestionably less dramatic than these, but a social cost is surely involved.

[13] Our gangs are definitely not the very fluid near-group phenomena which Yablonsky describes, although we can imagine our boys answering as his respondents did after they were picked up. See Lewis Yablonsky, "The Delinquent Gangs as a Near-Group," *Social Problems,* VII (Fall, 1959), 108–17; and Harold W. Pfautz, "Near-Group Theory and Collective Behavior," *Social Problems,* IX (Fall, 1961), 167–74.

[14] Solomon Kobrin and Harold Finestone, "Towards a Framework for the Analysis of Juvenile Delinquency," paper read at the annual meeting of the American Sociological Association, 1958 (dittoed).

This formulation has specific explanatory implications that may be illustrated by comparisons with Cloward and Ohlin's comment on the reduction of intergang fighting that comes about when detached workers become associated with gangs:

The reduction in conflict may reflect the skill of the social workers, but another explanation may be that *the advent of the street-gang worker symbolized the end of social rejection and the beginning of social accommodation.* To the extent that violence represents an effort to win deference, one would logically expect it to diminish once that end has been achieved.[15]

Instead of viewing the presence of the worker solely as symbolic of the interest of the larger society, we would also stress that his presence stabilizes what we have come to call "the leadership structure." And, in so doing, we believe it makes less frequent the need for status-maintaining aggressiveness by leaders. We believe that the gang also recognizes its obligation to the worker as a *quid pro quo* for services performed by the worker and for the additional status within the gang world that accrues to a gang by virtue of their having a worker.[16] Both of these points relate to status-maintaining mechanisms within more immediate systems—the gang itself and the gangs of the area—rather than to the "end of rejection" at the hands of a somewhat amorphous middle class society.

It is to be emphasized that we do not suppose the usual elementary approval and disapproval mechanisms are absent in the gang situation; it is more that we believe gang leaders to be particularly vulnerable when they try to use negative sanctions to maintain their rank. While we view the hypothesis as plausible, we believe it highly desirable to test it by purposive, experimental intervention in the functioning of on-going groups (e.g., by having a detached worker deliberately frustrate a leader). Because of the serious consequences that might follow from the resulting aggressions, we did not make such attempts with the groups under observation in the project.

In conclusion, we are concerned with a syndrome of behavior which is similar to what is popularly understood as scapegoating. In this case, aggression toward an out-group object is not a rarely

[15] Cloward and Ohlin, *op. cit.*, p. 176. Their italics.

[16] James F. Short, Jr., "Street Corner Groups and Patterns of Delinquency: A Progress Report," *The American Catholic Sociological Review*, XXIV (Spring, 1963), 13–32.

used last resort, it is a response to relatively minor status contention. Unlike authoritarian personalities who deny hostile feelings and displace them, there seems to be no complex transformation involved. The leader behaves directly but not as if he were an office holder who has automatically assumed control of group resources which he can then allocate to loyal followers. He soon learns that overt attempts to coerce members result in their withdrawing from the group and that his capacity to be aggressive can heighten group solidarity and the rewards of membership only if it is directed toward an out-group target. For such actions to result in the increase of status, there must be gratifications from the foray which are not regularly counterbalanced with disastrous consequences. The chapters which follow relate needs and gang process gratifications, and then in Chapter 11 we treat more generally the individual gang member's decision to join the "action." These later analyses delineate further the "givens" which are utilized by the gang leader in action to maintain his status.

CHAPTER 9

Sources of Threat, Group Norms, and Gang Delinquency

This chapter explores further the sources of status threat and other provocation to aggression, and the interplay of group norms and relations with the external environment with modes of status reaffirmation. In the process the scope of the mechanism described in the previous chapter will be extended to include gang members in addition to leaders.

The investment of gang leaders in their "rep" has been noted by many observers. Recognition by leaders of the relation between leadership status and delinquency in a form somewhat less subtle than that presented in the previous chapter is apparent from our own observational data:

Fred Hubbard called this afternoon to report a conversation on the West Side with Guy, leader of the Vice Kings. Fred noted that Big Jake, leader of the Potentates—a rival gang with which the Vice Kings often had been at war—had been "cooling it" over the fall and winter. However, Guy warned Fred that he "had better watch Big Jake" because "he has to do something." When Fred protested that Jake hadn't been humbugging and asked why Guy thought he had to "do something," Guy responded: "He's got to build that rep again. He's been gone. Now he got to show everybody he's back!" Fred told me: "I almost laughed at him—sounded like he had been talking to Doc Short. It was such a classic case I had to call you on it!"[1]

Note that both Guy and Big Jake were leaders of conflict-oriented gangs. With the exception of the "pill poppers" in Case 8, conflict was a major activity of most of the gangs involved in Chapter 8 cases. Among nearly all gangs studied, skill in fighting was a valued characteristic, whether or not the gang had a fighting "rep." An epi-

---

[1] Fred D. Hubbard is Director of the Program for Detached Workers. This note is a report of a telephone call from Mr. Hubbard to "Doc Short," 4/6/62.

sode involving aggressive behavior might occur as a result of the operation of the status threat mechanism among any of these gangs. This being the case, we must ask the question, "What distinguishes the *conflict-oriented* gang, and are aggressive episodes more likely to occur among such gangs than among the others, however they may be classified?"

The latter question must be answered in the affirmative. Some gangs are properly characterized as conflict-oriented, in the sense that conflict with other gangs is a major focus of group activity and a major source of status within the gang. These gangs are more often involved in aggressive episodes. Why this should be the case involves further discussion of the first question. Without attempting to account for the emergence of the phenomenon, we may describe our conflict-oriented gangs as *invested in their reputation for fighting vis-à-vis certain other gangs*. This investment gives the boys a group identity which provides incentive for conflict involvement and a basis for "threats" to leadership and to group status. The structure of these groups provides another clue to their orientation. Unlike other gangs, *they create roles expressive of their conflict orientation,* e.g., war counselor and armorer. Competition for these roles was observed among members of several gangs. This is not to say that the duties and privileges of such offices were clearly defined or performed. Instead of such formal role specifications and expectations, these roles tended to be the focus of ceremonial deference within the group. The existence of such roles provided yet another basis for individual status and group identity which were conflict oriented.

The following report by a detached worker illustrates the type of "guerilla warfare" typical among conflict gangs we have observed:[2]

. . . [I] was sitting there talking to Knights about things in general and again re-emphasizing my stand on guns, because they told me that they had collected quite a few and were waiting for the Vice Kings to come down and start some trouble. At one point I told them flatly that it was better that I got the gun rather than the police, and though they agreed with me, they repeated their stand that they were tired of running from the Vice Kings and that if they gave them trouble, from now on they were fighting back.

I had a chance to see what they meant, exactly, because while I was sitting there in the car talking to William, the remaining guys having gotten out of the car in pursuit of some girls around the corner, William

2 Incident report by Fred Hubbard, 3/26/61, and subsequent interview.

told me that a couple of Vice Kings were approaching. I looked out the window and noticed two Vice Kings and two girls walking down the street by the car. I didn't know them as Vice Kings because I only know the chiefs like Garroway, Pappy, etc. William then turned around and made the observation that there were about fifteen or twenty Vice Kings across the street in the alley and wandering up the street in ones and twos.

At this point, I heard three shots go off. I don't know who fired these shots, and no one else seemed to know, because the Vice Kings at this point had encountered Commando, Jones, and a couple of other Knights who were coming from around the corner talking to the girls. The Vice Kings yelled across the street to Commando and his boys, and Commando yelled back. They traded insults and challenges, Commando being the leader of the Knights and a guy named Bear being the leader of the Vice Kings. At this point I got out of the car to try to cool Commando down, inasmuch as he was halfway across the street hurling insults across the street and daring them to do something about it, and they were doing the same thing to him. I grabbed Commando and began to pull him back across the street.

By this time the Vice Kings had worked themselves into a rage, and three of them came across the street yelling that they were mighty Vice Kings and to attack Commando and the Knights. In trying to break this up, I was not too successful. I didn't know the Vice Kings involved, and they were really determined to swing on the Knights, so we had a little scuffle around there. I did see one Vice King who I did know—that was Jr. Smith—and I asked him to help me break it up. At this point, along the street comes Henry Brown, with a revolver, shooting at the Vice Kings. Everybody ducked and the Vice Kings ran, and Henry Brown ran around the corner. When he ran around the corner I began to throw Knights into my car because I knew that the area was "hot," and I was trying to get them out of there. Henry Brown came back around the corner and leaped into my car also. I asked him if he had the gun, and he told me that he did not, and since I was in a hurry, I pulled off in the car and took him and the rest of the boys with me.

This was a minor skirmish between two groups who had been feuding for some months. In conversation with the director of the research program at the University of Chicago, the worker continued his report, describing the behavior of the boys after the skirmish, when they were in his car:

In the car, Commando and the other boys were extremely elated. There were expressions like: "Baby, did you see the way I swung on that kid"; "Man, did we tell them off"; "I really let that one kid have it"; "Did you see them take off when I leveled my gun on them"; "You were great, Baby. And did you see the way I . . . ," etc. It was just like we used to feel when we got back from a patrol where everything went just right [the worker had been a paratrooper in the Korean conflict]. The tension was relieved, we had performed well and could be proud.

Here the status function of the conflict subculture is seen in bold relief. No doubt the Vice Kings, too, felt the thrill of the conflict. They had faced great danger and had a perfect alibi for not winning an unequivocal victory, viz., the fact that the opposition had a gun— and so, of course, did the Knights, for the worker intervened to prevent them from following up their advantage. Thus, participants on both sides of such a conflict can share the elation and the status-conferring glow of an encounter such as this. It is, in effect, *not* a "zero-sum game" in the sense that points won by a party to the conflict are not necessarily lost by his adversary. No one need necessarily be defeated; behavior in conformity with the norms of the subculture takes place and is rewarded, and law and order are restored. In this way society, too, shares in this non-zero-sum game. Lest we be accused of too sanguine a view of gang behavior, we note that boys may be defeated, individually and collectively, and much injury and property damage may and often does result from this "game."

Status threats to leaders represent a type of process which operates within the frame of group norms and values to precipitate some violent episodes of gang boys. It seems likely that the reaction of leaders to status threats is a special case of a more general process of "status management" which involves all gang boys and individuals and groups which have special meaning for them.[3]

Status management may be defined as behavior oriented toward the achievement of desired social positions or states of being, or the protection of desired social positions or states of being already achieved. In particular, it is our observation that the delinquent behavior of gang boys very often entails encounters by the boys with other persons, among themselves, with members of other gangs and with non-gang members, with girls, and with adults and adult-sponsored institutions. Some of these encounters involve status deprivation within the institutions and on the basis of the criteria of "respectable society." The great majority, how-

[3] See James F. Short, Jr., "Gang Delinquency and Anomie," in *Deviant Behavior and Anomie,* ed. Marshall B. Clinard (New York: The Free Press of Glencoe, Inc., 1964).

ever, appear to involve a boy's status as male, as a participant in a world of "fighting gangs," perhaps as a member of the "Egyptian Cobras," or as an aspiring adult, i.e., statuses which are of immediate concern to the boys in the on-going processes which engage their daily lives.[4]

Several of the classes of *status threat* which are covered in this broader conception are illustrated by events preceding, during, and after a "humbug" between members of several of our gangs.

The Humbug

The incident occurred in March, 1962, at the Chicago Amphitheater where a professional basketball game was being held. In all, five detached workers and members of their gangs were involved. The following report is taken from "incident reports" prepared by the workers and interviews with them subsequent to the incident.

Worker Jim O. met his group, the North Side Vice Kings, at 6:30 P.M. in their "area." The boys "had been drinking a little" and Jim suggested that they go with him to a professional basketball game at the Amphitheater. The boys piled into his station wagon. They "were in a pretty good mood but began to get restless while . . . being seated." Buck, the strongest leader of the North Side Vice Kings, was still under the influence of alcohol when they arrived at the Amphitheater, and upon arrival he seated himself near a younger group of boys, the Jr. Chiefs. According to the worker with the Chiefs, Buck was friendly to his boys, but was quite obnoxious to refreshment vendors and apparently was putting on a show for the younger boys.

Buck, who had recently turned 21 years of age, decided that he wanted to buy some beer. Jim O. told him that he couldn't drink beer when he was with the group at a Program-sponsored activity, but Buck bought the beer anyway. After a further exchange of argument in which Buck made much of the fact that he was 21, Jim took the beer away from him. Buck then became abusive to the worker and to other people around him. The other Kings now also became obstreperous. At this point, Jim O. announced that the entire group had to leave immediately. We pick up his narrative account:

All the fellows got their coats and we started to leave. As we got into the arena and on the main floor going toward the door, a group of fellows came into the door [South Side Rattlers] At this time I didn't know who they were. Buck started fat-mouthing at one of the fellows

[4] *Ibid.*, pp. 120–21.

in the group. At that moment the fellow put on a glove and Buck hit him. This started the whole incident. I was in the middle trying to stop it and get them out of the place; as I got five fellows together and put them out, I asked the police not to let them back in again, and started back to get the rest of the fellows. I looked up and they were back in the place again. By this time Bill G. [worker with the South Side Rattlers] walked in with a few fellows and they all looked up and started running toward the fight.

Bill G. reported that his boys "didn't know what to do" when accosted by Buck. When another of the Kings added to Buck's insults, Bull, leader of the Rattlers, returned in kind. One of the Kings then took a swing at Bull. Bill G. blocked this, but other boys crowded in and "suddenly, it happened. I don't know who passed the first lick, but within seconds both groups were at it."

When a third group, the Cherokees, came on the scene, the Vice King worker (Jim O.) reported: "No one stopped to get an explanation of what was going down. The fellows just looked up and saw the group fighting and they joined in." Rattler worker Bill G. reported that "The Cherokees came up just as the Kings managed to frighten the Rattlers into running—mainly because of two knives and what I think was a pistol. The Cherokees took over where the Rattlers had left off." Apparently this was not simply a matter of "collective excitement," however, because, as Bill G. notes, the "Cherokees . . . hated the Vice Kings" and Cherokee worker Charlie B. reports:

One of the Vice Kings, Buck, asked my boys which group were they from. Immediately there was a quick response from my boys yelling out "Cherokees!" Then he asked "Who is the president?" and Arthur yelled he was . . . Then one of the Vice Kings hit Arthur in the back of the head . . . this activated my group and the bigger boys, Arthur, Tommy, Moore, and Leon begain swinging back. The police broke this up to some extent, but there was small patch fighting here and there between these four and various Vice Kings. Well, I grabbed Leon to the side along with the smaller boys that were standing on the side watching, and the fight stopped. When the police came up to me I began explaining what was going on, but members of the Vice Kings came over shouting threats again while I was talking to the policemen and my boys. This just started the swing again.

A fourth worker, Leon W., came on this scene with a segment of his group, the Midget Vice Kings, just as the Cherokees joined in battle with the Vice Kings. Leon W. notes that the Vice Kings were "making all kinds of noises and repeating, "We're the mighty Vice Kings." When the Cherokees responded to this challenge, as described above, W's Midgets "immediately joined with the Vice Kings" in the fight.

The humbug was at last stopped, through effective action by detached workers and police. Three of the workers reported their boys' reactions *following* the incident:

Worker Jim O. (Vice Kings): My fellows said they were going back to the West Side and get some more Kings and their "stuff" [weapons] and come back to turn out the Amphitheater.

Worker Bill G. (South Side Rattlers): . . . I found them very upset. By this time they had had time to gain enough courage to fight the Vice Kings, and they wanted to go home to get their "stuff." I told them that I had asked for a police escort to our car because I did not want any more humbugs. A few of them objected, but most of them were quite happy to see the police walk up to our car. . . . On the way home, the fellows started to tease each other about running. . . . Interesting comments made by my boys were: "Those guys are crazy"; "The next time I go to a game I'm bringing my stuff"; "Why didn't their worker search them before bringing them"; "Mr. G., I want you to get me a list of the events in advance"; "Who has all of our shotguns?"

Worker Charlie B. (Cherokees): We talked about the incident in the car, and many of the boys spoke of war with the Vice Kings because of this event.

One of the groups (the Jr. Chiefs) never became involved in the fighting. It seems noteworthy that they were not involved in any of the status threats from other groups, or their workers, involved in the fighting. Of the other groups only the Vice Kings actually left the Amphitheater without seeing the game. As the game progressed, a third group of Vice Kings (the Juniors, who had not been involved in the earlier altercation) came in with their worker, George D., and innocently sat beside the Cherokees (who earlier had been fighting with the Vice Kings). Worker Charlier B. reports:

They sat down not knowing that a fight had taken place between the North Side Vice Kings and my boys, and there was no incident between us, but the boys were talking and mentioning that they were Vice Kings, and there was a little uneasiness during the game. Fortunately for George and myself, many of the boys in my group were friendly with boys in George's group, and they talked it over saying how they had been unjustly jumped upon when they came in. I don't know whether it was agreed by members of both groups, but there was nothing further done that evening.

We note several elements in this incident which were productive of threat: (1) the worker's public flouting of Buck's *adulthood,* and following from this, (2) his degrading of Buck in the eyes of his chosen audience, the Jr. Chiefs, and of his own group; (3) the threat to all of the Vice Kings when the worker decided that they all must leave. They were humiliated by being treated as a group of little boys who could not behave themselves sufficiently to remain in a public place. This was humiliating both in terms of their position in the gang world, again because the event was witnessed by the Jr. Chiefs, and in terms of their status in the public eye—they were being treated as "kids." (4) Both the Rattlers and the Cherokees responded to the Vice King challenge to their "rep," and we judge, their manhood.

Yet the fights were short-lived. All the boys except the Vice Kings, who were most central to the incident and who experienced the greater "status threats," were brought under control reasonably quickly and they witnessed the basketball game they originally had come for. The humbug provided grist for the mill of individual and group status within the status universe of fighting gangs. But, in the months which followed, no more "humbugging" between these gangs took place. The incident was relatively self-contained. It served to perpetuate the investment of these boys in their gang "rep," and it may have served the image of these boys as street warriors whose group norms required their participation in conflict with rival gangs. Without the detailed accounting of the incident, such an interpretation might seem reasonable. But, what happened to the norm after the fights were stopped? And why were they so easily stopped? Note, also, that not all boys participated in the fighting. With the exception of the Vice Kings, in *each* group there were some who never became involved. Careful review of the incident suggests that those most centrally involved were core members of the gangs, gang leaders and boys striving for leadership. Investment in individual and gang "rep," and in other statuses which are likely to be involved in the give and take of such an incident, apparently are variable among both groups and individuals. Certainly no gang norm required fighting of *all* boys, even under these provocative circumstances.

Group norms doubtlessly influence the behavior of gang members, but their influence on most members of the gang appears to be tenuous and largely situational. Further evidence of this fact is provided by the loose criteria of membership in most gangs, and by their fluid membership and low cohesion. Boys come and go for days or weeks at a time, and unless they occupy a particularly strong leadership or other important role in the group, they are hardly missed.

Criminals, Retreatists, and Response to Aggressive Threat

Whether conceptualized in terms of norms of the group or of customary ways of behaving, however, the subcultural orientation of a group cannot be ignored as an important influence on the behavior of a group. The previous chapter noted the very different reaction of two white groups to the "wade-in" Chicago beach incident. Here it seems clear that the retreatist orientation of the drug users was of fundamental importance in differentiating their reaction from that of the larger group which chose to react by violent means. The taunts hurled at the drug users included some very threatening reflections on their manhood, their bravery, and their status in the larger group. Their reaction was retreatist rather than aggressive.

Retreatism as a subculture. The contrast between our own group of retreatists and all other gangs under observation was striking. The basis of camaraderie among the drugs users was their common interest in kicks. Past and present exploits concerned experiences while high, and "crazy" behavior, rather than bravery or toughness. Use of pills and other drugs seemed virtually a way of life with these boys, interspersed with other kicks such as sex, alcohol, and "way out" experiences which distinguished them, individually and collectively. After several observations of this group in their area, a member of the research team reported:

The guys make continual references to dope. They talk about it much as a group of drinkers might talk about liquor. It comes up freely, easily in the conversation, a couple of remarks are made about it, who's taken it recently, how it affected this or that person, etc., and then it is dropped only to come up again before long. Today the guys made comments about dope and baseball. (You get the feeling that whatever the activity of the moment, the guys will talk about it in relation to dope—how taking dope affects their participation in the activity.) A commonly expressed notion was that so and so played baseball better when he was "high" than at any other time. Whether they believed this was hard to tell. It sounded much like oft-heard remarks that "I play poker better when I'm half drunk or high" (i.e., remarks made in the community at large). The remarks about dope are hard to record because they do not seem to express any attitude toward dope. They just seem to accept it in a matter of fact way—it seems to be so commonplace to them that the attitudes are often assumed and not felt worthy of expression. (At the same time it is true that comments expressing a positive attitude toward dope are not rare. The guys like to talk about their "highs," how much they have taken, how high they were, what they did while high, etc.) Perhaps one attitude is implicitly expressed, though, in these remarks; the attitude of acceptance.[5]

Five months later this same observer reported on a hanging session in which the group related "tales about some of the crazy and humorous things" in which various of the drug users had been involved.

The relating of these tales was greeted by laughter from all. Often the worker or observer would mention an incident and Butch would fill us in or correct us on details. Some of the incidents mentioned:

(1) The time Willie was so high he walked off a roof and fell a story or two and broke his nose. Worker thought he had been on a roof, while Butch maintained he fell from a boxcar. Butch said it was over a week before he went to the doctor. . . . Harry said he walked around the hospital in a crazy looking green coat whenever the guys went to visit him.

(2) The time Snooks, Baby, and Jerry climbed on a roof to wake Elizabeth. One of the guys reached through the window and grabbed what he thought was Elizabeth's leg and shook it to wake her up. It turned out to be her old man's leg and it woke him up.

(3) The more recent incident in which Sonny leaped over the counter to rob a Chinaman, who proceeded to beat him badly. When the police came, Sonny asked that they arrest this man for having beaten him so. He was doped out of his mind and didn't know what was happening.

(4) Walter got into an argument with a woman over whose car it was they were standing by. He insisted they call the police, and waited confidently until the police showed and took him away.

(5) Sonny tried to break into a building and was ripping off a door when the police found him.

(6) Some of the guys slept out in a car and woke the next morning to find the car was being pulled away. They asked the tower to stop just long enough so they could get out.

(7) One of the guys broke into a car and just about tore the door off doing so—this was a car with all the windows broken out—he was too high to notice.

[5] Field Observer Report (Whitney Pope), 5/5/61.

(8) One of the boys tried to start a car but just could not manage it. The car had no motor.

All laughed at these true tales. Butch even noted that he had been with the guy who broke into the car with no windows.[6]

Pope then observed that "these tales may be in the process of becoming legendary within the group. They are so characteristic of this group and describe it so well."

Though several of these boys had "grown up" together, they were not bound to each other by feelings of loyalty. Virtually their only common bond appeared to be use of drugs and the type of experiences which are recounted above. They did not really *share* drugs. Every boy was expected to "cop" (purchase drugs) on his own. In a peculiar way this was functional to the group, for although all of the boys who were financially and otherwise able to do so would get high, seldom were more than a few heavily under the influence of drugs at any one time. They liked to get high together, but boys who were not high appeared to enjoy the antics of others who were. They were really quite individualistic in their pursuit of kicks. Often the worker would find a boy off by himself, or with a girl friend or perhaps one other member. But these were not stable friendships. The group served the function of a sounding board for their common but individualistic interests—of moral support for a way of life.

For a variety of reasons these boys proved to be extremely difficult to study except by observation (by detached workers and field observers). On the basis of these reports, however, it is clear that the drug users were more alienated from their families and from other conventional institutions than were any of the other boys studied. So disorganized were their lives that it was difficult to trace the sort of continuity between conventional institutions and the group which was found in all other cases under study.

Reaction to Aggression. The orientation of the drug-using boys, and of a criminally oriented clique which also was a part of the larger group, is further informed by an incident which occurred during the spring of 1962. By this time a new worker had been assigned to the area, and other loose "hanging groups" were being worked with. The criminal clique, mentioned earlier in Chapter 4, consisted of eight boys. These boys had formed, according to Bobby, their leader, exclusively for the purpose of promoting theft activities. They were en-

[6] Field Observer Report (Whitney Pope), 10/12/61.

gaged in extensive auto stripping, burglary, and shoplifting—no "heavy stuff" such as strong-arming, robbery, or shakedown. The boys hung on the corner with the larger group, and when they did so were in no way distinguishable from this larger group. They were a clique only when they met away from the larger group, usually in each other's homes, to discuss and plan their theft activities. According to the worker assigned to these boys, "Bobby and his guys talk about what they are doing in one room, while Bobby's old man, who used to be some sort of wheel in the syndicate, talks to his friends about the 'old days' in the next room." The boys made it a point not to "clique-up" visibly on the street, and apparently their chief motivation for association with one another was the success of their predatory activities. In this way they were quite successful for a period of approximately two years. There is testimony that Bobby, in particular, enjoyed a considerable degree of police immunity.

The "incident" to be reported concerns a complicated series of encounters between a group of adults from a local tavern and the large white group, which included Bobby and his thieves, our retreatist group, and a larger number of boys who hung around the area, primarily in the Grenache Grill. One of the adults had struck one of the boys in the course of what started out to be a harmless request by one of the boys to "buy a punch" on a raffle card. The boys retaliated by smashing windows in the man's car. Two hours later the man returned with several of his friends, armed with wrenches, tire irons, pick handles, etc. They found four of the boys on the scene and proceeded to beat them badly. One of the four was Bobby, leader of the thieves. The worker reports the scene as he arrived:[7]

. . . they were bleeding: one kid lost most of his upper plate—it was smashed. They tried to run the story down to us. The driver of the car jumped out, threw open the trunk and said, "Let's go," and he had three bats and assorted tire tools. Bobby, the crippled kid, owns a little Ford, and he had already emptied it out—a few Grenache boys had come on the scene, and we had about 20 boys, including three of the four who had been beaten, just 15 minutes after the beating. One of the four was missing and he was supposed to be laying up in the alley, so we rounded the corner on foot, and he was just dragging himself out of the alley. This worker was hot and also grabbed a baseball bat. I suggested we get into the two cars and round up some more of the fellows before we went over to the tavern. About two-thirds of this group were young, which left just a few older muscle-bound boys from the area, and there was going to be blood. So I calmed down and realized there would be trouble. I said, "Let's gather up some more of the boys." So we jumped in the two cars and drove around the area. We rounded four corners and at each corner we got at least one full car. Within 45 minutes after the beating we had 60 boys and for the most part, at this time, they were the older boys.

Q: Any of the pot users in the group?

A: They will not fight. I discovered that Saturday.

Q: Want to go along and watch?

A: No. They were on the corner—they were aware of it and one of them ducked into a hamburger joint where they are supposed to be barred. Pete and Tootsie just disappeared. The other boys told me before that the pill poppers won't fight, and I found it to be true.

Again, the retreatist boys avoided violence. The worker's attention was diverted to the larger group, so we do not know whether the retreatists engaged in any group activity at this time, e.g., the drug use and card playing which occurred at the time of the "wade-in" incident. It is quite possible that they did not. The present incident was relatively spontaneous, whereas the wade-in was known and planned for well in advance. The thieves by contrast were much involved in the incident and its aftermath. The conflict simmered for several days, with the worker attempting to satisfy the boys' demands for revenge while avoiding overt conflict. Elaborate plans for attack were made but never carried out. The incident was a focal point of group activity for some time.

Here the provocation to aggression was aggression against group members, including the leader of the criminal clique. The fact that the criminal leader was among the victims perhaps made this a case of extreme provocation for the criminal clique. Certainly this was not simply a case of a leader's reaction to a threat to his *leadership* status. But neither can it be understood simply as retaliatory aggression. The aggressors against the boys were young men. Perhaps this was threatening in a manner which would not have been characteristic of aggression from another gang. In either case, retaliation would have been prescribed in this lower class cultural context. But the attack from adults—to whose status these boys aspire—was especially resented for it cast aspersions on their masculinity and relegated them to the status of "kids."

Status Threats, the External Environment, and Status Mechanisms within the Group

The status threat hypothesis now may be seen as a special case of the more general status argument. Note, however, that the locus of status concern has shifted from the social class system of the larger society to the face-to-face relationships of boys within a gang. We do not doubt that external systems are involved in problems of status management. Clearly they are. There appear to be at least three levels of such involvement:

(1) *Adult sponsored and controlled institutions of the larger society*, such as in schools, places of employment, and conventional social agencies, and in relations with the police and other functionaries representing adult "authority." These tend to be "middle class" in orientation in the sense specified by Cohen—that is, their criteria of status are based upon contributions of hard work, deferred gratification, and impulse control, and achievement of such objectives as good grades, exemplary conduct, saving one's money, and demonstrating leadership ability in conventional institutional endeavor. We do not have good observational data at this level, but we know that our gang boys have poorer school adjustment and worse police records than do nongang boys from their neighborhoods. They have very poor job adjustments, and local social agencies by and large find them very difficult to "reach" or serve in any way consistently. In all these aspects it appears that gang boys, more than other boys we have studied, have failed to achieve according to relevant institutional standards. The hypothesis that gang boys have found these institutions inadequate for their status needs is therefore not inconsistent with our data. The precise nature of these relationships is not clear from our data, however, and in any case independent data suggest that the boys are less "alienated" from conventional institutions generally than the reaction formation hypothesis would suggest. Consideration of two other external system levels may be even more appropriate to an understanding of gang boys' behavior than is this larger institutional level.

(2) *Lower class community "institutions"* in which gang boys participate, individually and collectively. Reference here is to encounters with lower class adults in quarter parties and pool halls (see Chapter 5), and in the informal neighboring and partying which is a part of everyday life, in Negro lower class areas in particular. The

counterpart in many white areas is the hierarchy of male social and athletic clubs, and the obvious social and political power, which are manifested by adults in the rackets and in politics.[8] The latter is emerging in the Negro community, but it is much less well established as a community tradition for Negroes.

Kobrin *et al.* studied seven street groups in a relatively stable mixed ethnic community where criminal and conventional elements were "integrated" among the dominant white (Italian) group in the manner described by Cloward and Ohlin.[9] Among these groups a hierarchy of status existed in which such ascribed status characteristics as ethnic identity, family power, and residential location were found to be as important in determining a group's status as were achieved status criteria such as fighting ability, notoriety, organizational competence, and sports competence.

Further, rankings on ascribed criteria were *more stable* than were rankings of achieved criteria. There was a high degree of consensus among group members, street workers, and other adult judges that in this community a group of "sophisticated delinquents" of Italian extraction, with family involvement in political organization and residing solely on "Italian streets," had the highest prestige of all groups. These boys ranked first also in sports competence, second in notoriety, but only third in fighting ability and organizational competence. Other delinquent groups in this community were less favored by ascribed status criteria and they were "notably unstable in their ranks on achieved status." The lowest-ranking group in terms of ascribed status ranked highest in fighting ability and notoriety, but very low in organizational and sports competence. This interplay of adult- and adolescent-status criteria in a more stable white community suggests a type of integration between group processes and the adult community, which supplements in important ways our more extensive information on Negro communities.

It is in such encounters at this level, for both Negro and white boys, that standards of adult behavior which are most appropriate to everyday life for the boys are inferred and directly inculcated. This

---

[8] See William Foote Whyte, *Street Corner Society* (Chicago: University of Chicago Press, 1943; 2d ed., 1955); and Solomon Kobrin, "Sociological Aspects of the Development of a Street Corner Group: An Exploratory Study," *American Journal of Orthopsychiatry*, XXXI (October, 1961), 685–702.

[9] Solomon Kobrin, Joseph Puntil, and Emil Peluso, "Criteria of Status among Street Gangs," paper read at the annual meetings of the American Sociological Association, 1963.

is the level to which the theory of "delinquency and opportunity" is addressed. And it is at this level that differences in the character of adult-adolescent relations, between "integrated" and "unintegrated" communities occur. Here observation strongly suggests that the gang boys recognize and respect the exercise of power at the local community level, whether it stems from legitimate or illegitimate sources. In most of these communities there is no such dramatic demonstration of legitimate power as frequently occurs in the illegitimate domain; witness the numerous gang-style slayings of hoodlums, and occasionally even of politicians. The byword among both Negro and white-gang boys is that "you can't beat the syndicate."

There are real differences in adult-adolescent relations among the communities under study, however. While their documentation is incomplete in our data, the following observations seem warranted. The "gap" between adolescents and adults is greater, but age-graded steps for achieving adulthood are more clearly demarcated in white than in Negro communities. This is true both in an "integrated" white community where acknowledged syndicate figures and their relatives are involved in local politics and business, and in a lower middle class white community where criminal elements apparently are not powerful locally. By contrast, in lower class Negro communities where petty crime, small-time "professional" burglary and robbery, drug traffic, and policy are rampant, neither legitimate nor criminal local adults are powerful politically, and economic affluence is illusive and undependable. Here the institutional structures for separating adults and adolescents appear to have broken down or never to have existed. There is competition among all age levels for excitement wherever it may be found—from a bottle, a battle, or a broad. Poolhalls are habituated by young and old alike, and it is hard to tell where life in the street leaves off and formal institutional life beings. In Homans' terms, a greater portion of behavior is "subinstitutional" than is the case in the white communities. We are inclined to attribute this to the lack of institutional organization and of formal institutionalized power. With Cloward and Ohlin, we expect this situation to change, as institutionalized power, both legitimate and illegitimate, increases in Negro communities. In the meantime, however, it is lacking, and the lack is compounded by fear and suspicion among themselves and of outsiders, both white and Negro, which is endemic among lower class Negroes.[10]

[10] Drake and Cayton comment extensively on the "ritual condemnation" of whites, high-status Negroes, and themselves which constantly recurs among lower

The precipitation of particular delinquency episodes cannot be understood solely or even primarily as a result of the functioning of this second level of the external environment of the gang. For conflict-oriented gangs in particular, the third level is of great significance.

(3) *The adolescent gang world,* with its networks of horizontal (across communities, e.g., East Side Cobras and West Side Cobras) and vertical (roughly age-graded, in the same community, e.g., Senior, Junior, and Midget) segments of a gang. It is almost definitional of conflict gangs that their destiny in some measure is controlled by the actions of other gangs or expectations thereof. Problems of status management are governed to some considerable extent by the state of feud or peace existing between rival gangs, by the threat of new gangs aspiring to ascendancy among local gangs, etc. Under conditions of threat from rival gangs (or of local adults at the second level, as witness the case of the "thieves" reported above), the criminal purpose of a clique or gang may be temporarily forgotten and replaced by aggressive goals.[11]

The gang is important in the resolution of status problems generated at each of these levels of the external environment. Indeed, it is their common concern with relationships at these levels which provides much of the *raison d'être* of the gang. Each level may, in turn, serve status-maintaining mechanisms within the group, as when a boy's defiance of the police, vandalism of a local institution, or "heart" in a skirmish with another gang enhances his status in the gang. The existence of the gang is crucial to an understanding of the manner in which status management is carried out by gang boys regardless of whether the threat originated from within or outside the group. The gang provides the audience for much of the acting out which occurs in situations involving elements external to the group, and it is the most immediate system of rewards and punishments to which members are responsive much of the time. It is the stimulation

---

class Negroes. Conversely, high-status Negroes decry the style of life of lower class Negroes. St. Clair Drake and Horace R. Cayton, *Black Metropolis: A Study of Negro Life in a Northern City* (Vol. II, New York: Harper and Row, 1962). Wilson remarks that among many thoughtful Negroes, "Expressions of distrust, cynicism, and even hostility against other Negroes are not infrequently encountered. The extent to which there is widespread private criticism by Negroes of Negroes as a race is remarkable, and more and more this criticism is being made public." James Q. Wilson, *Negro Politics: The Search for Leadership* (Glencoe: The Free Press, 1959), p. 5.

[11] See also Herbert A. Bloch and Arthur Niederhoffer, *The Gang, a Study in Adolescent Behavior* (New York: Philosophical Library, 1958), Part IV.

of relationships within the gang, or in any case involving other gang members, which most often precipitates delinquent episodes. Aspects of the external environment which are immediately relevant to delinquent episodes most often involve the levels of local community relationships and the gang world. At each level behavior, including delinquent behavior, arises in the course of patterns of interaction in the pursuit of in-process rewards of such interaction. The latter, it is apparent, often involve status concerns of gang boys, status within the gang and with respect to objects and activities valued by the gang.

CHAPTER 10

Explorations of Social Disability, Class, and Gang Status

In his classic analysis of street-corner society, Whyte quotes Doc as follows:

Fellows around here don't know what to do except within a radius of about three hundred yards. That's the truth, Bill. They come home from work, hang on the corner, go up to eat, back on the corner, up a show, and they come back to hang on the corner. If they're not on the corner, it's likely the boys there will know where you can find them. Most of them stick to one corner. It's only rarely that a fellow will change his corner.[1]

Whyte's comment is that, "The stable composition of the group and the lack of social assurance on the part of its members contribute toward producing a very high rate of social interaction within the group. The group structure is a product of this interaction." He continues, "Out of such interaction there arises a system of mutual obligations which is fundamental to group cohesion."

Whyte attributes corner boys' lack of social assurance to the limited range of social experiences of corner boys, with attendant rigidity in behavior patterning.

Each individual has his own characteristic way of interacting with other individuals. This is probably fixed within wide limits by his native endowment, but it develops and takes its individual form through the experiences of the individual in interacting with others throughout the course of his life. Twentieth-century American life demands a high degree of flexibility of action from the individual, and the normal person learns to adjust within certain limits to changes in the frequency and type of his interactions with others. This flexibility can be developed only through experiencing a wide variety of situations which require adjustment to

[1] William Foote Whyte, *Street Corner Society* (2d ed., 1955; Chicago: University of Chicago Press), p. 256.

different patterns of interaction. *The more limited the individual's experience, the more rigid his manner of interacting, and the more difficult his adjustment when changes are forced upon him.* (Italics added.) . . . gang activities proceed from day to day in a remarkably fixed pattern. The members come together every day and interact with a very high frequency. Whether he is at the top and originates action for the group in set events, is in the middle and follows the origination of the leader and originates for those below him, or is at the bottom of the group and always follows in set events, the individual member has a way of interaction which remains stable and fixed through continual group activity over a long period of time. His mental well-being requires continuance of his way of interacting. He needs the customary channels for his activity, and, when they are lacking, he is disturbed.[2]

While the nature of the disability (lack of social assurance) is similar among gang youngsters in the present study, its etiology appears to be different. Certainly the lack cannot be attributed to intensity and rigidity of interaction patterns with the same group. For the gang boys these patterns are not stable enough to produce such rigidity. There can be little doubt, however, that the gang boys also lack the variety of experience which increases role playing ability.

Doc's first point, at the beginning of this chapter, is apposite. The range of gang boys' physical movements is severely restricted. They are ill at ease when outside their "area," in part because of fear that they may infringe on a rival gang's territory, but in part due also to a more general lack of social assurance such as that to which Whyte refers. Without the base of stable composition of the group, the rate of social interaction within our gangs is lower than was the case with Whyte's corner groups. Mutual obligations, therefore, are tenuous among most gang members and, hence, according to the argument, group cohesion is low.

Excerpts from a detached worker's interview illustrate both the low degree of mutual obligation among gang members outside the arena of immediate interaction, and the sensitivity of one gang leader to the lack of social assurance of fellow gang members and of his girl friend. This leader clearly was more in command of the social graces than were the others, and he realized this fact, but the worker suggests that the leader, too, needed bolstering in this regard. In the following excerpt the worker is discussing his negotiations with Duke,

[2] *Ibid.*, pp. 263–64.

leader of the King Rattlers, concerning the disposition of tickets for the annual banquet of the YMCA of Metropolitan Chicago.[3]

A: When I first started thinking about the annual YMCA banquet, I knew I'd be able to get about five tickets, and I had planned on taking three boys and using the other two myself. I talked it over with Duke. First thing Duke suggested, he wanted me to get him a date with one of the YMCA girls from the downtown office. . . . I told him I thought maybe he'd be better anyway to take Elaine because. . . "You've never actually taken Elaine anywhere of importance. You've taken her to the show, but she's never been to a downtown affair."

Q: Is Elaine the girl who has Duke's two children?

A: She has a baby girl who is a year old and one that's three. Duke's never taken her to a real nice place, and I thought it would be nice if he asked her to go. He was real excited. "Okay, I'll ask her." So that was closed.

Then I had one extra ticket. I said, "Well, Duke, seeing that you and Butch get along real well, maybe Butch would go."

The first thing Duke said was, "No, no, we don't want to take Butch because he doesn't know how to eat out in company."

So naturally I smiled and said, "Crisake, he knows just as much as you do."

"No, he just don't know how to eat out in company."

Then he went all the way back to the time I took them to the Prudential Building. I suggested that we go in and get a cup of coffee, but Butch said, "No, we'd better go back to the area [home territory] and get a hot dog or Polish [sausage]." And Duke was all for it, too, because he didn't want to go in there either. On the "Top of the Rock" they did their sight seeing, but they didn't want to go into the little restaurant and get coffee. They didn't feel they were dressed, or something. They're real shy about going into a strange place that's real nice.

Earlier in the summer I took Duke, Butch, and Harry out to Lake Meadows, and they were real shy. They didn't want to go in because they felt they weren't dressed good enough. But I made them go in and at least have a cup of coffee. We went early. They had a little combo and I figured a guy could sit and listen to them play for maybe half an hour and drink coffee. 'Course, they went in the restaurant part. They didn't go in the other side where you can really hear the combo. They all felt the same way—they weren't dressed good enough.

Anyway, Duke didn't feel Butch was qualified. So I smiled and said, "Okay, how about Harry?"

"Hell no. Harry hasn't got enough clothes to go."

[3] Interview (Dryden), 2/11/60.

Harry only has one suit. I had mentioned the banquet to him earlier in the week, but he didn't know whether or not he could go—meaning that he didn't know whether he could get his suit out [of hock or the cleaners]. He didn't know whether he'd have any money. But Duke felt so strong about Butch's not going that I didn't push Harry. So I dropped it, and that was it.

On the way over there I did as much talking as I could about the meeting. I told them approximately what was going to go on, about the main speaker being President Eisenhower's doctor, and that there would be a lot of skits from the different YMCA's in the Metropolitan area. When we got to the amphitheater, I dropped Elaine, Alice [Duke's aunt and the worker's date for the evening], and Duke and I went to park the car. Duke asked me if I would pick him up a pack of cigarettes, so I told him I would. I told him to go in and check the coats. He looked around and finally came back because he didn't know where they were supposed to go. Then I found the tables and I put Duke and Elaine together.

Q: Did Duke comment at all about anybody else at the table or about the dinner?

A: Over-all, he had a real good time. He told his aunt and grandmother that he met Mrs. Hoot, or something like that. Really it was Mrs. Shoup. She's chairman of the Women's Auxiliary Board. I told Duke after we had left the amphitheater coming home that Mrs. Shoup has got enough money to bury you. What I meant was she is a good woman to know.

Also, I pointed out Mr. Grammercy. He was up on the stage and I wanted him to meet Duke real bad, because I told Duke quite a bit about Mr. Grammercy before—about his apartment on the north shore where I think he pays something like $1,700 a month. I wanted him to meet Mr. Grammercy real bad, but we couldn't meet him. I told him later on maybe I'd be able to introduce him.

Elaine complained because Duke insulted her and she couldn't eat her meat. Duke was trying to show her how to cut the meat. He said Elaine didn't know which hand to hold the knife in. She was real hungry and she ate everything but the meat, because Duke was rapping on her so much.

Q: I wondered why she kept looking around the table. She was very self-conscious.

A: Right. She felt real bad for not having eaten the meat. She didn't know whether it would have been appropriate to have Duke cut her meat or not. Duke said the meat was so tender he could cut it with his fork.

Duke and his girl friend were noticeably silent throughout the YMCA banquet. The accident of seating arrangements found them sitting at a table adjacent to the one where the worker sat. They never initiated conversation with the half dozen other guests at their table, and their responses to others' conversational efforts were brief and subdued. Throughout, Elaine seemed cowed by the experience, Duke less so, but obviously at some pains not to make a behavioral miscue. The two exchanged meaningful glances with one another during the course of the meal and the entertainment which followed. Their behavior was stiff and uncertain, quite in contrast to the generally relaxed and friendly atmosphere of the crowd.

Social Disability, Values, and That Old Gang of Mine

The lack of social assurance of gang boys was apparent from our very first contact with them and with the YMCA Program for Detached Workers. Workers reported frequently that their boys did not feel comfortable outside "the area" and that they were ill at ease in most social situations outside the gang context. It was an extension of the analysis of semantic differential data reported in Chapter 3, however, and an interpretation of data from a motivation opinionaire which directed our attention to an apparent lack of gratification even of gang membership and interaction, and hence to a hypothesis concerning a fundamental lack of social skills on the part of gang boys which seems even more crucial to an understanding of their behavior than does lack of social assurance.[4] It may be recalled from Chapter 3 that Negro gang boys evaluated "someone who is a member of your GANG" lower than did other boys, and also showed a greater tendency to evaluate themselves (SELF) higher than GANG. Even more revealing of gang boys' ambivalence concerning their peers, however, was a tendency, relative to the other boys, to endorse such apparently conflicting statements as: "Friends are generally more trouble than they are worth" and "You can only be really alive when you are with friends." In the treatment which follows we will attribute this apparent ambivalence to mutually reinforcing characteristics of gang boys, individually and collectively, which may be summarized in the term "social disability."

The coping ability of gang boys and their confidence in themselves —significant "social abilities"—may well be reflected in the disparity of private vs. gang values and behavior noted in Chapters 2 and 3. The disparity concerning the boys' individual and collective *family*

---

[4] As reported in Robert A. Gordon, "Social Level, Social Disability, and Gang Interaction," an unpublished paper being prepared for publication.

attitudes, and their individual attitudes and subsequent behavior is paralleled by similar observations concerning the world of *work*. On two widely separated occasions the following observations were made:

1. Fred commented on the similarity of his experience while conducting the family interviews with the Chiefs and a recent incident in the same area. Fuzzhead, a regular but low-status member of the Chiefs, approached Fred in a pool hall hangout and began to talk very seriously about his plans to get and keep a job so that he could provide for the girl he wanted to marry. Fred probed Fuzzhead and, finding him deadly in earnest, encouraged the boy in these ambitions and indicated his willingness to help him secure a steady job. In the midst of the conversation other Chiefs entered the pool hall and came over to where Fred and Fuzzhead were conversing. Upon discovering the topic of conversation they began ridiculing Fuzzhead's ambitions. Fuzzhead abruptly discontinued this discussion and despite Fred's encouraging words withdrew from the conversation.

2. This was my last field trip into the gang areas. Fred and I went first through the Chiefs' area where we found Billy sitting on a chair on the sidewalk in front of a pool hall, with one of his (illegitimate) children on his lap. I recalled his prophecy more than three years earlier that such a fate might come to pass.[5] Fred joshed with Billy about his failure to hold a job, and Billy, in turn, tried without success to borrow money from Fred. He allowed as how his "old lady" would give him some money.

   While we were chatting with Billy, others in the old Chiefs gang came on the scene. One of the boys pulled Fred off to one side and began telling him that he planned to get married but that he wanted to have a steady job first. Fred was skeptical but encouraging. When the other boys caught the drift of the conversation they began immediately to "razz" the boy concerning his ability to attract and support a wife. The boy dropped the subject completely.[6]

These boys' prospects for steady jobs were poor, despite their sincere desires and intentions. In addition to the instability of that segment of the labor market for which they were qualified, their associations on the street, even though the gang hardly existed any longer (as was the case with the Chiefs in the summer of 1962), was a deterring and disruptive influence. The influence of the gang clearly cannot be explained as a reaction formation against middle class val-

---

[5] Chapter 2, p. 47. Then Billy said, "Let me shut up 'cause I might be out walkin' my baby. You, too, Henry."

[6] Field report, August, 1962.

ues, nor can it, we believe, in terms of "delinquent norms." Boys in our gangs often were actively discouraged from the expression of conventional values in the gang context, chiefly by derision of individual ambitions and abilities, and espousal of group goals which were alternative but not necessarily anticonventional. Boys "rapped" with girls, and their choice of mates might be derided, but if a boy persisted in his choice and was successful, other members of the gang accepted the situation. Marriage was not tabu, as witness the marriages (common-law and conventional) of many active gang boys, but "making out with the broads" was a greater value on the street.

So, too, with employment. Detached workers were barraged by requests for jobs, but "hustles" of great variety were bragged about on the streets. Boys who had jobs were not derided for this fact—the Y program practice of giving favored treatment to gang leaders in securing jobs may have been a factor here—but life on the street was far removed from life on the job, and boys who were working knew full well that street life continued, whether or not they were there. One of the problems for these boys is the fact that the job as such is not an acceptable status alternative to the gang. For these boys the job situation is likely to be alien to those experiences he finds most rewarding. An example is the suspicion (in many cases justified) which gang boys experience on the part of plant security personnel:[7]

Ringo: Them plant policemen—you go down the hall, they ask you, "You got identification?" and "You work here?" and all that . . . well, I mean, they see you come into the building every morning and leave.

Jones: Like you're convicts, man.

Ringo: I told him, look here man, I ain't never been in no trouble.

Cooper: That's worse than being in the place [jail], isn't it?

Ringo: Yeah.

Cooper: At least in the place they don't ask you for no I.D.

Ringo: They know you're going to have your identification card.

Ross: Don't you think this is part of his job?

[7] "Youth Consultant Symposium on Jobs," YMCA of Metropolitan Chicago, mimeographed (spring, 1962). In the interview Ringo and Jones are gang boys, eighteen and nineteen years old, both with job experience through the Program for Detached Workers, both with unstable job histories. Both are core gang members, having occupied positions of considerable influence and leadership. Ringo, the youngest of the two, is married. Jones is single. Charles N. Cooper is Assistant Director of the Program for Detached Workers, and Benjamin Ross has at various times been a detached worker, Field Supervisor, and Employment Coordinator with the program.

Jones: What, to be bugging people all the time?

Ross: What would you do if you had the gig [job], would you sit up there and cool it?

Jones: Man, if you know I'm working here . . .

Ross: I mean, how many people they got working there?

Jones: Man, I don't know.

Ringo: Well, I know they've got lots of workers there . . .

Jones: The man, he knows who he wants to pick on. Now like I see you, Benny, if you don't look right, you look like you're going to do something wrong, well lookit, I'm not going to forget you, Jack. I guess that's the way we look to him.

Jobs for these boys tend to be neither challenging nor very well paid. When one of these conditions is improved, the other may cause trouble:

Ross: Have we ever gotten you a job that you think you might have stayed on for the rest of your life?

Jones: Yeah, this job at the laboratory, I was working at, was a nice job. I was learning how to do most of the things, and as I worked I was gradually catching onto everything and I took interest in it, but it was a small company. Well, it wasn't paying much from the start. Vallis explained that to me, and when I went for an interview with the owner of the company, he told me that it was a small company but that I would be starting with the company and I could grow with the company, and he said that in the first three months I would get a raise, and then after the first six months I'd get a raise. I think I worked about four and a half months and I was looking for my raise . . .

Ross: What happened?

Jones: The cat, he says, "All right, all right, tomorrow." Two weeks later he gave me a nickel raise. About then it was time for me to get the second raise, my six-month raise. And he fired me.

Ross: Why did he fire you?

Jones: I was getting on the cat's back.

Cooper: You got your first raise.

Jones: About thirty-eight dollars. I was making about $1.20. I was making thirty-six at first, my take home pay. And he gave me a nickel raise.[8]

[8] The notion that one should "live fast, die young, and leave a beautiful corpse" might be romantically attractive to a few gang boys, but it would also be regarded as the height of folly. The very few boys who persist in extreme aggression or other dangerous exploits are regarded generally as "crazy" by the other boys.

Even in the rare cases when pay is adequate, job challenging, and with a good future, the lure of the gang may spell disaster. In the spring of 1962 the director of the Program for Detached Workers reflected that after three years not one of the Chiefs was employed, despite the fact that every one of them had been employed at one time or another, some two or three times through efforts of the employment coordinator. This was sheer frustration for the director, who had worked hard and well with these boys when he was their worker, later as field supervisor, and now as director of the Program. He was especially disappointed with Walter, one of two high school graduates among the Chiefs. Walter was a likeable boy, not given to aggression or excess as were many of his fellow Chiefs. The Program had secured for him a good paying job at a large cosmetics firm, and he had impressed his employer and other workers with his industry. After awhile, however, he began to be tardy and he missed work a few days. As a consequence, he was fired. Said the director, "Walter was always one of the boys. It's hard for such a guy to make it. Only the guys who stay on the fringe of the gang, or leave it altogether, have much of a chance to make it."

Gang boys do not reject the validity of job responsibilities, but life on the streets is not conducive to meeting these responsibilities:

Ross: Suppose you had a factory gig for yourself and you say I'm going to hire me some studs, give them a break because I know how it was when I was coming up, and you hire these cats. What would you expect of them?

Jones: I'd expect them to get there on time and do their work.

Ross: And if they didn't, what would you do?

Jones: Fire them.

Ross: Would you give them a break, would you talk to them or what?

Jones: That's understood—I'd talk to them.

Ross: For how long? Or would you walk in and tell the cat, "Look baby, if you're late one more day, you going to be in the wind; I ain't paying you for coming in late."

Jones: If a person is a nice worker, even if he does come in late, if he can get his work out and not slacking on the job, I don't give a damn what time he got there.

Here Jones clearly indicates his lack of awareness or appreciation of the interdependence of tasks in modern industry—a not too abstract idea, but one very little understood by these boys.

Ross: What would you do in the case of Smith? This joker went down to the gig and the first night he stood around and he looked, 'cause you figure he's learning. And the second night he went down and looked, and you figure he's still learning. And the third night, and he stood in the same spot, and he looked . . . would you fire him?

Jones: I'd give that cat a week's pay and tell him to leave town.

Ross: So what you're trying to tell me is that the cats do not miss the gigs on Monday morning because they tore up [got drunk].

Jones: Aw, maybe on a Monday.

Ross: But not during the rest of the week.

Jones: There you go. Once you get past Monday, Benny . . .

Cooper: You're just liable to make it.

Ross: What did Billy tell me the other night? "I know damn well I'm going to make it tomorrow because it's Friday and Friday is pay day." But you will miss a Monday morning or be late on Monday morning?

Jones: Well, you're trying to get over a weekend, drunk or whatever you've been doing. Especially, Jack, if those broads have been keeping you up all night.

Ross: It ain't always the Thunderbird, sometimes it's them broads.

A dependable supply of money is seductive, however, and even the gang *may* exert a favorable influence on job *getting,* if not on job stability:

Ross: This is what I wanted to ask you . . . Do you get some group pressure, you know, like Billy. I'd have swore up and down that Billy would never get a job. Do you think that Billy got a job because the rest of the fellas were working around there and he sort of got bugged or something?

Jones: They are riding Billy too hard, you see; Billy is a person that loves money. He'll do anything, even work.

Ross: That's what I was trying to find out, you know, if with the majority of the cats working, do you feel like maybe this makes the rest of them want to work. If there ain't nobody working, then the rest of the cats want to quit their jobs.

Ringo: If everybody's working, then they'll try to get a job. If you're out loafing, they're with you; if they've got somebody to drink with, they're with you.

* * *

Jones: Once you get used to that money coming in once a week, Jack, it's hard to get over.

Ringo: If you think that you are going to work next week or something, you ain't worried. But when you get fired and ain't got nothing coming in, that's the time to worry.

Jones: Boy, that money is habit-forming, Jack.

Finally, family responsibilities, when they are taken seriously, influence employment attitudes of gang boys just as anyone else:

Ross: Do you have any kids?

Ringo: One.

Ross: Is your wife working?

Ringo: Nope.

Ross: How long you been out of work—three days?

Ringo: Three days. I went out to Mailway, Carson Pirie and Scott. I'm in the habit of working now—I don't feel right just freeloading no more.

Ross: Did you talk to Vallis (employment coordinator) yet?

Ringo: No, Al (detached worker) has been talking to Vallis. He's been down two days straight, you know. Vallis sent word he's going to try to do something for me. I was thinking about going to the relief board for a couple of days, you know. Around about Christmas time, too, you know. My old lady she just got out of the hospital; she wants this, she wants that . . .

Ross: How old is the baby?

Ringo: About five weeks.

But, the "glamour" of family responsibilities is short-lived. The harsh realities of "making both ends meet" with low wages and minimal skills soon assert themselves. A young husband and father, even with the best intentions, is likely to chafe under restrictions imposed by wife and family. The lure of the street is not easily forgotten, and it is culturally supported.

There is no reason to believe that gang boys' performance on the semantic differential and their behavior in conversation with detached workers is any less real than are gang norms and behavior. Indeed it is quite possible that the boys' abstract evaluations of conventional and deviant images and their earnest discussions of the future with detached workers are in a sense "more real" than is the culture of the gang. With very rare exceptions, even the most ardent gang boys do not conceive of the gang as "forever." Much of gang behavior represents a striving toward *adult* status, and older gang boys soon come to put down gang fighting as "kid stuff." Other forms of delinquency which may be more integral to their particular form of lower class culture are not so easily put down, as we have seen. Harsh reality intervenes, also, to make conventional adjustments difficult to achieve. It is easier as well as more status-giving to continue the gang ways and the ways of lower class culture, particularly for boys who possess few of the skills which equip them for achievement outside of these systems and for boys caught up in the status system of the gang.

The apparent paradox of gang boys' allegiance to competing value systems really is not a paradox at all. Their coping ethic simply confirms that value systems do not apply consistently to all situations, or to all roles. Different situations and different roles require different values and different behavior patterns. The reality of contradictory value systems, so endemic to modern society, is especially acute for adolescents who must learn abruptly that they are no longer children and that they are supposed to behave as young men and women while foregoing many of the privileges of adulthood. The ambivalence of adolescents generally, and of gang boys in particular, with respect to parental values, for example, is attested to by a host of studies, past and present. Like Shaw's "jack roller," many adolescents long both for nurturance and security, and for freedom and adventure.[9]

The relation between values and behavior is further complicated by a time perspective. It may be useful if we conceptualize gang life as a *career phase*, much as did Shaw earlier and in the terms of reference of the literature on professions.[10] Thus, for example, Becker *et al.*[11] report that medical students talked idealistically of the medical profession when they were alone with the investigators but they

[9] See Clifford R. Shaw, *The Jack-Roller: A Delinquent Boy's Own Story* (Chicago: University of Chicago Press, 1930). Cf. Erik H. Erikson, *Childhood and Society* (New York: W. W. Norton Co., 1950); Frederick Elkin and William Westley, "The Myth of Adolescent Culture," *American Sociological Review*, XX (1955), 680–84; S. B. Withey and E. Douvan, *A Study of Adolescent Boys* (Ann Arbor: University of Michigan, Survey Research Center, 1955); E. Douvan and C. Kaye, *Adolescent Girls* (Ann Arbor: University of Michigan, Survey Research Center, 1957); and James Coleman, *The Adolescent Society* (New York: Free Press of Glencoe, Ill., 1961).

[10] See Clifford R. Shaw, *The Natural History of a Delinquent Career* (Chicago: University of Chicago Press, 1931); cf. Sutherland and Cressey's discussion of "Behavior Systems in Crime," in Edwin H. Sutherland, *Principles of Criminology*, rev. by Donald R. Cressey (6th ed.; New York: J. B. Lippincott Co., 1960).

[11] See Howard S. Becker, Blanche Geer, Everett C. Hughes, and Anselm Strauss, *Boys in White: Student Culture in Medical School* (Chicago: University of Chicago Press, 1961).

never did so when other medical students were around. Idealism was an important factor in their choice of medicine as a career and in terms of their hopes and aspirations for the future. Some problems of student life and their later decisions concerning the choice of general practice or medical specialty would call forth other, sometimes quite different, values. In all of this the candor of the medical students seemed unquestionable.

A basic difference between gang boys and medical students is that for gang boys career phases are less clearly demarcated, and commitment to or involvement in gang life hampers achievement of values held with respect to future phases. For medical students each phase equips for the next—they "grow into" successive stages. Gang boys are expected to "grow out of" gang life and into adaptations for which the gang in many respects has been poor preparation. This is not to deny Miller's contention that certain aspects of gang life are functional to subsequent lower class adult life:

Some school-connected experiences such as football—with its long, tedious practice periods and drills, interspersed with a weekly battle that calls for a sharp focus of all physical skills and strength in concentrated measure and for a short duration—find analogies in lower class life and in certain kinds of lower-class occupational roles. A dull, slow, and typical week in this subculture frequently culminates in a "night out on the town" and by "hanging one on." It should also be noted that a substantial portion of the labor force today (about 50 per cent) still consists of laborers, unskilled workers, and routine factory operatives. Most of these jobs are filled by lower-class individuals. Graduates of the street corner, as they grow and assume their roles in the world of work, have been prepared to operate within these interactional milieus, for their street-corner and occupational groups share similar sets of ideas, principles, and values. The job routines of the fireman, trucker, soldier, sailor, logger, and policeman reflect the occupational rhythmic pattern characteristic of lower-class community living, street-corner activity, and football—long periods of routine activity broken by intense action and excitement. As one views occupational needs of the future and, at the same time, analyzes the prevailing features of street-corner society, the following conclusion emerges: *The essential outlines, values, and language patterns; the emphasis on "smartness"; the regard for strength and physical prowess, all appear to remain functional, adjustive, and adaptive for these youngsters.*[12]

[12] William C. Kvaraceus, Walter B. Miller, *et al.*, *Delinquent Behavior: Culture and the Individual* (New York: National Education Association of the United States, 1959).

Gang life is not conducive to punctuality, dependability on the job every day, discipline, and consistency in job performance, however— all basic requirements of modern industry and of the jobs to which Miller refers. To the extent that the gang is delinquent, or defined as such by the larger community, its "rep" may damage the prospects for conventional job and other types of adjustments. Thus, a gang leader complained to the Program for Detached Workers that he had been picked up by the police and held in jail for several days "on suspicion" of a crime for which he was in no way responsible. The young man admitted that his *past* behavior may have warranted the suspicion, but this did not alter the fact that the police action placed his current job in jeopardy.

The failure of individuals to make satisfactory adjustments in any institutional sphere inevitably handicaps their ability to achieve future goals. Our gang boys fail often in school, on the job, in conventional youth-serving agencies, and in the eyes of law enforcement officials (and therefore in the public eye). They fail more often in each of these respects than do the non-gang boys we have studied, both middle and lower class. These failures, combined with limited social and technical skills, and blocked legitimate opportunities, constitute an overwhelming handicap for the achievement of the goals they endorse.

It is possible at this time to add to the social disability hypothesis preliminary observations from the personality assessment and one general observation of gang boys compared with other boys studied. From the former, data suggest that gang boys are less self-assertive (in this conventional test-like situation), they are more reactive to false signals than are the other boys, they tend to be slightly more neurotic and anxious, less gregarious, and more narcistic.[13] The possible cumulative effect of these differences is more impressive than are the individual findings, for they add up to boys who have less self-assurance and fewer of the qualities which engender confidence and nurturant relations with others. It seems likely that these characteristics heighten status insecurities of gang boys in many contexts. For example, our psychological testing team observed that gang boys were much more sensitive to how others were answering questions, completing instruments, and performing various tasks than

[13] From a report by Desmond S. Cartwright, "Psychological Test Differences Between Gang Boys and Others: Summary Prepared for Advisory Group Meeting" (August, 1962, dittoed).

were the other boys, and they appeared to be more anxious concerning their own performance relative to others. When we talked to gang boys about the research program, they indicated a special sensitivity to why *they* were being studied. We had to take special precautions in these respects, both to protect the anonymity and the integrity of responses and to assure gang boys that they were not being singled out for any peculiar and derogatory reason. Their public image is of concern to them and, like so many things, is a source of ambivalent feeling. Newspaper headlines and other mass-media references to the gang often are a source of prestige among and within gangs, but they are the *raison d'être* also for changes in gang names, e.g., from Vice Kings to Conservative Vice Kings, from Cobras to Executives.

It is unlikely that gang experience, with its constant challenge to boys to prove themselves tough, adept with the girls, "smart," etc., in any substantial way alleviates status insecurities or their related social disabilities except insofar as gang experience better equips boys to respond successfully to gang challenges. These skills are not calculated to enhance gang boys' status prospects outside the gang, however. And so the cycle is perpetuated.

The carefree image of "that old gang of mine" as a solidary group —all for one and one for all—and the notion that the gang prepares a youngster for adult roles, are tarnished, to say the least, by this interpretation. One suspects that this image derives from nostalgia concerning their own childhood of former members of gangs or of middle class individuals (including sociologists) whose interpersonal skills are more highly developed than are those of our gang boys. Careful observation of lower class gangs has been extremely limited and in most cases superficial. It is unlikely, for example, that Thrasher was able to receive more than a casual impression of the nature of interpersonal relations among the 1,313 Chicago gangs which he surveyed.[14] The romantic note sounded in discussions of the wanderings of gang boys away from home and school, and references to the hangout as the gang boy's castle may reflect the vicarious gratifications of adult investigators and their own childhood fantasies to a greater extent than they do the perspectives of gang members. To be sure, it is a mistake to read into the behavior of youngsters the motivations of adults, and elements of fantasy are involved in the behavior of gang boys today, as they were at the time of Thrasher's

[14] Frederic M. Thrasher, *The Gang* (Chicago: University of Chicago Press, 1936; abridged, with a new introduction by James F. Short, Jr., 1963).

classic study. But the behavior and the fantasies of gang members today are less like Sir Galahad and King Arthur and more like the power plays of syndicate hoodlums and racial bigots among their adult contemporaries.[15]

Thrasher was acutely sensitive to the necessity for accurate communication between adults and adolescents, and he urged that "to understand the gang boy one must enter into his world with a comprehension, on the one hand, of this seriousness behind his mask of flippancy or bravado, and on the other, of the role of the romantic in his activities and in his interpretation of the larger world of reality" (p. 96). Our quarrel with this interpretation is not that fantasy plays no role in the world view of gang youngsters, but that even these fantasies are sharply restricted by harsh realities of life and by the spectacular successes achieved by a very few,[16] rather than by fairy tales of an earlier and middle class generation. Hero worship, yes, but romantic fantasy, no.

Our argument, further, is that the "seriousness behind his mask of flippancy or bravado" reflects fundamental lacks in social skills and other socially rewarded abilities which are characteristic of the majority of gang boys. Far from being "blythe of heart for any adventure" (Thrasher, p. 86), there is among these boys a deadly serious character in their fantasies and even in their horseplay. And while their fantasies concerning gang membership and prowess may be adventurous, their fear of the world outside "the area" and of association with persons beyond the rather narrow circle of their acquaintance suggests the need for security as a motivation rather than new experiences.

While this argument varies considerably from Thrasher's *interpretations,* it is consistent with much of his data. Thrasher noted the generally unstable character of gang membership and structure, and the short-lived nature of many gangs. These facts, and the ability of gang boys to survive and find food and shelter by various means while wandering the city streets or otherwise away from home impressed Thrasher as evidence of their *independence.* It may be questioned, however, whether this type of existence was adequate preparation either for psychological maturity and general well-being, or for social and other skills. It should be emphasized that we are not arguing that the gang is devoid of play and interpersonal gratifica-

[15] Cf. Lewis Yablonsky, *The Violent Gang* (New York: Macmillan Co., 1962).
[16] Such as popular entertainers and sports figures, politicians, and hoodlums.

tions. Quite the contrary, it is likely that gang membership offers these youngsters a larger measure of these types of rewards than does any alternative form of association of which they are aware and which is available to them by virtue of preparation and other reality considerations. Many gangs have a history of long association, some extending over periods of more than a generation. Further, close and systematic observation of our most highly delinquent gangs reveals much camaraderie and genuine friendship. These are often very unstable, however, for a variety of reasons. There is, for example, the underlying tone of aggression which characterizes so much of the interaction within the gang. There is a threat which hangs over even the closest of friendships that one may have to prove oneself against one's friend, perhaps as a result of forces within the gang but extraneous to the friendship. Status within the gang is subject to challenge from many quarters, and status threat may disrupt even close friends. There is, over all, the atmosphere of mutual distrust of "insiders" as well as "outsiders" which pervades much of lower class culture. The gang boy is likely to come to the gang suspicious of the motives and the dependability of human relationships generally—a suspicion that carries over to the gang itself, and to which the gang contributes in terms both of interpersonal relations within the gang and external to it.

Yet the gang is not characterized by *desperation* in search of stable human relationships, nurturance, and security. It seems, rather, to have worked out a reasonably realistic solution to problems. The gang boy in many respects is a pragmatist, not "driven" to accept personal relationships which are less than satisfactory, but accepting them, nonetheless, with the expectation that while they may fail him, he will share in-process rewards which offer a considerable measure of gratification.

Similarly, with few exceptions, gang boys do not appear to be "driven" to the excesses involved in their delinquencies, e.g., aggression, alcohol, and sex. These, too, may be seen in part as situationally determined, arising in the course of interaction on the street. Once experienced, inherent gratifications may be pushed to extremes in part because other types of gratifications are so elusive and undependable. Only in our retreatist group did the boys seem "driven" to excess, in the sense that they were obsessed with the search for "kicks," through drugs in great variety and through personal experiences which carried a strong element of self-destruction—witness the character of their "lore" as described in Chapter 9. For the most part, however, the behavior of these boys appeared less determined by personal idiosyncrasies than by the demands of status and role within the context of the immediate situation. Their social abilities, or the lack of them, determine in important ways the nature of the problems to which they respond and the coping mechanisms at their disposal.

The Roots of Social Disability

The importance to personality development of relations with other persons is a much honored theme in the behavior sciences. From the perspective of role theory, however, interpersonal relations are involved not only in development of personality; in important ways, they come to *constitute* personality. Thus, Brim has noted, "that what is learned in socialization, is interpersonal relationships. To express it slightly differently, much of personality is learned interpersonal relations. . . ."[17]

Observations from an experimental nursery school for lower class Negro children at the University of Chicago suggest that at the age of four and one-half these children are less able to maintain nonaggressive close physical bodily contact with their age mates than are children from middle class homes. The early development of these children appears to be a product of a combination of harsh socialization practices, frequent cautions about a threatening environment, and little cognitive development or verbal skill.[18]

Variations in the socialization practices of these A.D.C. mothers were related to the popularity of the children among their peers and to I.Q. changes registered over the thirteen-week nursery school experience. The finding of most general interest from this study is that these two independent variables were very differently related to the character of the mothers' relations with their children.[19] Specifically, use of *verbal* (vs. physical) means of discipline was positively related to I.Q. gain, but unrelated to sociometric popularity; while children

[17] Orville J. Brim, "Socialization Through the Life Cycle," revision of a paper prepared for a conference on this topic, sponsored by the Social Science Research Council, May, 1963 (mimeographed).

[18] For preliminary documentation of this program, see Fred L. Strodtbeck, "The Reading Readiness Nursery: Short-Term Social Intervention Technique," Progress Report to the Social Security Administration (Project 124), the Social Psychology Laboratory, University of Chicago, August, 1963.

[19] *Ibid.* (1964).

with strict (vs. lax) mothers were popular but undifferentiated with respect to I.Q. gain. The irony in these relationships is that the rationale for strictness most often employed by these mothers is that they wish to help their children to do well in school. A factor described as maternal warmth and acceptance of dependency was negatively related to I.Q. gain, but positively associated with popularity. Aggressive children tended to be less well liked.

While it would be unwise to bridge so large a gap on the basis of such limited evidence, the similarity of observations concerning popularity among peers of lower class nursery school and gang youngsters is suggestive. Nurturant non-aggressive boys are rewarded with popularity. The fact that these characteristics are negatively related to I.Q. gain in the nursery school situation suggests still another reason for gang boys' poor performance in school. Caught between the need for friendship and for long-range gains in the form of institutionalized learning, the very young child is likely to choose the former. The aggressive child, on the other hand, is not likely to meet with favor on the part of harried teachers in overcrowded schools, and so does not achieve the gain made possible in the experimental nursery school situation.

Thus, while it cannot be doubted that later experiences in adolescent and adult groups give specific content and order to the display of aggression, and condition its provocation, this early linking of child socialization and aggressive posture suggests that aggressive behavior is not a simple function of later experiences. The early development of aggression as a characteristic means of interpersonal interaction, with its sociometric consequences, should they be confirmed by more systematic research, would add to observations of social disability which flow more directly from gang participation, whether of stable corner boys, à la Whyte, or of our more delinquent and less stable gangs.

The gang presents a boy with a dilemma similar to the school: group norms place a high value on toughness and the ability to fight, yet aggressive behavior waged injudiciously makes one unpopular with peers. To succeed within such narrow boundary conditions requires great skill indeed, skill which most of these boys lack. The "status game" tends not to be played well by these boys, but it *is played*, with gusto, most often in the form of body-punching, signifying, and other forms of pseudo-aggressive behavior— pseudo-aggressive because few boys are hurt in such encounters, despite their intensity. The game takes such a form, we argue, because the boys' social disabilities, compounded by status uncertainties, preclude other games requiring higher order skills.

A further hypothesis to account for the limited social skills of gang boys concerns the narrow range of their social experience within as well as outside the family. The two areas of experience are mutually reinforcing in this respect. The family does not equip the child with role-playing facility adequate to the demands of such institutions as the school, and unsatisfactory experiences in school further narrow the range of role-playing opportunities which later facilitate job success—"getting along" with employers and fellow workers, and more than this, "getting along" in new and strange situations generally. The ability to move easily from one role to another and to adjust rapidly to new situations is a much cultivated art in modern urban society, particularly among upwardly mobile persons. This ability is inculcated in their children by middle class parents at an early age, and this may prove to be one of the major differentiating areas of early family experience between gang and non-gang boys within the lower class. Certainly the range of favorable role-playing opportunities in school has proven to be greater among non-gang than gang boys. 15.3 per cent and 20.5 per cent of Negro and white lower class, non-gang boys, respectively, were found to have achieved successful school adjustment, compared to 9.9 per cent of the Negro and 9.5 per cent of the white gang boys. The contrast is even more striking with respect to *un*successful school adjustment: NLC = 22.5 per cent, WLC = 24.0 per cent, NG = 46.8 per cent, WG = 42.7 per cent.[20] The negative opportunities through unfavorable contacts with police, courts, and correctional institutions, and association with delinquent peers also have been greater for the gang boys.[21]

Middle class parents teach their children to be sensitive to behavioral requirements of a variety of situations—to role play in an appropriate manner even though the situation may be new to them. They are taught by example and by direction to be sensitive to the nuances of behavior expectations, to look for cues as to what is appropriate behavior and what is not. "Company" is different from

[20] The data are reported in Jonathan A. Freedman and Ramon J. Rivera, "Education, Social Class, and Patterns of Delinquency," paper read at the annual meetings of the American Sociological Association, 1962; and in James F. Short, Jr., "Gang Delinquency and Anomie," in *Anomie and Deviant Behavior*, Marshall B. Clinard, ed. (New York: The Free Press of Glencoe, Inc., 1964).

[21] The data are summarized in Chapter 12, Table 12.1.

"family," entertaining "the boss" is an important educational experience for it teaches socially approved means of relating to authority as well as something about situationally shifting requirements of dress and manners.

We cannot document systematic differentiation of gang from non-gang family experiences of this nature. In addition to the balance of favorable and unfavorable experience in other institutional contexts which was referred to above, however, we know also that more non-gang than gang boys of both races report having contact with high-status adults and they less often choose local (and therefore lower class) occupational role models than do the gang boys.[22] These are further indications of the broader range of social experiences shared by non-gang boys.

Intelligence. We may speak directly to the question of the intelligence of gang and non-gang boys. Whether or not differential experiences of this nature are responsible, it is the case that gang boys had lower scores on measured intelligence than did non-gang boys studied in the Chicago project. Intelligence was measured by a "culture free" method, a standardized arithmetic test, and by vocabulary, memory, and information tests designed especially so as not to bias the tests against lower class and gang subjects.[23] A general intelligence factor was extracted from intercorrelations of other tests. On all six intelligence measures available from these procedures, *gang boys scored lowest,* followed by lower class non-gang, and then by middle class boys. I.Q. estimates, based upon transformation of culture-free test scores for the six population groups are presented in Table 10.1.

[22] "High-status adults" were defined as those having occupations above the mean national socioeconomic (or occupational-prestige) level as determined by the Duncan index. See Ramon Rivera and James F. Short, Jr., "Occupational Goals: A Comparative Analysis," in *Juvenile Gangs in Context: Theory, Research, and Action,* Malcolm W. Klein and Barbara G. Myerhoff, eds. (Youth Studies Center, University of Southern California, Conference Report, 1964).

[23] Standard tests from the Institute for Personality and Ability Testing were employed. See R. B. Cattell and A. K. S. Cattell, *Handbook for the Culture Free Test of Intelligence,* Vol. II (Champaign, Ill.: University of Illinois Press, 1958); and R. B. Cattell *et al., Handbook for the Objective-Analytic Personality Batteries* (Champaign, Ill.: University of Illinois Press, 1955). Specially designed tests were prepared by Desmond S. Cartwright and Kenneth I. Howard. Findings are presented in greater detail in Kenneth I. Howard, Alan E. Hendrickson, and Desmond S. Cartwright, "Psychological Assessment of Street Corner Youth: Intelligence," unpublished manuscript, Youth Studies Program, University of Chicago, 1962.

These findings are impressive because of their consistency and the care with which the test program was developed and administered. They offer convincing evidence that the gang boys were disadvantaged with respect to intellectual ability of the sort which is rewarded by the institutions of conventional society. We need not enter into the nature-nurture controversy concerning measured intelligence. The point is that the school in particular, but other institutions as well, reward the "bright" child and that with respect to this variable, the gang boys are handicapped. Measured intelligence clearly cannot explain all of the variation in behavior among these boys, but it is an important component of the social disability of

TABLE 10.1

I.Q. ESTIMATES FOR LOWER CLASS GANG AND
NON-GANG BOYS, AND FOR MIDDLE
CLASS BOYS, BY RACE*

Social Class and Gang Status	Negro	White
Lower class gang..........	69.0	85.0
Lower class non-gang......	74.0	91.5
Middle class.............	96.5	111.0

* Adapted from Kenneth I. Howard, Alan E. Hendrickson, and Desmond S. Cartwright, "Psychological Assessment of Street Corner Youth: Intelligence," unpublished manuscript, Youth Studies Program, University of Chicago, 1962.

these boys.[24] That other factors influence selection for gang membership and behavior is equally clear from the very low I.Q. measure obtained for lower class, Negro non-gang boys.

Leaders, Girls, and Gangs. Whyte observed that among his street-corner boys, "The members do not feel that the gang is really gathered until the leader appears." This does not appear to be the case among the gangs we have studied; yet, leaders perform in ways which are very important to the other boys, individually and collectively. Some leaders are so powerful that they are referred to by the boys as leaders even during prolonged absence from the gang, e.g., a stretch in the service or in jail. Even among gangs with such powerful leaders, it is the case that boys in any segment of a gang, when

[24] Reiss and Rhodes also report that delinquents are less intelligent than non-delinquents when social class is held constant. See Albert J. Reiss, Jr., and Albert Lewis Rhodes, "Delinquency and Social Class Structure," *American Sociological Review,* XXVI (October, 1961), 720–32.

gathered together, are likely to identify themselves as members of a gang, and, more importantly, to be identified by others as members of the gang. The gang, *in toto*, does not often gather. Hence, the gang has in fact gathered when any number of members are gathered.

Field observation suggests that there is a tendency for smaller group segments to come together around those in leadership positions, but even in these cases it is likely that there will be a number of separate interactions, e.g., around a playground or restaurant hangout, in and outside an apartment, etc. One of the reasons for this is the presence among many gangs of girls on the occasion of most evening gatherings. This, in turn, relates to a difference in function of the adolescent gang as compared with the adult groups Whyte studied. As was indicated in Chapter 2, the adolescent gang is an arena for heterosexual activity, in many cases exploitative and in many cases for courtship purposes. Here is where the boys first "try their wings" in relations with girls. Whyte's young men apparently were less involved in these processes, though they were hardly lacking in heterosexual interest, as Whyte eloquently demonstrated in his description of "A Slum Sex Code."[25]

The point is that, despite the availability of willing females, these boys tend not to be sophisticated in relations with girls. They are largely ignorant of the biology of sex, and though they may "make out" with what many middle class boys might regard as enviable frequency, sex is a matter of much concern and some anxiety to them. The pressure of the gang compounds the matter, for it is less easy for gang than for non-gang boys to withdraw from sexual competition, by excelling in some other endeavor, for example.

The evidence on this point, while somewhat sketchy, is convincing. Baittle reports that among the gang boys he studied intensively, sexual matters were a source of much anxiety to all the boys regardless of the nature of their sexual experience.[26] Miller and his associates describe the physically aggressive interaction of boys and girls as being "aggressive in form only" in the sense that the *object* of such aggression is quite the opposite of aggression, namely to

[25] William F. Whyte, "A Slum Sex Code," *American Journal of Sociology,* XLIX (July, 1943), 24–31.

[26] Reported to a Ford Foundation sponsored Faculty-Agency Seminar on Juvenile Delinquency at the University of Chicago, 1960. See also Brahm Baittle, "Psychiatric Aspects of the Development of a Street Corner Group: An Exploratory Study," *American Journal of Orthopsychiatry* (October, 1961), pp. 703–12.

encourage friendly relations. The rough and tumble of "accidental" bumpings, wrestling, and body punching between boys and girls is a means of establishing liaisons for many youngsters who are embarrassed at their own ineptness in relations with the opposite sex.[27] A detached worker with the "female auxiliary" of a gang of Negro boys refers to this "mock fighting" as "one of the most frequently pursued activities between the boys and girls while on the corner. This play appears to be a form of sexual excitation, invitation, or, at times, prologue. I have rarely witnessed a girl flirt with a boy or be seductive in any other way."[28]

Some gangs contribute to the dilemma of the boys by sanctioning exploitative sexual behavior, while at the same time regarding with cynicism and disdain nurturant relations between boys and girls in the courtship process. Hence, on the corner, at least, the boy has little alternative but to behave aggressively toward girls. This doubtless is related in part to age. Among some older gangs, the "lover" is given great prestige, and "technique" with girls becomes less physically aggressive and more verbal—one's "rap" with the girls is a criterion of status within the gang.

Among the gangs we studied, the relatively high incidence of sexual intercourse, particularly among Negro boys, and the value placed on sexual prowess by at least one of the gangs, The Chiefs, has been noted in previous chapters. Detached workers' reports suggest that "making out with the girls" was highly valued among all the gangs studied and received much attention in the endless conversations on the corner. Yet, a field observer from our research team reported the following incident among members of the King Rattlers, a gang noted for their sexual exploits:[29]

About a half an hour later Roy was talking with Billy over on a couch which was placed under the bay windows in the front parlor. I could not hear what they were saying but after a few minutes they went over to the worker and Billy asked him a question, and the worker, after talking to them for a second, told them to "Call Larry (field observer) over to the side and tell him about it." Billy, the worker, George, and

[27] Walter B. Miller, Hildred S. Geertz, and Henry S. G. Cutter, "Aggression in a Boys' Street-Corner Group," *Psychiatry,* XXIV (November, 1961), 283–98.

[28] We are grateful to Robin Sheerer, detached worker, for these and other observations as a participant in seminar work at The University of Chicago during the summer of 1962.

[29] Field observer report (Lawrence A. Landry), 2/26/60.

Roy then came over to me and Billy said after calling me into the dining room:

"Tell 'em something. Ain't it true that you can have intercourse with a woman during the time she's menstruating without her getting pregnant?"

Larry: "Yeah." (The worker is laughing and Roy is listening with great interest.)

Billy: "It might be a little messy—get a little blood on you, but she's wide open. One time Duke and I were screwing this girl and I couldn't get it in; I stood back and spit on it and it went in." (Billy gave this last part with animation.)

Though it was not specifically stated, the inference here clearly was that Roy did not understand the menstrual cycle.

Roy had fathered one illegitimate child and had a second child well on its way, yet he had little knowledge about the biology of reproduction.

Another research observer reported on a conversation with a young gang leader well known for his prowess as an auto thief.[30]

Sometime later after we had returned to our seats, Sherman came back and sat with me. He said that he wanted to ask a question and he wanted an answer from "someone intelligent."

Sherman: "When you are trying to 'make' a girl, you don't tell her direct what you want but you hint around—What do you do—how do you say it?"

Answer: Well it depends on how well you know her and where you are—this is something you may want to avoid—but your approach is different depending upon the situation, your acquaintance with the girl, and the type of girl—."

The question was asked in a straight-forward manner and I tried to give him an answer in a similar fashion without the moral overtones, but pointing to the realistic problems encountered by youth as a result of such behavior.

Sherman showed considerable interest in the discussion. To show his understanding of the need for finesse in "making" a girl, he asked my opinion of some poetry he had composed while in jail. He recited a verse or two. The ideas and words used to express them revealed some thought on the matter.

Skill in "rapping to the girls" and in "making out" is highly valued among the gang boys and it often happens that boys with these skills are leaders. The relative ineptness of most boys in relations

[30] Field observer report (John Moland), 5/21/62.

with girls stands in sharp contrast to the few who possess such skills.

Though systematic data are not available, detached workers and research observers agree that gang girls, especially those who hang with Negro gangs, also are considerably disadvantaged by social disabilities as well as objective opportunity. The girls are not, by and large, attractive by conventional standards either with respect to physical appearance or behavior. A research observer from the Youth Studies Program describes a group of thirteen- to sixteen-year-old Negro girls who hang with a gang of boys as "a loud, crude group of girls who not only curse and are sexually active, but who take no pride in the way they dress. They will come out on the streets or to the community center one day dressed fairly well . . . but on other days, they will turn out with their brother's pants on or jackets, and their hair will not be straightened nor combed and they will look one big mess."[31] Like the boys, the girls are not articulate concerning their problems or possible ways of coping with them. Programs which seek to teach the girls how to dress, use cosmetics, and comport themselves find eager recruits, but sometimes with grotesque results which are comical despite their underlying pathos. Our observer reports a scene at a West Side community center:

. . . We walked up a long flight of drab stairs and entered a huge, almost barren, depressing looking room. At this time, there were about twenty girls prancing up and down the room, pretending to look and be like mannequins. But the sight of these girls was almost grotesque. They were dressed in a mannish manner; men's suit jackets, dirty sweaters and blouses, their hair was in disarray and their street-corner slouch was very much in evidence. Or I should say their toughness. Leading the prancing was a model-teacher who looked not like a model at all, although she was an attractive brown-skinned Negro woman who possessed some very unmodellish curves. The girls tried to imitate her, failed, and giggled. This seemed to me to be a very normal, girlish reaction.

Three weeks later, in an apartment hangout of the Vice Kings and their ladies, the observer reported:

. . . the model is still coming to give the girls modelling lessons. Both Alice and Lottie decided to show me how they had learned to walk and to sit. The boys started making jokes about their modelling lessons. But the girls proceeded to show me. They did the exact walking procedure that I saw the model teach them. They made no mistakes. However, their postures were as poor as ever and their heads still jutted forward, shoulders sloped and a gang girl "tough girl" lope. It was obvious to me that they did not realize that posture counts as well as learning this walking procedure.

Our observations in Chicago have been confirmed by Rice in New York.[32] His group, the Persian Queens, also slouched, looked at their sweater buttons as they talked, did their hair poorly, and suffered the concomitant decrease in self-esteem because of their ineptitude. On one occasion, when the Persian Queens tried to compose a three-line letter of gratitude to a beauty operator who had fixed their hair, they got out a "Dear Madame." The rest of the composition effort became hopelessly involved over their feeling that it was not proper to thank a benefactor directly, and, between them, they failed to find the appropriate circumlocution. Rice's impression was like that of our observer: it seemed as if nothing much ever happened at the meetings.

Thus, both boys and girls are caught in a cycle of limited social abilities and other skills, and experiences which further limit opportunities to acquire these skills or to exercise them if acquired. These disabilities, in turn, contribute to the status dilemmas of these youngsters and in this way contribute to involvement in delinquency. In the final section of this chapter a more direct relation between social disability, gang behavior, and some delinquent episodes is suggested.

Social Disability and Gang Behavior

Theoretically and empirically it appears plausible that gang boys are dependent upon each other for a large share of interpersonal gratification. Yet we have suggested that the gang is less than satisfactory as a source of nurturance and other gratifications. Other recent studies are consistent with this interpretation, though they do not bear specifically on the issue of gang membership as such. Thus Bandura and Walters report that their non-aggressive control boys were "warmer toward peers" than were the aggressive boys, and Rothstein finds that delinquent boys are less likely to regard loyalty and trustworthiness as attributes associated with high social status.[33]

---

[32] Robert Rice, "The Persian Queens," *The New Yorker* (October 19, 1963), pp. 153 ff. See also Harrison E. Salisbury, *The Shook-Up Generation* (New York: Harper and Brothers, 1958). See especially Chapter 4.

[33] See Albert Bandura and Richard H. Walters, *Adolescent Aggression* (New York: Ronald Press Co., 1959); and Edward Rothstein, "Attributes Related to High Social Status: A Comparison of the Perceptions of Delinquent and Non-Delinquent Boys," *Social Problems*, X (Summer, 1962), 75–83.

Even more revealing, perhaps, Bandura and Walters also found aggressive boys more conflicted and anxious about manifesting dependency behavior than were the control boys.

Because adolescence is a period of emancipation from childhood dependency relations, dependency needs are difficult to express for most if not all adolescents. They are especially difficult for gang boys, however, for they are likely to be interpreted as an expression of personal weakness. The lower class focal concern of *toughness* pervades gang life, as evidenced by the highly aggressive nature of within-group interaction on the street and in many other social contexts such as at skating parties, quarter parties, and athletic contests.[34] The latter provide an instructive contrast between gang boys on the street, or even in a designated and equipped recreation area, and most non-gang boys. Athletic contests in a school setting or on a sandlot generate much camaraderie and feelings of loyalty to fellow teammates and to the student body, if such there be. The game is played hard by all, and, while there may be occasional charges and actual incidents of cheating or fighting, the game is likely to proceed according to the rules and to be carried to a conclusion according to these rules. Observation suggests that this is much less true of gang boys. Athletic contests are more frequently marred by conflict, among team members as well as between teams. Kobrin notes that adolescent gangs in an area very near one of our white gangs were "so completely committed . . . to the value of victory that the rules of the game seemed to have a tenuous hold on their loyalties. It was not unusual for them when stern adult supervision was absent to avoid impending defeat in a sports contest by precipitating a fight."[35] Among our gang boys the threat of violence during and after athletic contests was ever present, among participants and spectators alike. After one particularly heated contest, twenty shots were fired by members of one gang at their rivals, as a result of an altercation over basketball officiating. No one was arrested for the incident, and fortunately, no one was hurt. We have noted, also, an exaggerated tendency by gang boys to *rationalize* failure by invoking by way of explanation factors beyond the boys' control, e.g., "We

[34] See Walter B. Miller, "Lower Class Culture as a Generating Milieu of Gang Delinquency," *Journal of Social Issues,* XIV (1958), 5–19; and Miller, Geertz, and Cutter, *op. cit.*

[35] Solomon Kobrin, "Sociological Aspects of the Development of a Street Corner Group: An Exploratory Study," *American Journal of Orthopsychiatry,* XXXI (October, 1961), 688.

were so high we were almost blind when they beat us," or "They ran in a bunch of old guys—practically pros—or we'd 'a' beat 'em."

Importantly, for gang boys the *institutional* basis for bonds of loyalty among teammates and their supporters is lacking. The gang lacks the advantage of a major institutional function in which athletics and other activities are ancillary, albeit important. Even among high schools and colleges, athletic contests sometimes are marred by unruly crowd behavior, and followed by pitched battles between supporters of opposing teams, or riots of revenge or celebration. Institutional controls usually prevent such excesses, however, and supporters of both winning and losing teams customarily share rewards which make them unnecessary in any case. For the gang boy, athletic contests differ in this respect from gang fights such as were described in Chapter 9. In athletic contests there is likely to be no substitute for winning—no school fight song for expressing one's feelings, or sobering school hymn following the game, no homecoming parade, or dance afterward where old acquaintances are renewed and the pains of defeat can be salved by other bonds in common. A "moral victory" is not even in the vocabulary of most gang boys. The gang is neither cohesive nor dependable enough to provide solace in times of defeat. There is excitement galore, and identification with team members during athletic contests, but nowhere to go if the contest is not won.

Gang boys' problems in this regard we suggest, are in part compensated for by involvement in delinquency. Reference to Thrasher again is appropriate. In discussing group control in the gang he observes that "A stable unity does not develop in the diffuse type of gang . . . until it becomes solidified through conflict." More recently Jansyn's study of a white gang with whom he worked as a detached worker is apposite. Jansyn found that group activity, both delinquent and non-delinquent, and delinquent behavior by individual members occurred most frequently following *low points* in a "solidarity" index which he constructed for the group on the basis of independent observations. His interpretation is that these activities represent responses to declines in group solidarity. That they were successful in this respect is indicated by the continued rise in solidarity which was observed following these behaviors.[36]

[36] See Leon Jansyn, "Solidarity and Delinquency in a Street Corner Group: A Study of the Relationship between Changes in Specified Aspects of Group Structure and Variations in the Frequency of Delinquent Activity," unpublished Master's thesis, University of Chicago, 1960.

It may prove to be the case that increased opportunity for expression of dependency needs and their gratification is one of the chief benefits derived from organized athletic activity such as that which is sponsored by detached-worker programs. The YMCA Program for Detached Workers in Chicago attempts to promote team effort and loyalty by staging tournaments and leagues of several types of athletic activity. A project newspaper publicizes the results of such play and occasionally one or more of Chicago's major dailies reports on them. Observation of basketball, pool, and softball games indicates that for most groups a high degree of enthusiasm is generated and the boys do generally receive interpersonal gratifications regardless of the outcome of the contests. It should be noted, however, that some groups have proven very difficult to organize into stable teams. Detached workers with the more delinquent gangs, especially, often have to forfeit games because team members fail to show up for games, or do so under the influence of alcohol or in some cases of drugs. The retreatist boys were never effectively organized into athletic teams, and much of their conversation concerning their own involvement in athletics related to how much better they played while "high." Finally, as noted in the previous chapter, in order to compensate for status threats involved in defeat in athletic contests, the YMCA finds it necessary to provide numerous trophies so that all may share to some degree in these glittering and tangible rewards of team play.

Field observation confirms, albeit unsystematically, that delinquency creates situations in which dependency needs among these boys may be met. This is apparent, for example, in the account of the boys' reactions to conflict behavior in Chapter 9. It is even more clearly evident among the retreatists, who protect and care for members who are helpless under the influence of drugs or who have suffered debilitating injury. Boys who are in danger of wandering into traffic patterns will be restrained. When police arrive on the scene the other boys will attempt to shield from view a boy who is obviously under the influence. Again from Chapter 9, concern for the boys who were beaten by adults, and the righteous indignation of the gang over this assault molded that amorphous group, including the criminal clique, into a unit bent on retaliation. The fact that the worker was able to prevent the boys from carrying out their planned assault of the responsible adults suggests that the chief (latent) purpose of their wrath may have been interpersonal gratifications experienced by the boys in the course of the incident. A new bond of loyalty existed among the boys as never before. The fact that it was short lived underlines the unstable basis of such gratifications among these boys and the necessity for contriving repeated instances in which dependency needs may be satisfied.

The tentative nature of the social disability argument should be clear. Should the hypothesis prove correct, it will provide an important and previously missing linkage between broad categories of individual pathology and group process in the causation of behavior. Family data from our project to this point unfortunately are inadequate to elucidate hypothesized differences between gang and nongang boys in social disabilities such as those on which we have focused. Later research hopefully will contribute such information.

CHAPTER 11

Aleatory Risks versus Short-Run Hedonism in Explanation of Gang Action

The central question raised in this chapter relates to the motivation of gang boys to expose themselves to the risks of serious incidents arising from delinquent activity. We can conceptualize their action as a game played for small reward with little risk of loss, save that when the loss does occur it involves great costs. The argument suggests that the participation is rational, rather than impulsive, and that the critical element in the understanding of the motivation involves the recognition of the chance, or aleatory process, by which consequences—both good and bad—are allocated.

In a critique of "near-group theory," Harold Pfautz makes reference to a report from the present study which conceptualizes certain factors in delinquency episodes as "aleatory" in nature (see Chapter 2).[1] Pfautz incorrectly identifies our position as referring to "those aspects 'which are beyond understanding or, potentially, prediction.'" He goes on to say that our "formulation only emphasizes the contingent, episodic, and non-routinized nature of this 'collective behavior.'" While the report in question specifically stated that we did *not* refer to factors "beyond understanding or potentially, prediction," we recognize that we had not written, nor thought, as

This chapter was first published in *Social Problems,* XII (Fall, 1964), 127–40.

[1] See Harold W. Pfautz, "Near-Group Theory and Collective Behavior: A Critical Reformulation," *Social Problems,* IX (Fall, 1961), 173. The report referred to is "Street Corner Groups and Patterns of Delinquency," a Progress Report on Research Grant M-3301 to the National Institute of Mental Health, March, 1961. For a revised edition of this paper, see James F. Short, Jr., same title, *The American Catholic Sociological Review* (March, 1963), particularly on pp. 20–21. The language in the latter publication conforms more closely to this analysis than does the original paper. The authors owe a debt for the original use of the terms to Edwin Sutherland, with whom Strodtbeck studied, and for the stochastic phrasing to marginal comments by Albert K. Cohen on an earlier manuscript.

clearly as we should have. It was our intention to suggest that understanding could be greatly deepened by a conceptualization of delinquent behavior which stressed the joint relevance of motivated and aleatory considerations.

This chapter carries the early argument further. We shall first review how we encountered the problem and then present a utility-risk paradigm proposed as a solution. In separate supporting sections, the role of cultural responses to potential violence and the absence of satisfying interpersonal peer group relations will be introduced as factors which predispose one to play at the utility-risk game.

This perspective has implications for a definition of delinquency and leads to predictions concerning subsequent movements to the rackets, or away from the corner. In contrast with Merton's deviance paradigm, the present model postulates striving for status within the group rather than class mobility and explains continued participation in incidents of group action rather than distribution of delinquency in the social order.

Risk and Illegitimacy

We first encountered the problem of assessing the rational in contrast with chance elements in corner-boy behavior in an analysis of parenthood among the Chiefs.[2] Illegitimate fatherhood was conceptualized as an "outcome" of several distinct components of behavior:[3]

A kind of two-step stochastic process is involved. First there is the probability that a given boy will engage in extramarital intercourse with a given frequency. Secondly, there is the probability that these actions will eventuate in illegitimate parenthood. The term "aleatory" refers to the independence between the first and second probabilities.

The first probability is dependent upon the cultural tolerance of intercourse, the intrinsic pleasures of intercourse, etc. However the full matrix of costs of payoffs is conceptualized, it is clear that, for the class of actions involved in the first step of this process, the outcome of the second step has little consequence. It makes little difference whether or not the boys become fathers, and for this reason, the outcome probabilities of the second stage are given little thought at the time of the first action. In this way, the incidence of illegitimacy becomes a function of the amount of time spent "at risk," and the explanations of variance among individuals is, so far as we can tell, independent of intentions or expectations about parenthood.

<hr/>

[2] See Chapter 2.   [3] *Ibid.*

This explanation evolved in the course of two years' observations during which the number of illegitimate fathers among core members in the group increased from three to nine out of twelve boys. Almost without exception, the Chiefs individually expressed attitudes supporting the virtues of fidelity in marriage, small families, hard work and thrift, and keeping one's sons in school. Despite these verbal attitudes, the boys became school dropouts, job failures, and fathered illegitimate children for whom they assumed little if any responsibility.

The Chiefs' "area" was characterized by high physical deterioration, illegitimacy, juvenile and adult crime, and was a known center of drug traffic and use. The attitude of the adult community toward illegitimacy was, in general, permissive, and ample evidence of sexually unconventional role models among adults of both sexes could be found. Group norms placed a high value on sexual exploits and treated with derision the stable attitudes and expectations expressed in individual interviews. Yet, illegitimate paternity did *not* confer status in the gang, and there was no indication that the boys actively sought to become fathers.

Even in this first conceptualization, our use of the term "aleatory" did not restrict it to events which are independent of the actions of the persons involved. It was incidentally true that the events in question were not for this stratum punished by society. However, we now wish to go beyond this feature and direct the argument to instances of serious aggression in which the outcome is not desired either by the boys or the community, and for which serious consequences, like imprisonment, may result from the response by the larger society. We do not say that all cases of serious aggression result from action with such an aleatory element, but that, in terms of etiology, those which do should be distinguished from cases in which serious injury is the clear intent of the actor.

Specifically, it is our hypothesis that much of what has previously been described as short-run hedonism may, under closer scrutiny, be revealed to be a rational balancing, from the actor's perspective, of the near certainty of *immediate* loss of status in the group against the remote possibility of punishment by the larger society *if* the most serious outcome eventuates. Viewed this way, one does not hold that punishable behavior occurs because the youngsters are blind to the possibility of unfortunate consequences. We assume they realize that intercourse may result in paternity and that the bluff of an enemy may fail. Nor is it necessarily the case that delinquents generally value violent outcomes which society views with alarm. They risk these undesired outcomes because, from their perspective, the rewards and probabilities associated with risk taking appear to outweigh the disadvantages. In a very special way they gamble and, sometimes, lose.

Status and Sudden Violence

To make clearer how involvement comes about, we call attention first to the way in which seeking leadership in a gang provides certain and immediate gratification, if one is successful, but in the process, confers a heightened exposure to risks at times of violence. To illustrate this process, we include a brief account of Duke and the King Rattlers.[4] This case also indicates the existence of important background considerations which are otherwise unacknowledged but, as will be shown, should be recognized as preconditions for the general explanation.

Duke's gang had a well deserved "rep" for conflict, and also engaged in systematic strong-arming and other illegal means of acquiring money (some of which involved co-operation with the girls in a local house of prostitution—to the extent of not rolling their customers until after the girls had made the mark), some pot smoking, and a good deal of heavy drinking. Though small in stature, Duke was a powerful leader in the rough and tumble of street-corner life. He was "cool" in his relations with other gangs and with adults in the community. He exercised a strong influence on other boys in the group who respected his organizational ability, his coolness in crisis situations, and the fact that he was capable of quick, decisive action when the occasion demanded it.

Close to Duke in the leadership clique was Harry, a hard drinking, quick to fight, expert strong-armer, who effectively restrained any tendency toward aggressive dominance within the gang but could always be counted on for assistance in out-group encounters. Duke and Harry thus complemented each other in their differing leadership styles. Duke, the stronger leader, was cool and cunning. He spent fewer hours on the street with the boys than did Harry, partially because of his attachment to one steady and several part-time

---

[4] Case materials are taken from interviews with detached workers of the YMCA who were in contact with the gangs, or from field notes by research team members who reported on their contacts with boys or workers.

girl friends, and at times seemed standoffish in his relations with the gang. Harry, by contrast, was forever with the gang and more "one of the boys." He was less cautious in involving himself in episodes of violence and often in trouble with the police.

Duke, Harry, and a few other boys constituted a leadership clique among the Rattlers. These boys supported one another in a loose sort of way. When there was no trouble, these boys were hardly distinguishable from the remainder of the group. Their worker commented:[5]

Just to see them [the officers] on the street you wouldn't think there were any [leaders]. . . . This stuff of officers don't go on the street. *Everybody's* body punching from Duke on down . . . [but] it's like [when] these guys are all on the street, they won't make a move unless Duke tells them.

The incident to be examined involved a fight between Harry and another boy and his brothers, not members of the Rattlers. We do not know the circumstances which led to the altercation, but we do know that it took place in the middle of the crowded main street in King Rattler territory, and Duke was a spectator. The detached worker with the Rattlers tells the story:[6]

A: . . . He [Duke] wasn't directly involved in the fight. He said that Harry had a fair fist fight with one of the brothers . . . [but] then another brother jumped in to two-time Harry. Then Billy [another Rattler] took on this other brother and they were going to it. When the third brother jumped in, the other two Rattlers stood back, and Duke came on with the revolver. Now the revolver [wasn't Duke's, it had] passed through everybody's hands—all the Rattlers' hands. The revolver was brought to this fight by this boy who isn't even in the King Rattlers. But the gun didn't belong to this boy. It belonged to his friend who again isn't in the Rattlers. The revolver passed all the hands and Duke ended with it. He jumped in the middle of the street and fired one shot up in the air, and no one responded. He told me they started closing in on him so he fired low. He wasn't firing at any particular person, but he wanted to keep the brothers off of him, and he didn't know he shot anybody other than a woman, and he felt real bad about it. But he said that he just got excited. This is the first time that he's ever put himself in that position. He said, "They just closed in on me all of a sudden." And he just started firing away.

<hr />

[5] Interview, 9/17/59 (Dryden).   [6] Interview, 10/1/59 (Dryden).

Q: Did he hit more than one person?

A: He hit three. The youngest brother is 19 and the other ones are 20 and in the 20's. One was on crutches. I think he broke his left leg. Duke shot him in the right leg below the kneecap, and the other brother got shot in the arm. The woman got shot in the arm.

Q: Was he actually aiming to hit any of these people?

A: I don't know. He did say that he shot a warning shot.

Q: That just doesn't sound like Duke.

A: No, it doesn't, and none of the policemen can understand that. Why Duke? 'Cause Duke usually won't get himself involved; he'll direct everything from the outside. The gun was knocked out of Duke's hand by the fellow with the crutch. Now Duke says he doesn't believe he shot anybody but the woman. [He maintains] the gun fired after it hit the ground.

Q: Does he know how many times he shot?

A: He said he shot three times. The gun was fired five times. But no one wanted to admit anything else. Duke will admit that he fired the gun three times. He says he shot one warning shot and then he just blasted away until the gun was knocked out of his hands.

Duke's leadership role was originally achieved, not by being recklessly disposed to use a gun, but by standing up to aggression directed toward him by members of the King Rattlers before he became a member of the gang. Once in power, he proved to be cool in crisis situations, *up to the point when action was required.* Then, he would strike hard and fast. Under these circumstances he was fearless and effective. He possessed, in addition, other valued skills and characteristics which fitted him for a leadership role in this kind of group. He could dance well enough to "turn out" most anyone in the neighborhood—other dancers typically cleared an area for him and his partner. He dressed "sharp" and "made out" with the girls. He did not needlessly cause other boys to lose face when he directed decisions within the gang. For these qualities he was rewarded with deference, both within the gang and within the larger neighborhood, by adults and young people alike.

Unlike our earlier analysis of out-group aggression in response to leadership threats,[7] there is no evidence that Duke precipitated this incident to deal with a challenge to his rank, or that status threats of any sort were involved in Duke's initial action. Once the situation crystallized, however, there was a clear expectation that Duke would

---

[7] Cf. Chapters 8 and 9.

take charge. Duke did not "just happen" to get the gun—it was passed to him. Once it was in his hands, it seems likely that Duke's perception of the norms of the group along with the exigencies of the violence he faced, strongly determined that he use the gun. In this sense, his actions arose "in line of duty," as part of the leadership role.

The Utility-Risk Paradigm

Once the incident has occurred, so much is lost relative to possible gain that one is tempted to regard Duke's behavior as a conditional response elicited by the stimulus situation rather than as a cognitively mediated response arising after rational assessment of choices. Only after the incident is formulated into a utility-risk paradigm

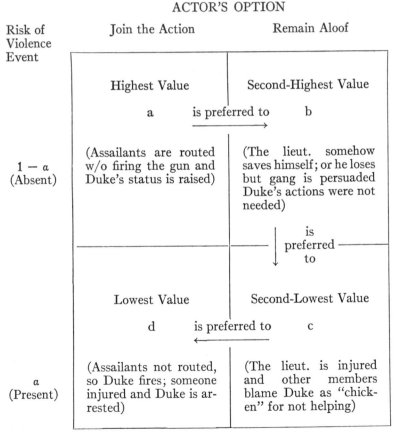

ACTOR'S OPTION

Risk of Violence Event	Join the Action	Remain Aloof
	Highest Value	Second-Highest Value
	a is preferred to b	
1 − a (Absent)	(Assailants are routed w/o firing the gun and Duke's status is raised)	(The lieut. somehow saves himself; or he loses but gang is persuaded Duke's actions were not needed)
		is preferred to
	Lowest Value	Second-Lowest Value
	d is preferred to c	
a (Present)	(Assailants not routed, so Duke fires; someone injured and Duke is arrested)	(The lieut. is injured and other members blame Duke as "chicken" for not helping)

FIG. 11.1.—Matrix of behavior options

in which Duke's actions coincide with the rational choice does the probability of cognitive mediation seem clear. Consider the matrix in Figure 11.1.

The figure conceptualizes the situation as a two-person game, the actor against the environment, with columns representing options available to the actor. Rows represent the occurrence or non-occurrence of a violent event after the actor makes his choice. Each cell contains a description of the outcome and the value placed on it by the actor.

Figure 11.1 shows four alternatives (a, b, c, and d) as Duke might have defined them in terms of his experience. These alternatives do not, of course, exhaust the courses of action or the outcomes which were possible in this incident, nor do they necessarily represent those which actually occurred to Duke. The paradigm does not represent the freezing of alternatives such that decision making and action processes become locked into discrete units. It is known that, under pressure, individuals narrow the range of alternatives which they consider in reaching decisions, but it is our belief that in on-going activities such as occur on the street, behavior is a continuing process of adjustment to elements in the situation such as those being described. The paradigm simplifies exposition of the process. Returning to it, therefore, we assume that an actor will be able to rank the utilities associated with the four alternatives in a set, V(a), V(b), V(c), V(d), where V refers to values assigned various outcomes, and that an alternative will be chosen only when the associated utility is larger than that for any other alternative in the set. The utility of an outcome is, however, not solely a function of its subjective preferability.

To describe the subjective utility (μ) one must associate with each alternative not only a preference value (V) but also a subjective estimate of the likelihood of the event occurring. The subjective probabilities, like ordinary objective ones, can be symbolically represented by a number (ψ) between zero and one. Subjective expected utility involves, therefore, a combination of preference and probability.

$$\mu(a) = V(a)\psi(1-a)$$
$$\mu(b) = V(b)\psi(1-a)$$
$$\mu(c) = V(c)\psi(a)$$
$$\mu(d) = V(d)\psi(a)$$

To denote the alternatives of joining or not joining the action, we will write aαd and bαc. The expression aαd indicates that the highly desired outcome "a" materializes if risky alternative α does not occur, and that "d" materializes if α does occur. With these conventions we may now write a description of the two alternatives open to Duke as in Figure 11.1.

Join: $\qquad \mu(a\alpha d) = V(a)[1-\psi(\alpha)]+V(d)\psi(\alpha)$

Remain Aloof: $\mu(b\alpha c) = V(b)[1-\psi(\alpha)]+V(c)\psi(\alpha)$

From these equations, in which it is assumed that the preference ordering, i.e., $a > b > c > d$ is independent of the judgment of the likelihood of the outcome[8] one can deduce a series of empirically testable statements.

For example, if α were an event which never occurred, then one would always choose the first column, the option to join the action.

TABLE 11.1

PROBABILITY STEP FUNCTION FOR
THE PARADIGM MATRIX

Probability of Consequences Being Avoided		Luce's Empirical Estimates of Probability of Joining the Action
0.00	≈ 0.20	0.00
0.28	≈ 0.41	0.18
0.41	≈ 0.46	0.59
0.46	≈ 0.58	0.89
0.58	≈ 1.00	1.00

On the other hand, if α always occurred, one would always choose the second column, the option to stay aloof. Stated in somewhat more general terms, if the risk of violence or *some other undesirable outcome* were not present, then boys would always join the action because this makes possible the most highly valued outcome. If serious violence, or other extremely undesirable outcome, always resulted when the action was joined, boys presumably would always remain aloof. Thus, as the probability of undesirable outcome (α) moves from zero to one, the probability of joining the action moves from one to zero.

Under conditions of the model here utilized, the sole assumption necessary for the prediction of choice is that $a > b > c > d$ strictly hold. The absolute magnitude of the differences are immaterial, so long as "a" is more preferred than "b," etc. This contrasts with other

[8] R. Duncan Luce, *Individual Choice Behavior* (New York: John Wiley, 1959), pp. 78–90.

game theoretic models in which the play is directly influenced by the magnitude of the difference of the preferences.

More conventional decision-making experiments by Luce suggest that, in a situation of this sort, the probability of α and the probability of choosing the first column do not define a continuous ogive curve,[9] as one might expect from psychophysical data, but will show a step-wise, discontinuous relationship (see Table 11.1). Luce's analysis would lead one to conclude that, when the probability of $1 - \alpha$ was perhaps as high as 0.4, the actor would consistently join the action and expose himself to the risk of "d."

The Culture and the (α) Consequence

The selected lower class values to which street-corner gangs give heightened emphasis increase the destructive potential of gang behavior. In Chicago, particularly in the Negro slums, guns are valued as defensive weapons, and sometimes for offensive purposes. The boys are afraid of guns, and Duke, in the incident described, might well have expected that the combatants would respond immediately to his demand to stop the action when he brandished the gun. Characteristically, when one gang has guns and another does not, the gang without guns flees the scene of the battle, and with good reason. Among adults in these neighborhoods, parents are known to tell their children to "keep the gun handy" when they are home alone; at other times a child may be told to bring a gun along when meeting a parent at a bus stop after dark. Guns are not perceived as objects of sport, as in hunting or target shooting, and there is little support in middle class society or in the mass media for their use in active defense. The rationale appears to arise from widespread fear that sudden violence may be perpetrated—almost at any time—and that the police power will not be effective to stop it. The fear is not wholly unrealistic; women are assaulted near train stations, unoccupied apartments are broken into, and by official estimate there are more armed robberies in Chicago than anywhere else in the United States. Ownership of a gun (or control to the degree that it can be produced for a rumble) is both sought and, if attained, status conferring. Having guns available in turn increases the possibility that others will feel them necessary and that they will, eventually, be used.

[9] R. Duncan Luce, chapter in *Social Science Approaches to Business Behavior*, George B. Strother and Richard D. Irwin, eds. (Homewood, Ill.: Dorsey Press, 1962).

Public drinking on the street, in the pool halls, taverns, and at "quarter parties," complicated by the interpersonal strains of a frequent succession of sex partners, produces episodes of violence where short-lived demonstrations of toughness are appropriate. The toughness of lower class urban Negroes[10] is quite unlike the Yamato Damashi of Japanese culture which places emphasis upon the ability to withstand pain and work hard no matter what the challenge. In the culture of the gang, themes which suggest superego elements associated with patrilineality are absent. There is little emphasis upon being able to suffer and endure.[11] For the most part, the emphasis is upon being able to avoid all pain, and to injure and dominate without risk through superior weapons and numbers. Hence the seriousness and irreversibility of certain actions which arise in inner-city gang delinquency are in this way related to the availabilty of guns, but not this alone. There is a pervasive sense of threat, an emphasis upon aggressivity, and the absence of heroic or masochistic battle ethics.

Our conservative estimate is that not more than one in five instances of potential violence actually result in serious consequences. When serious consequences arise, these are discovered by the authorities in only approximately one-fifth of the cases, and this figure is less than one in ten when the injury is inflicted in individual and group fighting.[12] For average Negro gang boys the probability of arrest for involvement in instances of potential violence is probably no greater than .04, and for the very skillful this figure might fall to .02. However estimated, the probability of avoiding serious outcome appears to be sufficiently large to make the option of joining the action quite attractive.

More than this, once the decision to join the action has been made and rewarded a few times, the actors are not assumed to be motivated to alternate in the way subjects guessing which of two lights will be lighted are reported to do. In such experiments it has been demon-

[10] See Walter B. Miller, "Lower Class Culture as a Generating Milieu of Gang Delinquency," *Journal of Social Issues,* XIV (1958), 5–19.

[11] The only significant exception to this is the tendency among retreatist gangs to engage competitively in apparently self-destructive activities. Members of such a gang included in the present study took drugs to the point literally of "knocking themselves out" and engaged in delinquent episodes which inevitably led to incarceration, embarrassment, or personal injury. Their "folklore" revolved around discussion of kicks and of "way out" behavior under the influence or in pursuit of drugs. This group is discussed at greater length in Chapter 9.

[12] See John M. Wise, "A Comparison of Sources of Data as Indexes of Delinquent Behavior," unpublished Master's thesis, University of Chicago, 1962.

strated that the naïve subject in a sequence rewarded seven-tenths of the time tends to converge toward giving the rewarded option seven-tenths of the time—a strategy which is inferior to taking the more frequently rewarded option all of the time.[13] For the case in question, we assume that while one or two episodes of violence with serious injury (α) might take a boy out of circulation, it would not materially reduce his selection of the option to play once he were back with the gang. The source of the motivation to join the action becomes more intelligible when one views the role of the gang action in reducing the isolation of the individual boy.

Street-Corner Peer Relations and Behavior Options

To the extent that predictable friendship networks exist, we assume that threats of corner life are reduced. Field observation and other data from the present research program suggest, however, that the search for satisfying friendships often is thwarted and the uneven quality of corner relationships gives rise to uneasy tension between unmet needs to affiliate and fear of involvement. The result is an uncertainty about identification which is periodically resolved by a precipitate "joining" in group action.[14]

We note the tendency to distrust all "outsiders" beyond one's own intimate associates. There is a common disposition to exploit each situation to one's personal advantage, and, as is characteristic of many persons at the bottom of the social and economic ladder in a variety of cultures, to assume that others are similarly motivated.[15] For inner-city, Negro gang boys in particular, the exploitative skill which is part of a trickster-trader, easy-money tradition is poorly developed. As a result, the fearfulness of being conned or exploited is reinforced by a projection of desires which they lack the ability to carry out. Thus, torn between needs for affiliation and suspicion, the youngsters alternate between gullibility and suspiciousness of others with regard to long-term involvement.

While the desire to avoid involvement with strangers loses out very easily to a gregarious need for friendship, friends often make demands which at times cannot be met or if met, cannot be repaid. There is a

---

[13] David G. Hays and Robert R. Bush, "A Study of Group Action," *American Sociological Review*, XIX (December, 1954), 693–701.

[14] Evidence on this point is discussed in Chapter 10.

[15] Edward Banfield, *The Moral Basis of a Backward Society* (Glencoe, Ill.: Free Press, 1958).

rapid shift of residences in dwelling units in which fear of actual injury at the hands of newcomers motivates the avoidance of over-involvement. The tensions with usurious landlords and the defensiveness before bill collectors, A.D.C. investigators, police, and other agency representatives creates an atmosphere in which other potentially legitimate sources of support, as well as neighbors, are defined as part of a hostile out-group. The result is that, for the adolescents, a liaison which is as informal as standing on the corner with other boys comes to be sought precisely because it requires so little formal commitment or exposure. The sociability pattern turns on being near, but not being a part of, a kind of adjacency to events which can be easily transformed to active milling when a crisis arises.

It would be inconsistent for this "adjacency" pattern to be observed and for there to be, at the same time, a tight organization. When a crisis is brewing or a decision is being made about a trip or a ball game, the centrality of boys with leadership roles becomes visible and activated. But most of the day-to-day interaction seems to arise more from transfer to the corner of emphases upon drinking, dancing, food, sex, and money from the parent lower class culture than from distinctive norms or special discipline of the group. So far as standing in the group is concerned there is so little of the formal apparatus of institutionalized leadership that the day's gains evaporate with the passage of time. As a result, all boys are in jeopardy of radically changing their standing if they elect to "stand aloof" in an incident such as that described above. If a leader does play it "cool" and others choose not to follow, he loses control over the action even though he would be touched by the negative consequences if matters turn out badly. Taken together, we view these considerations as creating the social basis for the vulnerability which leads to electing the "join the action" option.

The Personality and Situation Paradox

One implication which follows from the inclusion of risk factors in the delinquency sequence relates to a question concerning a theoretically adequate definition of the delinquent. Can one say a boy is transformed from a non-delinquent to a delinquent by the aleatory outcome of his action, or does the essential delinquency begin at the earlier point when he elects to join the action? A long tradition in criminology cautions against generalizations about crime which are based solely upon persons who have been apprehended and incarcerated.[16] The point at issue here is similar. It underlines the need for knowledge about those who join the action without regard for the aleatory play of circumstances which bring a particular boy to the attention of the larger society.

At a superficial level this distinction only calls attention to the fact that "a"-type careers of joiners who have not been hit (as in "d") by the play of chance are included among non-delinquents in many research designs. While this is unfortunate it is less fundamental than decisions concerning relative contributions of, on the one hand, the delinquent's personality and, on the other, the payoff paradigm which, by its operation, at least in some percentage of cases, produces delinquency.

Since the subjective probability that event "α" will occur if the actor joins is influenced in part by the objective probability of "α" and in part by the actor's personality; and since the subjective preference is influenced in part by the actor's personality and in part by how those around him respond, both personality and the process represented by the payoff paradigm inevitably are implicated. More generally, the role of personality factors should be greatest when (1) the objective possibility is obscure or unknown; (2) the value of an event is *not* affected by reactions of other people; and (3) when there are many events (courses of action) to evaluate and choose from. The role of personality factors is reduced when (1) the objective probability is clear, evident, and cannot be ignored, (2) the value of an event depends on reactions of others, and (3) there are few choices open.

The conditions for conflict delinquency give little latitude for differential response due to personality once it is established that an actor attributes a given degree of legitimacy to the payoff paradigm. In general the situation will be one in which personality makes little difference save when the personality factor at issue relates to the capacity to become "involved." For example, we have found that boys with "scoutish" self-descriptions are more involved in conflict than are boys who describe themselves as "cool aggressive," and boys who are "clean" are more involved than those who are "athletic." We have suggested[17] that this is the case because "cleans" among the latter must compensate for the lack of status-rewarding athletic skills,

---

[16] Cf. Frank Tannenbaum's classic discussion of this issue in *Crime and the Community* (Boston: Ginn and Co., 1938), pp. 17 ff.

[17] See Chapters 6 and 7.

and because the characteristically responsible interpersonal relations which are the mark of the "scouts" place them in positions of group centrality and influence, and therefore of vulnerability to joining the utility-risk game. The imperfect correlation of self-concept and behavior arises because boys with widely differing self-concepts at least seek to maintain and perhaps increase their status in the group.

Rackets and Risk Elements

The utility and risk paradigm can also be associated with more deliberately chosen options which are to a greater degree coerced by the larger society—rather than peers. This can be illustrated by the later career of Duke, whose role in the street shooting was previously described.

Shortly after he secured a job as messenger boy with a large department store, Duke married the girl who had borne him two children out of wedlock. He liked the job from the start, and he performed well. Despite the fact that he had less than an elementary education, the position gave him a good deal of personal responsibility which he accepted easily. He became very much involved in the firm's employee profit-sharing plan. He was buying new clothes and furniture, and making payments on an automobile. After nearly a year of successful employment, Duke was promoted to another job with more pay. He was reluctant to make the change to the other department, and almost immediately began to be late for work and to miss entire days. He was fired after only a few days on the new job.

Shortly thereafter, while he was also collecting unemployment compensation, he made a connection with "policy" operators in the area and became a "runner" for the organization. With these two sources of income he was, of course, making a good deal more money than his department store job had paid him. At last report he was still working in "policy" and his wife had secured a job. He has expressed some interest in legitimate employment, but with his limited education and skills it seems unlikely that he can ever obtain a job which would provide as much income as does policy.

We view Duke's decision to join the action, i.e., push numbers, as being determined in part by the fact that his legitimate job had given him the "opportunity" to get so deeply into debt that he would not be able to meet his payments even with the increased pay of the promotion (b). Without the messenger's uniform and opportunity for shifting, pleasant but peripheral contacts which his messenger job had involved, it is likely that he feared his lack of education would be more unequivocally known. He might well have reasoned that he would have little chance for further promotion (c).

The rackets option had the immediate bonus of unemployment compensation plus earnings, a chance to float and be personable with many different contacts a day (a), but with the possibility that at some time he would be picked up by the law (d). Here, however, the "d" outcome no longer has its place in the $a > b > c > d$ order of the model. It is now preferred to "b" and "c" because the penalties for pushing numbers are small in contrast with the rewards, and, in the event of arrest, Duke could possibly expect some legal help from those in control of policy operations.

For the Negro gang boys who drift away from the gang into lower class jobs, the "stay aloof" option is in part determined by the decrease in the importance of maintaining their rank in the group of what eventually becomes younger peers (i.e., $b\alpha c > a\alpha d$). Since the average gang boy doesn't have the opportunities for racket jobs which Duke's personal skills had won for him, the legitimate rewards of steady work such as spending money and credit become determinatively important. Thus while leave-taking from the gang via both the rackets and lower class occupations is describable by different utility and risk states of the basic model, it is important to note that, with leave-taking, the original ordering, $a > b > c > d$, is necessarily broken.[18]

Discussion

In conclusion, we return to the related questions of what we mean by the term "aleatory" and what we suggest as an explanation of the disposition of gang boys to join in the action in instances in which serious delinquency results. For our data in particular, we conclude that the disposition to join the action is not satisfactorily explained by the degree of deviance in values or neurotic or irrational tendencies of gang boys. We argue that the disposition to expose oneself to the risk of serious trouble should not be described as short-run hedonism, for we believe that the abandon in actions suggested by the term *hedonism* is misleading.

The alternative explanation recognizes the role of three parties in the action situation: the gang, the society, and the actor. We view

[18] Cases in which a young man is employed to engage in violent activity, e.g., a "hired gun" would *not* break the $a > b > c > d$ chain.

the status-maintaining mechanisms of the gang as working continuously. The culture of the gang concentrates energies in activities which are outside the level of awareness of the larger society except in those instances in which serious consequences result. The possibility of serious consequences is increased by the easy availability in lower class culture of offensive weapons, widespread feelings of threat, and the absence of codes of honor surrounding aggressive behavior. The typical delinquent gang is not perceived as highly integrated, and the most serious outcomes of gang action are viewed with concern both by the gang and by the larger society.

The dynamic mechanism by which these elements are related involves the collective effects of a narrowing of attention at times of heightened in-group interaction and out-group conflict. At the moment of truth, the field of potential responses becomes narrowed to joining the action or staying aloof. For any given incident a good proportion of the boys do stay aloof, but those who are leaders, or are within striking distance of leadership roles, are particularly responsive to the immediacy and implication of the group response for their status.

The paradigm represents an intersection of two fields of influence: the group and the larger society. Both are essential. The implications for status in the gang reinforce the involvement in activities which, on occasion, lead to serious consequences. The capacity of the larger society to strike back after serious incidents creates the tension. To maintain the conditions under which rational choice to join the action can occur, two conditions must be met: (1) the aleatory play of circumstance by which an action leads to serious consequences should not be subjectively perceived as too frequent (say, less than about four in ten); and (2) joining must be relevant to status within the gang sought by the actor, or required of him by virtue of role expectations.

In this framework, the term *aleatory* is narrowly restricted to the risk that an action, which in itself is below the threshold of concern of the larger society, will result in an outcome of such severity as to bring about punishment of the actor by agents of the larger society. So long as the utilities are ordered $a > b > c > d$ and the $P(\alpha)$ is low, the actor will elect to join the action. If the action is not joined, rank, which flows through familiar social exchanges of the group, will, in some degree, be sacrificed. Against this near certain loss of rank in the group, the actor assumes the low risk of serious trouble with society and gambles to win the group reward.

CHAPTER 12

The Group-Process Perspective

Our inquiry has taken us somewhat afield of theories which guided the initial research designs. We set out to bring data to bear on the theories of Cohen, Cloward and Ohlin, and Miller. Some of our chapters (3, 4, and 5, for example) do this quite directly, but the study has generated a considerable body of data relevant to these theories which has been laid aside as we have worked on what we believe to be a somewhat unique contribution, namely the group process level of explanation, which complements and in some instances calls for modification of the other theories.

The degree of emphasis upon delinquency episodes rather than delinquency rates which this has entailed was not fully anticipated in the original research plans. We did have the foresight to know that we wanted continuous data through time—literally a window through which we might watch corner groups in action. Unlike many delinquency studies, we were interested in mundane as well as delinquent activities for the obvious but often ignored reason that even the most delinquent youngsters engage in delinquent activities for only a small fraction of their waking hours. If we needed any convincing on this point, the availability of some of Walter Miller's materials could leave no doubt. Unlike Miller, who has worked with such great patience to tease insights from empirical observations at considerable distance in time from their collection, we wanted to work in vivo. We even naïvely hoped that we would be able to collect information about boys, evolve micro-detailed functional theories, then plant a role player or make some other intervention in the manner of a true experiment. We never succeeded in being sufficiently on top of our action commitments to make suggestions for intervention solely in the interest of research questions.

It was perhaps an unrealistic expectation that an action program in its years of growth and role definition in the parent organization could have the leisure or the latitude to engage in experimentation to clarify theory rather than practice. During these principal years of the study, however, "opportunity-structure" theory served as the guiding theoretical conception for the detached-worker program. Leaders of the YMCA program were convinced that in the neighborhoods of greatest concern, local community resources could not be organized to suppress delinquency without greater support from the outside than was implicit in the theory or explicit in the community experiments of the Chicago Area Project.[1] They believed, also, that the Association could translate the needs of the corner boys to the business and industrial community in such a way as to bring new resources to the inner city. By this linkage it was hoped that boys could be given new motivation to understand and move toward participation in a world which would not be closed to them by school failures or altercations with the law, a world which could compete successfully with illegitimate status opportunities and which would be gratifying in other ways. Moreover, the program sought actively to prevent school dropouts and other barriers to successful accommodation with the larger society. The fact that the program was operating along lines suggested by the Cloward and Ohlin formulation created an atmosphere in which detached workers became sensitive to status processes in a way similar to the concern with psychodynamic processes characteristic of social workers trained in the case work tradition.

It is important that this *Geist* be understood, for it makes clearer the nature of the research and action collaboration and the opportunity for creative development in both. It would be incorrect to say that the research program exercised a controlling influence on the action program—or vice versa. We attempted to respond sympathetically to the research opportunity presented by shifts in the detached-worker program, though much of our work required only the continued entree to gangs provided simply by continuation of the program. On the other side, it may be noted also that the detached-worker program has responded to research findings.[2] The status-threat hypothe-

---

[1] See Anthony Sorrentino, "The Chicago Area Project after Twenty-Five Years," *Federal Probation*, XXIII (June, 1959), 40–45; and Solomon Kobrin, "The Chicago Area Project—a 25 Year Assessment," *Annals of the American Academy of Political and Social Science*, CCCXXII (March, 1959), 19–29.

[2] See Charles N. Cooper, "The Chicago Y.M.C.A. Detached Workers: Current Status of an Action Program," *Juvenile Gangs in Context: Theory, Research, and Action*, Malcolm W. Klein and Barbara G. Myerhoff (eds.), Youth Studies Center, University of Southern California, Conference Report, pp. 125–34.

sis "made sense" immediately to leaders of the program and to the workers. A "consultant program" in which gang leaders were recruited (and paid) by the YMCA to aid the detached workers was begun in 1961. As the experiment developed, the role of consultant was elaborated in function and in status so that it was possible for boys to move from Field Assistant (at $10 per month) to Field Consultant ($20 per month) and then to Senior Consultant ($30 per month). The latter position was created in part to move boys away from intimate group involvement and into adult roles. A fourth position, of Part-Time Worker, was created primarily for local adults who could assist detached workers in a variety of program functions. In a few instances gang boys have "graduated" from the gang to serve as Part-Time Workers. In these actions the program sought to harness status concerns with broadening the horizons of gang boys and mobilization of school and job opportunities. It is in this way congenial both to the Cloward and Ohlin analysis and to our concerns with within-group rank and status in the larger society. Further efforts to document and to evaluate the program is a part of continuing relations between the research program and the YMCA.

The detached workers varied in the degree to which their reports, even with repeated and supportive interviewing, created clear and persuasive accounts of their experiences. They very shortly began to look forward to their weekly interviews "at Research" as a time for discussion not only of what happened on the street, but of how they felt about the various domestic and job cross-pressures to which they were subjected. While these open-ended reports have proved to be stubborn materials to summarize and exploit, the detached workers' reports as informants (see particularly Chapter 4) responding to standardized instruments have been a particularly valuable source of data.

The presence of observers from the university in the field with the detached workers enabled us to parallel techniques developed by Whyte in Boston[3] and by Ohlin and Cloward in their studies of delinquency treatment institutions, just as the use of detached-worker informants enabled us to parallel Miller. Many of the points throughout the book have been drawn from reports of these observers, and other techniques of study such as field interviews with boys also owe much to their good sense and persistence. In all, observers, detached workers, persons carrying out the personality assessment routines,

[3] William F. Whyte, *Street Corner Society* (Chicago: University of Chicago Press, 1949).

and the administrative staffs at the YMCA and the university were members of a young organization. Even though the clarity of function of a mature bureaucracy was not present, there was at all times sufficient independence of research from service operations that research was freed from any obligation to justify the service aspects of the program.

The Opportunity Perspective

To complement detached-worker interviews and observer reports, a program of systematic interviews with the boys was undertaken. The interviews, designed to elicit the boys' perception of legitimate educational and occupational opportunities, are discussed elsewhere in

TABLE 12.1

PERCEPTION OF OPPORTUNITIES AND OFFENSES
KNOWN TO THE POLICE, BY SIX POPULATIONS

Legitimate Educational and Occupational Opportunities (Low–High) (0–22)	Perception of Illegitimate Opportunities (High–Low) (0–18)	Perception of Adult Power and Helpfulness (Low–High) (0–8)	Total Opportunities Score* (Low–High) (−18–30)	Mean Number of Offenses Known to Police, per Boy (High–Low)
NG (9.0)	NG (11.4)	NG (4.5)	NG (2.1)	NG (3.14)
WG (9.3)	NLC (9.5)	WG (4.7)	WG (5.0)	WG (2.73)
NLC (11.0)	WG (9.0)	NLC (5.6)	NLC (7.1)	NLC (0.47)
WLC (13.7)	NMC (8.2)	WLC (5.6)	WLC (12.6)	WLC (0.31)
NMC (15.6)	WLC (6.7)	NMC (6.2)	NMC (13.6)	NMC (0.06)
WMC (20.2)	WMC (3.5)	WMC (7.4)	WMC (24.1)	WMC (0.02)

* Total Opportunities Score is designed to reflect both legitimate and illegitimate pressures toward delinquency, and is obtained by adding together legitimate educational and occupational opportunities and adult power and helpfulness scores, and from this sum subtracting illegitimate opportunity scores. Hence it is expected to be negatively correlated with delinquency.

greater detail.[4] They cover both the boy's own experience and his perception of "the area where you hang out" concerning integration of criminal and non-criminal values, opportunities to learn criminal techniques, visability of criminal careers, elite criminal opportunities, and general adult power and helpfulness in relation to teen-agers.

It may be seen that the *ordering* of our race-by-class-by-gang-status boys according to the degree to which opportunities are perceived to be closed (the "Total Opportunities Score" in Table 12.1)

[4] James F. Short, Jr., Ramon Rivera, and Ray A. Tennyson, "Perceived Opportunities, Gang Membership, and Delinquency," *American Sociological Review* (February, 1965), pp. 56–67.

is exactly the same as the order obtained by the number of offenses known to the police. Within race, perception of legitimate educational and occupational opportunities as absent, perception of illegitimate opportunities as present, and perception of adult power and helpfulness as lacking are ordered in the same manner also as offenses known to the police. This is true despite the fact that within gangs, opportunity scores do not predict behavior; that is, they do not have stable correlations with individual behavior, either as measured by police contacts or by detached-worker ratings (our behavior factors). Thus, the opportunity scores reaffirm Cloward and Ohlin, document the weight of social and structural variables appropriate to the explanation of differential rates of behavior, but do *not* explain within-gang variations.

Similarly, the disparity between boys' occupational aspirations and their expectations has been found to order these groups in much the same manner as their police contacts.[5] These scores, taken as an index of "position discontent," are consistent with Cohen's and with Cloward and Ohlin's account of the social distribution of delinquent subcultures.[6] Again, however, neither police contacts nor detached-worker behavior ratings are systematically related to within-gang variations in "position discontent." We conclude, therefore, that other variables, at other levels of explanation, are required to explain variations in within-gang behavior.

The Group-Process Perspective

We have turned to the face-to-face context of behavior for further guidance and precision. We accept in principle the idea that structural differentiation in the culture of the larger society gives rise to subcultures of social classes characterized by conditions of life which are productive of differential rates of criminal behavior. The focus of this book is on hypotheses relating to mechanisms by which norms and values associated with structural variation become translated into behavior. Between *position in the social order,* including detailed

[5] See James F. Short, Jr., "Gang Delinquency and Anomie," in Marshall B. Clinard (ed.), *Deviant Behavior and Anomie* (New York: The Free Press of Glencoe, 1964).

[6] Support for Cloward and Ohlin at this level is not unequivocal, however. Other indexes of "position discontent"—disparity between both boys' aspirations and expectations and their fathers' achieved occupational levels did not order the boys in the same manner as extent of police contacts. The data are discussed in *ibid.*

knowledge of the subculture which this implies, and *behavior* there intervene processes of interaction between individuals in groups.[7] For delinquency theory, we feel it is particularly important to link peer-group process and community relations. It is these group-community interactions which impart to delinquent behavior so much of its apparently *ad hoc* character.

The fortunate linkage of our research operation to a detached-worker service program compelled a deeper appreciation on our part for what might be considered *ad hoc* "opportunities." Whatever the effectiveness of the detached worker in his applied role, it seems to arise from his monitoring of the flow of events rather than his effectiveness in changing personality or values of gang boys. From a methodological standpoint, surrounded as we are with efforts to evolve models of behavior which operate over great stretches of time, this entailment of *ad hoc* opportunities from the community milieu and within-group process may seem to be an excessively circumstantial approach. The point is perhaps well taken, for in the literal sense of the word, "circumstantiality" is intended—like Murray,[8] we require a specific recognition of a short-run but frequently recurring situational press. An important part of the argument of this book may be viewed as an effort to increase the consciousness, perhaps the scientific status, of contingencies of action.[9] For our part this effort has not involved a head-on confrontation such as would be involved in the elaboration of classificatory typologies. It has emphasized rather the importance of understanding the actor's adaptive strategies as

[7] A similar point has been emphasized with respect to leadership and the flow of influence in fashion, marketing, and public affairs among women. See Elihu Katz and Paul F. Lazarsfeld, *Personal Influence: The Part Played by People in the Flow of Mass Communications* (Glencoe, Ill.: The Free Press, 1955). See also, in the present context, Albert K. Cohen, "The Sociology of the Deviant Act: Anomie Theory and Beyond," *American Sociological Review* (February, 1965), pp. 5–14.

[8] H. A. Murray, *Explorations in Personality* (New York: Oxford University Press, 1938).

[9] Matza's recent theoretical essay views delinquency as a result of choices among behavior alternatives somewhat as we do, but primary stress is upon the lessening of control mechanisms by the temporary removal of moral and legal restraints via their neutralization and "drift." By "drift" Matza refers to lack of commitment either to convention or crime, not in the sense of an actor totally free to choose, but of a person responding to pressures without the constraining influences of commitment and self-control. Though Matza's perspective is not incompatible with ours, we have attempted to describe and analyze more specific influences and mechanisms than are implied in the concept of "drift." See David Matza, *Delinquency and Drift* (New York: John Wiley and Sons, Inc., 1964).

they might be elicited and their consequences augmented in given situations. To make this clearer, we will review in slightly reorganized form some of the materials of the earlier chapters.

Macro- to Microstructural Continuities

We note that realities of social structure—class and ethnic differentiation and the operation of ecological processes—place severe limitations on the realization of cultural universals, such as the high value placed on material wealth and status achievement in important institutional contexts as school and the world of work. At the individual level, failure to achieve these goals begins early in life for many lower class and ethnically disadvantaged persons—the socialization skills of the parents are defective in terms of preparing children to meet the achievement criteria of the larger society.

This process is complicated by the existence of subcultures with distinctive ethnic and lower class characteristics, and by youth subcultures, which are delinquent in a variety of ways. But subcultures of all types have both historical and contemporary roots. They serve to insulate their adherents from experiences which might make possible achievement of many "respectable" goals by "respectable" steps toward their achievement, and to evolve values which compensate, in some measure, for failure or the likelihood of failure. Conceived somewhat more broadly, the social gratification of peer-group participation gives rise to we-feelings which, in some degree, operate as a compensation for failure in every strata of society and at every age.

Important *goals* of the larger society are quite successfully communicated, as Merton suggests,[10] and so also are values concerning legitimate means for their achievement. Evidence from a variety of sources, e.g., the Flint Youth Study and our own, suggests that disadvantaged youngsters do not become alienated from the goals of the larger society, that even the gang ethic is not one of "reaction formation" *against* widely shared conceptions of the "good" life.[11]

We have called attention to the public nature of drinking and "party" behavior, shifting sexual and economic liaisons, a high incidence of guns and the acceptance of violence as a means of settling

[10] Robert K. Merton, *Social Theory and Social Structure* (rev. ed.; Glencoe, Ill.: The Free Press, 1957).

[11] Cf. Martin Gold, *Status Forces in Delinquent Boys* (Ann Arbor: University of Michigan, Institute for Social Research, 1963).

disputes as the way in which groups and institutions which are the primary carriers of lower class, ethnic, and delinquent subcultures create high risk of involvement in actions with severe consequences. Because field observations did not extend to our middle class youngsters, we are less able to document the precise nature of the constructive sociability and work opportunities which are absent for lower class and especially for gang youngsters. It is our conviction, however, that for the latter, the relative absence of middle class achievant opportunities and concerns leaves a kind of vacuum which becomes occupied with other time-filling expenditures of energy built around capacities for gratification through interaction with the gang.

Juxtaposition of the "typical" with "what is not present" is required to appreciate fully the cognitive consequences of continued and narrowly circumscribed existence in a given environment. We note, for example, that one of the principal ways in which a person is motivated to use elaborated language in persuasive form is by involvement in situations in which some common resources are being used for an agreed upon, collective objective. In the system of relations of the middle class home, such discussions must be very extensive to insure the rapprochement of such diverse matters as need to paint the house v. a better car, or orthodontia v. music lessons, etc. The necessary phasing of expenditures in the presence of reasonable certainty that needs can be met if a plan is abided by is a natural introduction to future time orientation. When resources of the lower-lower class family are too meager to go around no matter what is done, the children of such families miss an important opportunity for development of verbal skills which come from participating in discussions of resource allocation.[12]

Despite the many hours together on the corner, most of the gang boys gain no verbal skills which in any sense compensate for academic shortcomings. Quite the contrary, our perception of the status process is that, in the absence of an intervention by an outside agency, the natural gang leadership will direct the energies of the gang to the heightening of affective feelings and stress on matters such as distinction of dress, dance style, prowess in fights, etc., which have virtually no relevance for the job world or other long-term goals. In an earlier paper, Gordon drew upon Allport and Homans in suggesting that "if a group lacks a task, purpose, or mission as a result of not being integrated into a demanding external system—as

---

[12] These points are elaborated in Fred L. Strodtbeck, "The Hidden Curriculum in the Middle Class Home," in *Urban Education and Cultural Deprivation*, C. W. Hunnicut (ed.) (Syracuse: Syracuse University Press, 1964), pp. 15–31.

may in fact be the case for street-corner gangs—then it would fail to generate a major part of the rewards and sentiments which its members might expect to gain from it."

One solution is to adopt or contrive tasks which justify dependence between members and call for cooperation in a common enterprise. Criminal ventures (which for this purpose need not be purely utilitarian), gang warfare, and the search for the "fix" and "kicks" would be means within the organizational capabilities of gang members of providing such shared and demanding problems. Still another solution, not mutually exclusive with the first, is to compensate for the absence of normal in-course rewards by emphasizing assurance rewards such as style of dress, nicknames, sharing, permissiveness toward acting-out, body-punching privileges, and so on. None of these, of course, really compensates for the lack of genuine warmth and care from others which presumably makes the whole problem of reward so crucial for gang boys. Nevertheless, it would appear that the power of delinquent tasks to energize bonds between gang members would be especially attractive to boys who miss warm ties with others, lack the resources to stimulate them by example, and who have doubts as to the quality of response to be expected from others under ordinary circumstances. The normal exigencies of such activities may be relied upon to drive members closer together without exposing themselves to such accusations and anxieties as might be triggered by openly dependent behavior in the absence of some compelling external event.[13]

The point is more subtle. The process of interaction within a group transforms culture. The subterranean aspects of the culture elaborated by middle class adolescents is linked to the work world by its very opposition to it.[14] But the parent culture of the gang boys, particularly the Negro gang boys, does not offer a structuring which is meaningful to oppose. One might guess that church folk could be paired against delinquent folk in the Negro community, but the classic work of Drake and Cayton makes clear that this is not the case. They comment as follows:

The physical "world" of Bronzeville's lower class is the world of store-front churches, second-hand clothing stores, taverns, cheap movies,

---

[13] Robert A. Gordon, "Social Level, Social Disability, and Gang Interaction" (an unpublished paper being prepared for publication). See Floyd H. Allport, "A Structuronomic Conception of Behavior: Individual and Collective. I. Structural Theory and the Master Problem of Social Psychology," *Journal of Abnormal and Social Psychology,* LXIV (1962), 1–30; and George C. Homans, *The Human Group* (New York: Harcourt, Brace and Co., 1950).

[14] See David Matza and Gresham M. Sykes, "Delinquency and Subterranean Values," *American Sociological Review,* XXVI (October, 1961), 712–19.

commercial dance halls, dilapidated houses, and overcrowded kitchenettes. Its people are the large masses of the poorly schooled and the economically insecure who cluster in the "worst" areas or nestle in the interstices of middle-class communities. The lower-class world is complex. Basic to it is a large group of disorganized and broken families, whose style of life differs from that of the other social classes, but who are by no means "criminal" except so far as the children swell the ranks of the delinquents, or the elders occasionally run afoul of the law for minor misdemeanors. Existing side by side with these people is a smaller, more stable group made up of "church folks" and those families (church and non-church) who are trying to "advance themselves." In close contact with both these groups are the denizens of the underworld—the pimps and prostitutes, the thieves and pickpockets, the dope addicts and reefer smokers, the professional gamblers, cutthroats, and murderers. The lines separating these three basic groups are fluid and shifting, and a given household may incorporate individuals of all three types, since, restricted by low incomes and inadequate housing, the so-called "respectable" lowers find it impossible to seal themselves off from "shady" neighbors among whom they find themselves. The "church folks," despite their verbal protests, must live in close contact with the world of "sin."[15]

Strodtbeck's recent work in the reading readiness nursery indicates that Aid-to-Dependent-Children mothers, whether from "shady" or "church-oriented" backgrounds are consistent in the degree to which, in the socialization of their children, they earnestly attempt to keep their children out of trouble.[16] This heightened concern with trouble, coupled with the lack of resources to meet her own material and emotional needs, drains the mother's energies and exhausts whatever capacity for playful role-taking may have been available to her for the socialization of her children. Her own lack of knowledge and imagination concerning such opportunities as do exist, personal problems, and her overriding concern for keeping her children out of trouble cause her to deal with her children in ways which stifle the curiosity so necessary for the child to do well in school—an explicit goal sought by these mothers. Thus, even the non-delinquent empha-

[15] St. Clair Drake and Horace R. Cayton, *Black Metropolis: A Study of Negro Life in a Northern City* (New York: Harper and Row, 1962), Vol. II.

[16] See Strodtbeck, *op. cit.*, and Fred L. Strodtbeck, "Progress Report, the Reading Readiness Nursery: Short Term Social Intervention Technique" (Social Psychology Laboratory, University of Chicago, August, 1964, multilith).

sis among the unstable poor is self-defeating of the cherished goal of school success, and the lack of school success in turn defeats the objective of keeping out of trouble.

The nursery school materials are rich with detailed illustration of weak hopes for betterment through the child's education embedded in the distrust and helplessness themes so characteristic of the unstable poor.[17] We cannot be certain that there are experiences of this sort in the early childhood of our gang boys, but the chain of inference linking similar experiences at five to a career on the corner at fifteen is not implausible. Yet the old message that delinquency begins in the family is more disavowed than reaffirmed by our analysis. Insofar as it is present, it emerges in a new form. We firmly believe that need dispositions which are requited by gang membership arise in the interaction between the lack of preparation for school-type achievement in the home and the absence of access to alternative adaptations to failure in the schools. We see this syndrome re-enacted in later encounters of countless variety in local and larger communities. By the time boys acquire the identity associated with gang membership, a police record, or dropping out of school, the process of selectivity for failure is established. Conversely, those whose socialization confers verbal facility and achievement skills are better equipped to cope with the demands of school and other "middle class institutions." While a delinquency episode may bring a boy dramatically to attention, the fact to be emphasized is the slow, cumulative nature of a process in which minor differences in experience can greatly change the probability of serious involvement in delinquency. Thus, in contrast with gang members, the non-gang boys appear to be well on their way to limited success, at least so far as this may be inferred from school and police records.

The selective processes which separate gang and non-gang youngsters extend beyond the influences which might be expected, as for example, gang v. other friendship groups, the school v. the corner, and favorable v. unfavorable relations with the police. Interviews with the boys indicate that gang members are less favorably disposed toward adult incumbents of legitimate roles such as teacher, religious

[17] See the excellent analysis and review of the literature reported in Albert K. Cohen and Harold M. Hodges, Jr., "Characteristics of the Lower-Blue-Collar Class," *Social Problems* (Spring, 1963), pp. 303–34.

leader, policeman, businessman, and politician than are their non-gang, lower class counterparts.[18]

When the boys were asked to nominate the four adults with whom they have the most contact, gang boys nominated fewer adults and those whom they nominated came from lower status occupations than did those nominated by either lower or middle class, non-gang young-sters.[19] When samples of these adults were interviewed it was found that far fewer of the adults nominated by the gang youngsters said they had been spoken to by the boys concerning problems at school. The percentages of nominated adults reporting school-related conversations are:

Negro gang = 39	White gang = 37
Negro lower class	White lower class
non-gang = 85	non-gang = 78

In addition, non-gang nominees, more often than gang, stressed middle class objectives for the boys when they were questioned about their conception of "a good life" for the youngsters who had nominated them. All of these findings suggest at least a diffuse but consistent support for an achievant, conventional life orientation, a support which increases the likelihood that these goals will be more frequently achieved by non-gang youngsters. Not all the non-gang boys will succeed, of course, nor will all of the gang boys fail. Our present argument requires only that success and failure be related in the manner specified to variables and processes such as those to which we have drawn attention. At issue are experiences which are not exclusively present for either gang or non-gang youngsters. It is rather that their distribution is heavily skewed in the directions we have indicated.

Life Chances, Gratifications, and Decision-Making

Since we think in terms of a moving balance of contemporary experience, we are concerned with both the opportunities which present themselves and the strategy of decision-making carried out in the

[18] James F. Short, Jr., Ramon Rivera, and Harvey Marshall, "Adult-Adolescent Relations and Gang Delinquency: An Empirical Report," *Pacific Sociological Review* (Fall, 1964), pp. 59–65.

[19] James F. Short, Jr., Harvey Marshall, and Ramon Rivera, "Significant Adults and Adolescent Adjustment: An Exploratory Study," revision of a paper presented at the 1964 meetings of the Pacific Sociological Association (mimeographed).

interest of gratification. In preceding chapters we have dealt both with the initiation of actions and with "joining" or "not joining" actions in process. For example, a benign search for "companionship" with habitues of bars and pool halls may be moderately rewarding, but the relationships are specific to the bar and they are likely to be tenuous. They provide the gratifications of companionship only so long as one does not burden them too greatly. Since substitutes to gang participation are not easily available, old hanging patterns are slowly relinquished even when the number of effective friendships is greatly reduced by the breakup of some earlier "gang." Many "join the action" on the corner only in the sense that they are "close by." They can relinquish with little cost the low level of gratification which this entails, if entangling "exchange relationships" arise. Thus, it works out that the strategy of being "on the corner" and *not* being involved is a cheap way to obtain opportunities for involvement without there having been any commitment in advance. In fact this is not the case, because there is a continuing risk to those with delinquent backgrounds that they will be picked up on suspicion, or become more seriously involved. Unlike the earlier period of more intensive dependence upon the corner, however, there is no loss of status for not joining. Hence, when the delinquent culture becomes the parent lower class culture, the participant substitutes wariness of being conned for his earlier efforts to gain status in the group.

The lower class street ethic of sexual exploitation of females by males and of economic exploitation of males by females lessens the probability of emotional gratification related to sexual relations and heightens the probability of undesirable consequences such as venereal disease, illegitimate children, "broken homes," and involvement in violence in the course of sexual competition. Miller's discussion of the translation of "focal concerns of lower class culture" into delinquency involvement is relevant. Involvement in "trouble" often is the price of affiliation and prestige within the one-sex peer group and, apropos of the social disability thesis, a means of achieving "the covertly valued desire to be 'cared for' and subject to external restraint, or the overtly valued state of excitement or risk."[20] The fine line between assault or other serious violence and the characteristic display of "toughness" on the corner, disguising "strongly affec-

[20] Walter B. Miller, "Lower Class Culture as a Generating Milieu of Gang Delinquency," *Journal of Social Issues,* XIV (1958), 8.

tionate feelings towards other men,"[21] is difficult at best to maintain. Provocations to violence and appropriation of property occur often in the course of the display of "smartness." And the search for "excitement" against the background of the colossal boredom of "hanging" with "nothing to do" involves high risks of delinquency involvement.[22]

Situations in which one can have fun and not be responsibly involved tend to entail heightened exposure to risks of failure of conventional institutional constraints. For example, bar room "brawls," the availability of alternative kicks, and "accidents" while intoxicated have the surface appearance of "opportunities" detached from repercussions from failure to discharge responsibilities of marriage, family, or the job.

During the period this project has been in process, important extensions in the theory of exchange[23] have occurred which are relevant here. The original phrasing assumed that human interaction was motivated by a desire for profit in the tangible or intangible rewards exchanged between persons during relatively short time intervals. According to Homans, the motivation for elementary subinstitutional behavior is social, the source of reward is another person; it is voluntary; contact is face to face; the behavior precedes or transcends formalized role behavior. More recent work by Gouldner and Blau has been addressed to the integration of relationships between persons who are pursuing non-common goals. These analyses suggest that exchanges which create unspecified expectations require a binding norm of reciprocity to tide participants over the period in which the time and nature of reciprocal action is unspecified.

When two people first enter interaction, they are willing to risk very little. For our analysis, it is important to stress that the absence of effective organizational constraints, housing mobility, and job shifts reduce the duration of relationships. More fundamentally, in

21 *Ibid.*, p. 9.

22 Playwright Arthur Miller also has commented on the boredom component of gang delinquency. See his "The Bored and the Violent," *Harper's Magazine,* CCXXV (November, 1962), 50–56.

23 George C. Homans, *Social Behavior: Its Elementary Forms* (New York: Harcourt, Brace and World, 1961); John W. Thibaut and Harold H. Kelley, *The Social Psychology of Groups* (New York: John Wiley and Sons, Inc., 1959); Alvin W. Gouldner, "The Norm of Reciprocity: A Preliminary Statement," *American Sociological Review* (April, 1960), pp. 161–77; and Peter M. Blau, *Exchange and Power in Social Life* (New York: John Wiley and Sons, Inc., 1964).

terms of exchange theory, since the value of A's attention to B is evaluated in terms of the sum of values A has foregone while giving attention to B, simple nurturant sociability tends to be undervalued by those who need it most. If you are committed to a number of activities, your time becomes more precious. The more socially engaged A becomes, the more he is foregoing to be sociable with B, and the more B appreciates it, assuming he is sufficiently engaged socially to understand.

The elaboration of pluralistic institutional commitments enriches interpersonal relations in two ways. Scarcity of time causes nurturant episodes to be more valued, and the expectation of continued access to one another due to the constraint of formal role relations increases the degree to which the time and nature of reciprocation can be unspecified. During moratoria on exchange, while interaction and some degree of imbalance exists, social relations take on their most complex and fascinating form. The avoidance of overt hostility (avoided because the network of indebtedness is endangered by impulsive behavior) is reinforced by the elaboration of normative constraints. Very subtle verbal skills are required to indicate that the value of a gift received is not the equivalent of a gift given, and then to clear the way for a rapprochement on the next exchange.

Adults engaged in this prototypic social game teach their children by example, and at times explicitly. When adults do not actively "play" such games it is virtually impossible for them to teach their children. If their children are to learn, they must learn from rewards and punishments received in peer-group relations. From the perspective of our analysis, we would guess that earlier analyses of young children have overemphasized what is learned *de novo* in child peer-group relations.[24] Conversely, they may have underestimated the degree to which children's play activities involve opportunities to use modes of interrelation and evaluation which they have observed

[24] Bordua has criticized recent formulations concerning gang delinquency for neglecting family influences on the boys. See David J. Bordua, "Some Comments on Theories of Group Delinquency," *Sociological Inquiry* (Spring, 1962), pp. 245–60. The greater freedom accorded lower class adolescents outside the family has been documented, but making this point does not free the investigator from the obligation to take into account familial influences. See George Psathas, "Ethnicity, Social Class and Adolescent Independence from Parental Control," *American Sociological Review* (August, 1957), pp. 135–91. Nye's study attests to the poorer parent-child adjustment in lower socioeconomic families. See F. Ivan Nye, "Adolescent-Parent Adjustment: Socio-Economic Level as a Variable," *American Sociological Review* (June, 1951), pp. 341–49.

among adults.[25] We find that the capacity of lower-lower class gangs to elaborate and enforce norms of reciprocity is very much below what might be required to sustain the group if alternative forms of gratification were available. In short, they seem not to teach what is supposed to have been learned in groups.

Intertwined with early and ongoing socialization experiences and related social disabilities, with "opportunities," group process, and the structure of social action is another class-linked characteristic which predisposes some to "join the action," others to hold back, or better still, to avoid situations involving such choices. We refer to the *short-term orientation* of those at the very bottom of the social class ladder—the concern with problems of the moment, because they are so pressing and omnipresent, and with such opportunities as may be found for temporary relief from these problems. S. M. Miller has remarked of the "unstable poor" that:

Lower-class life is crisis-life, constantly trying to "make do" with string where rope is needed. Anything can break the string. Illness is most important—"Got a job but I got sick and lost it"; "We managed until the baby got sick." The great incidence of physical afflictions among the poor—frequently unknown to the victim—are obvious to any casual observer. Particularly striking are the poor teeth of many. The tendency of lower class people to somaticize their emotional difficulties may be influenced by the omnipresence of illness.[26]

The "unstable poor" are vulnerable to many crises, any one of which may "break the string"—seasonal unemployment or other job layoffs, disabling injury or accident, criminal victimization, arrest. Efforts to plan, to control the remoter effects of their actions, are

[25] This may account in part for differences in findings and interpretation between ourselves and the Sherifs, who emphasize adult-youth conflict and the autonomy of peer groups in terms of group norms and their influence on adolescents. Their data and ours indicate broad areas of agreement among children and parents, as well as some areas of disagreement. See Muzafer Sherif and Carolyn W. Sherif, *Reference Groups: Exploration into Conformity and Deviation of Adolescents* (New York: Harper and Row, 1964); Ray A. Tennyson, "Family Structure and Delinquent Behavior," in *Juvenile Gangs in Context*, Malcolm W. Klein and Barbara G. Myerhoff (eds.), a Conference Report from the Youth Studies Center, University of Southern California, 1964 (mimeographed), pp. 56–70. See also Clay V. Brittain, "Adolescent Choices and Parent-Peer Group Pressures," *American Sociological Review* (June, 1963), pp. 385–91.

[26] See "The American Lower Class: A Typological Approach," *Social Research* (Spring, 1964). Republished in the Syracuse University Youth Development Reprint Series, pp. 1–22.

repeatedly frustrated. The string will not stretch, and it is too easily broken. More frequently than members of other classes, they find themselves confronted with situations not of their own making and beyond their control. The future is even less predictable and less dependent on present actions. Thus, the payoff matrix is likely to be approached by such persons in terms of short-run consequences rather than possible future gains.

By contrast, the future is more predictable, more within the grasp of middle class persons, and of those of the lower class who manage to escape or avoid the social and economic insecurities of the "unstable poor." Thus, in effect, participants in different class subcultures approach the payoff matrix with different orientations toward risk. Even when the realistic probabilities and the values of the cells are the same (as they are *not between* classes, but likely to be for gang and non-gang lower class youngsters) decisions will vary as a result of varying orientations toward risk. An actor's estimate of the subjective probabilities in any situation is determined in part by whether he has learned to regard the future as predictably dependent upon short-run decisions, or as independent of these.

Orientations toward the interdependence of short-run decisions and long-run outcomes tend to be self-fulfilling and self-reinforcing. Belief in interdependence reinforces planning for and anticipation of long-run consequences and increases the probability that immediate actions will produce desired effects. The feedback in turn increases confidence in one's ability to control, or at least to influence significantly, one's future. The converse also is true: Belief in the independence of one's present behavior and future well-being discourages planfulness, increases the probability that unhoped for consequences will in fact occur. And the feedback decreases confidence in ability to anticipate or deal effectively with the future.

Viewed in this way, the status of short-run hedonism as an explanatory construct, which was challenged in the earlier chapter by the aleatory phrasing, now re-emerges in somewhat different form. It is important to stress that there is no positive value placed on decision-making in terms of short-run consequences, nor is such decision-making simply a "realistic" adaptation to the circumstances. Decisions to "join the action" are seen to grow out of culturally patterned experiences which have failed to teach that long-run consequences are subjectively dependent on short-run decisions. To be biased in the middle class sense toward "deferred gratifications" means that one's cognitive grasp of the relatedness of experience has been expanded. Cognitive convictions about the reality of events not immediately present or subject to verification turn on cultural support from others. When there is consensus about such matters, decisions can be made which anticipate the continuity of relations in the broader universe. When such matters have to be "cleared" or defended *ad hoc*, it places a heavy burden upon the actor. Conversely, cultural *support* for these biases means that decisions based on them do not have to be "cleared" with others *with whom they are shared*. They understand because they share, and in the sharing ensure that it will be so.[27]

If we are to account for known observations, it must be the case that non-gang, lower class youngsters, and some lower class adults, are somehow protected from influences summarized in this chapter. While systematic family data are lacking to document the case, it follows that non-gang youngsters have not been prevented from learning the verbal and social skills necessary for conventional achievement to the same degree as gang boys; they have learned to be more planful of their time, particularly as concerns their investment in the future. While their chances are better, as judged by every index we have available, avoidance or engagement remain actuarial matters.

One other point needs to be made before we close. Our data are drawn chiefly from Negro gangs, and the implications of theoretical points we have made appear to be more characteristic of the Negro gangs we have studied than of the white. If these points are to be significant, it must be the case that families torn by economic stress, fear, and helplessness are unable to impart to their children the necessary skills and achievant orientation for adjustment to the demands of conventional institutions. To the extent children lack the means for achievement, they are likely to be caught up in the web of community and gang influences we have described.[28] To the extent that a child

---

[27] We are indebted to Albert Cohen for his counsel regarding this point.

[28] Preliminary observations from a study of Negro gangs in Los Angeles suggest at least that the social disabilities of these boys are a good deal less serious than is the case with our boys. The area in which these Los Angeles boys live looks very much like the community settings of our Negro *middle* rather than our lower class boys. The institutional setting in the Los Angeles communities is more conventional and less like the lower class varieties we have described. The study is under the direction of Malcolm W. Klein, Youth Studies Center, University of Southern California. Helen E. Shimota is Senior Research Associate for the study.

acquires the lower class, culturally patterned bias against planful behavior, he will be drawn to situations where the "action" is likely to involve choices which crucially affect his ability to stay out of trouble. To the extent that his own abilities to relate in nurturant ways to others are highly developed, he will gain from many, relatively brief, high commitment group activities. The greater the plurality of groups, the greater his latitude to arrange his membership so as to increase his gratification—and, if the desire to avoid delinquency is present, to avoid trouble. We have shown that the probability of his becoming involved in trouble will depend on the types of groups with which he associates and on role relations within these groups. To the extent that members of these *groups* are characterized by extensive social disabilities, group effort will involve individual and collective attempts to create symbols and situations which will allow for—perhaps even demand—the gratification of dependency needs with only the shallow commitment these youngsters are capable of expressing.

Friendships and loyalties which derive from social process on the corner may in some instances prove to be as binding and lasting as any. But the unstable gang context, serving as an arena in which status threats are played out, tends to undermine these friendships and loyalties and makes them shorter lived and less binding. Our encounter with delinquent gangs convinces us that it is not simply a "middle class" bias which leads to the conclusion that their lives so often are miserable; and, by the same logic, it is not just latter-day "dogoodism" which convinces us that much can be done to remedy their situation.

Index

Activities, self-reports of: limitations, 144–46; data collection, 165–66; description of factors, 166–68; relation to delinquency involvement (racial differences), 169–72; relation to self-description and observed behavior, 172–79

Adolescent-adult relations: concerning sexual behavior, 36; adult role models, 37–39, 108–9, 273–74; delinquency-supporting (racial differences), 107–15; in lower class institutions, 108–12, 115, 190–91, 212–14; contact with high-status adults, 237, 275–76

Advisory group, ix

Age of boys studied, 15, 49, 96

Aggressive behavior: involving status threat, 185–215 *passim;* child socialization, 234–35; pseudo-, 235, 239–40; and dependency needs, 243–46. *See also* Conflict *and* Violence

Alcohol: incidence of drinking, 82; correlation with other behaviors, 86–89, 92; in corner-boy activities, 104; at "quarter parties," 110; in "hanging" situations, 36, 112; and conflict, 203

Aleatory elements: in illegitimate parenthood, 44–45, 249–50; and gang behavior, 248–64; involving violence, 250–59; and delinquency involvement, 277

Allport, Floyd H., 272, 273 n.

American Documentation Institute, 49, 52

Anderson, Gene, 19 n., 210 n.

Anomie, 3, 269 n.

Anxiety: of gang boys, 230; and illegitimate parenthood, 38

Arrest rates of boys, 258, 268–69

Athletic, as self-description, 119–22,

131, 160–62; relation to conflict behavior, 174–76, 179–81

Athletics: incidence of behaviors, 82–83; classification of, 84; correlation with other behaviors, 85–86; as stable corner activities, 87–89, 92; character-building value, 161–62; self-reports of, 166–72; and social disability, 244–46

Attitude-clique differentiation, and self-description, 125–35, 138

Attitudes: toward marriage and family, 29–32, 36, 222–27; legitimacy of, 59–65, 70–71, 73–74; paired-comparison measures, 146–59; toward employment, 222–27. *See also* Values *and* Self-description

Authority protest: as behavior factor, 89–100 *passim;* racial comparisons, 102–3; relation to self-descriptions and self-reported activities, 179

Auto theft: incidence of, 82; as authority protest, 89, 90, 92, 100; as criminal behavior, 90, 98

Bach, Henry, 19 n.

Baittle, Brahm, 9 n., 239 n.

Ball, John C., 142 n.

Bandura, Albert, 243, 244

Banfield, Edward, 259 n.

Baseline assessment, 20; of behaviors, 81

Becker, Howard S., 228

Behavior, delinquent. *See* Delinquent behavior

Behavior, observed: types and incidence of, 81–83; racial differences, 81–83, 93–96, 102–13 *passim;* factor analysis of, 87–97; delinquency valence of factors, 87–93; interrelation of factors, 96–100; and delinquent subcultures,